ZAGAT SURVEY

Back in 1979, we never imagined that an idea born during a wine-fueled dinner with friends would take us on an adventure that's lasted three decades – and counting.

The idea – that the collective opinions of avid consumers can be more accurate than the judgments of an individual critic – led to a hobby involving friends rating NYC restaurants. And that hobby grew into Zagat Survey, which today has over 350,000 participants worldwide weighing in on everything from airlines, bars, dining and golf to hotels, movies, shopping, tourist attractions and more.

By giving consumers a voice, we – and our surveyors – had unwittingly joined a revolution whose concepts (user-generated content, social networking) were largely unknown 30 years ago. However, those concepts caught fire with the rise of the Internet and have since transformed not only restaurant criticism but also virtually every aspect of the media, and we feel lucky to have been at the start of it all.

As we celebrate Zagat's 30th year, we'd like to thank everyone who has participated in our surveys. We've enjoyed hearing and sharing your frank opinions and look forward to doing so for many years to come. As we always say, our guides and online content are really "yours."

We'd also like to express our gratitude by supporting **Action Against Hunger,** an organization that works to meet the needs of the hungry in over 40 countries. To find out more, visit www.zagat.com/action.

Nina and Tim Zagat

ZAGAT®
CELEBRATING 30 YEARS

New Orleans
2009

- Dining
- Nightlife
- Attractions
- Hotels

LOCAL EDITORS
Todd A. Price and Mimi Read
SENIOR CONSULTING EDITOR
Sharon Litwin
STAFF EDITOR
Karen Hudes

Published and distributed by
Zagat Survey, LLC
4 Columbus Circle
New York, NY 10019
T: 212.977.6000
E: neworleans@zagat.com
www.zagat.com

ACKNOWLEDGMENTS

We thank John Abajian, Cary Alden, Doug Brantley, Patricia Chandler, Lois and Crozet Duplantier, Bart Everson, William A. Fagaly, Ross Kelley, Charlie London, Barbara Mollere, Andrea Price, Alex Rawls, Steven Shukow, Scott Simmons and Jacqueline Sullivan, as well as the following members of our staff: Christina Livadiotis (assistant editor), Amy Cao (editorial assistant), Brian Albert, Sean Beachell, Maryanne Bertollo, Jane Chang, Sandy Cheng, Reni Chin, Larry Cohn, Bill Corsello, Alison Flick, Jeff Freier, Shelley Gallagher, Andrew Gelardi, Michelle Golden, Justin Hartung, Roy Jacob, Garth Johnston, Ashunta Joseph, Natalie Lebert, Mike Liao, Dave Makulec, Andre Pilette, Kimberly Rosado, Becky Ruthenburg, Aleksandra Shander, Jacqueline Wasilczyk, Donna Marino Wilkins, Liz Borod Wright, Sharon Yates, Anna Zappia and Kyle Zolner.

The reviews published in this guide are based on public opinion surveys. The numerical ratings reflect the average scores given by all survey participants who voted on each establishment. The text is based on direct quotes from, or fair paraphrasings of, participants' comments. Phone numbers, addresses and other factual information were correct to the best of our knowledge when published in this guide.

Contents

About This Survey

Here are the results of our **2009 New Orleans Survey,** covering 704 of the city's finest restaurants, nightspots, attractions and hotels. Like all our guides, this one is based on the collective opinions of avid consumers – 3,877 all told.

WHO PARTICIPATED: Input from these enthusiasts forms the basis for the ratings and reviews in this guide (their comments are shown in quotation marks within the reviews). Among this group: 48% are women, 52% men; 10% are in their 20s; 22%, 30s; 23%, 40s; 27%, 50s; and 18%, 60s or above. Collectively they bring vast experience and knowledge to this Survey. We sincerely thank each of these participants – this book is really "theirs."

HELPFUL LISTS: Our top lists and indexes can help you find exactly the right place for any occasion. See the lists that begin each section: Dining (pages 7–15), Nightlife (pages 93–94), Sites & Attractions (page 114) and Hotels (page 124). We've also provided 78 handy indexes.

OUR EDITORS: Special thanks go to our local editors, Sharon Litwin, the senior vice president of the Louisiana Philharmonic Orchestra and founding president of the Crescent City Farmers Market; Todd A. Price, a food and travel writer and frequent contributor to the *New Orleans Times-Picayune*; and Mimi Read, who writes about food, architecture and design for national magazines.

Z ABOUT ZAGAT: This marks our 30th year reporting on the shared experiences of consumers like you. What started in 1979 as a hobby has come a long way. Today we have over 350,000 surveyors and now cover airlines, bars, dining, entertaining, fast food, golf, hotels, movies, music, resorts, shopping, spas, theater and tourist attractions in over 100 countries.

INTERACTIVE: Up-to-the-minute news about restaurant openings plus menus, photos and more are free on **ZAGAT.com** and the award-winning **ZAGAT.mobi** (for web-enabled mobile devices). They also enable reserving at thousands of places with just one click.

VOTE AND COMMENT: We invite you to join any of our surveys at **ZAGAT.com.** There you can rate and review establishments year-round. In exchange for doing so, you'll receive a free copy of the resulting guide when published.

AVAILABILITY: Zagat guides are available in all major bookstores as well as on **ZAGAT.com.** You can also access our content when on the go via **ZAGAT.mobi** and **ZAGAT TO GO** (for smartphones).

FEEDBACK: There is always room for improvement, thus we invite your comments about any aspect of our performance. Did we miss anything? Just contact us at **neworleans@zagat.com.**

New York, NY
January 2, 2009

Nina and Tim Zagat

What's New

It's been three years since Hurricane Katrina tore through New Orleans. Over 25% of the community has yet to return and may never come back. Still, a huge amount of restoration has taken place. Locals and tourists alike, eager to move the city forward, are again enjoying its culinary and cultural charms. But in light of the economic storm battering the nation, they're taking precautions: for example, 32% of surveyors say they're paying more attention to menu prices, and 25% are choosing less expensive restaurants. Fortunately, with one of the lowest average meal costs in the U.S. – $28.52 vs. the national average of $34.31 – the Big Easy makes it a cinch to dine affordably.

AROUND TOWN: A flurry of post-Katrina museum activity brought the French Quarter's buzzing **Audubon Insectarium** and the CBD's **Southern Food & Beverage Museum,** which includes admission to the **Museum of the American Cocktail.** In 2009, the home base of the **New Orleans Jazz National Historical Park** is set to move into the renovated **Perseverance Hall** in Louis Armstrong Park.

HOTEL UPGRADES: Most hotels have reopened post-Katrina, usually in spiffed-up form. Two exceptions: the still-shuttered Hyatt Regency (awaiting redevelopment); and the historic Fairmont, which is to relaunch in June 2009 under the **Waldorf-Astoria** banner and carrying its original name, the **Roosevelt.** It will be home to über-chef John Besh's highly anticipated **Domenica,** featuring an Italian menu with fresh pastas and wood-fired pizzas.

SMART BITES: Many of this year's new restaurants are low on ceremony and high on savvy thanks to their emphasis on small plates (the preferred dining style for 24% of respondents). The CBD's **Rambla** (from the **Cuvée** crew) offers communal dining over tapas, while Mid-City's **Arabesque** provides a global mélange of meze. In the French Quarter, the newly revamped **Wolfe's** (fka Peristyle) augments its Contemporary Louisiana cuisine with a special small-plates menu at happy hour, while **Iris** (recently relocated to the **Bienville House**) boasts inventive bar bites to match its cocktails.

CROWD-PLEASING COMEBACKS: Several much-missed eateries, including the French Quarter's arty **Café Sbisa** and Uptown's iconic **Charlie's Steak House,** finally reopened their doors this year to the delight of loyal locals. **Ruth's Chris Steak House,** aiming to appease critics of its post-Katrina departure, returned with plenty of sizzle to the city proper in fancy new digs at **Harrah's.**

PERFECT POURS: While New Orleans still loves its dives, the thirst for well-made cocktails is gaining ground at sleek new nightspots like the French Quarter's **Bar Tonique** (an offshoot of **The Delachaise**) and the CBD's **Bar UnCommon.** With 55% of surveyors opting for mixed drinks on the weekends, it makes sense that even a low-key addition like Bucktown's **Live Bait** offers over 100 labels of rum.

New Orleans, LA
January 2, 2009

Sharon Litwin
Todd A. Price
Mimi Read

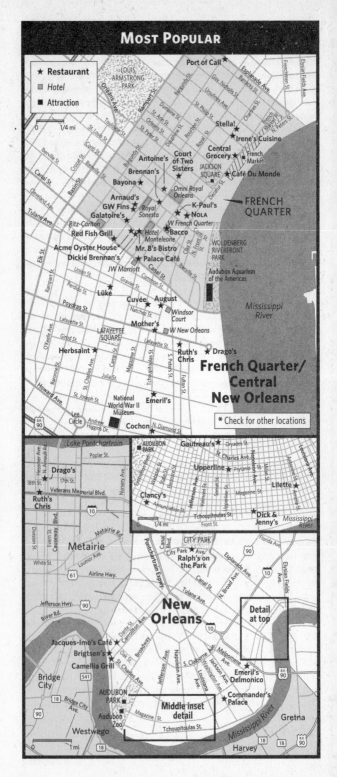

MOST POPULAR

★ Restaurant
▪ Hotel
■ Attraction

LOUIS ARMSTRONG PARK

Port of Call ★

Esplanade Ave.

Stella! ★

Irene's Cuisine ★

Antoine's ★
Court of Two Sisters ★
Central Grocery ★
French Market

Brennan's ★
JACKSON SQUARE
Café Du Monde ★

Bayona ★
Omni Royal Orleans ▪

FRENCH QUARTER

Arnaud's ★
GW Fins ★
Galatoire's ★
K-Paul's ★
Royal Sonesta ▪
NOLA ★

Ritz-Carlton ▪
W French Quarter ▪

Red Fish Grill ★
Bacco ★

Acme Oyster House* ★
Hotel Monteleone ▪

Dickie Brennan's ★
Mr. B's Bistro ★
Palace Café ★

JW Marriott ▪

WOLDENBERG RIVERFRONT PARK

Audubon Aquarium of the Americas ■

Lüke ★

Cuvée ★
August ★

Windsor Court ▪

Mississippi River

Mother's ★
W New Orleans ▪

Herbsaint ★

Ruth's Chris ★
Drago's ★

French Quarter/ Central New Orleans

National World War II Museum ■

Lee Circle
Andrew Higgins Dr.

Emeril's ★

Cochon ★

* Check for other locations

AUDUBON PARK

Gautreau's ★

Lake Pontchartrain

Drago's ★
17th St.
Veterans Memorial Blvd.

Upperline ★

Ruth's Chris ★

Lilette ★

Clancy's ★

Metairie

Dick & Jenny's ★

Mississippi River

CITY PARK

Ralph's on the Park ★

New Orleans

Detail at top

Jacques-Imo's Café ★

Brigtsen's ★

Camellia Grill ★

Bridge City

Emeril's Delmonico ★

Commander's Palace ★

AUDUBON PARK

Middle inset detail

Audubon Zoo ■

Westwego

Mississippi River

Gretna

Harvey

40,000 places to eat, drink, stay & play – free at ZAGAT.com

Most Popular

1. Commander's Palace | *Creole*
2. Galatoire's | *Creole/French*
3. Bayona | *American*
4. Café Du Monde | *Coffee/Dessert*
5. August | *Continental/French*
6. Acme Oyster | *Seafood*
7. Emeril's | *Contemp. Louisiana*
8. Jacques-Imo's | *Creole/Soul*
9. K-Paul's | *Cajun*
10. NOLA | *Contemp. Louisiana*
11. Brigtsen's | *Contemp. Louisiana*
12. Brennan's | *Creole*
13. Antoine's | *Creole/French*
14. Stella! | *American*
15. Mr. B's Bistro | *Contemp. LA*
16. Arnaud's | *Creole*
17. Drago's | *Seafood*
18. Clancy's | *Creole*
19. Cochon | *Cajun*
20. Herbsaint | *American/French*
21. Mother's | *American/Cajun*
22. Emeril's Delmonico | *Creole*
23. Upperline | *Contemp. Louisiana*
24. Bacco | *Italian*
25. Irene's Cuisine | *Italian*
26. GW Fins | *Seafood*
27. Central Grocery | *Sandwiches*
28. Dickie Brennan's | *Steak*
29. Dick & Jenny's | *Creole/Eclectic*
30. Red Fish Grill | *Seafood*
31. Ralph's on Park | *Contemp. LA*
32. Ruth's Chris | *Steak*
33. Lüke | *French*
34. Court of Two Sisters | *Creole*
35. Camellia Grill | *American*
36. Palace Café | *Creole*
37. Cuvée | *Continental/Creole*
38. Gautreau's | *American/French*
39. Lilette | *French*
40. Port of Call | *American*

It's obvious that many of the above restaurants are among the New Orleans area's most expensive, but if popularity were calibrated to price, we suspect that a number of other restaurants would join their ranks. Thus, we have added two lists comprising 90 Best Buys on page 15.

KEY NEWCOMERS

Our editors' take on the year's top arrivals. See page 158 for a full list.

Arabesque | *Eclectic*

Creole Skillet | *Contemp. LA*

Daniel's on the Bayou | *Creole/Italian*

Gimchi | *Japanese/Korean*

Hostel | *French*

Il Posto Café | *Italian*

La Famiglia | *Creole/Italian*

Lago | *American*

Pellicano | *American*

Rambla | *French/Spanish*

West Indies Cafe | *Pan-Latin*

Wolfe's | *Contemp. LA*

Ratings & Symbols

Zagat Top Spot	Name	Symbols	Cuisine	Zagat Ratings			
				FOOD	DECOR	SERVICE	COST

Area, Address & Contact

Z **Tim & Nina's** ◗ *Creole*   ▽ 23 | 9 | 13 | $15

Garden District | 6400 Tchoupitoulas St. (Laurel St.) | 504-555-3867 | www.zagat.com

Review, surveyor comments in quotes

"Definitely no croc", this Garden District "gargantuan gator house" "fries, sautés and flambés" its specialty into "more than just a swamp thing"; the decor looks "dredged from the bayou" and service "could be snappier", but the cooking's so "sharp" that boatloads of locals "wrestle to get in."

Ratings

Food, Decor and **Service** are rated on the Zagat 0 to 30 scale.

0	–	9	poor to fair
10	–	15	fair to good
16	–	19	good to very good
20	–	25	very good to excellent
26	–	30	extraordinary to perfection
	▽		low response | less reliable

Cost

Our surveyors' benchmark estimate of the price of a dinner with one drink and tip. Lunch is usually 25 to 30% less. At prix fixe-only places we show the charge for the lowest-priced menu plus 30%. For **newcomers** or survey **write-ins** listed without ratings, the price range is shown as follows:

I	$25 and below	E	$41 to $65
M	$26 to $40	VE	$66 or more

Symbols

Z	Zagat Top Spot (highest ratings, popularity and importance)
◗	serves after 11 PM
Ⓢ	closed on Sunday
Ⓜ	closed on Monday
⊄	no credit cards accepted

See also the Ratings & Symbols key in each section.

Index

All establishments are listed in the Alphabetical Index at the back of the book.

Top Food Ratings

Excludes places with low votes, unless indicated by a ▽.

28	Brigtsen's | *Contemp. LA*
	Stella! | *American*
	Bayona | *American*
	Dakota | *Amer./Contemp. LA*
	Gautreau's | *American/French*
	August | *Continental/French*
27	Clancy's | *Creole*
	K-Paul's | *Cajun*
	Commander's Palace | *Creole*
	La Provence | *Creole/French*
	La Boca | *Argentinean/Steak*
	Cypress | *Creole*
	Galatoire's | *Creole/French*
26	Herbsaint | *American/French*
	Dick & Jenny's | *Creole/Eclectic*
	Vizard's | *Contemp. LA*
	St. James Cheese | *Continental*
	Upperline | *Contemp. LA*
	Jacques-Imo's | *Creole/Soul*
	GW Fins | *Seafood*
	Lilette | *French*

Ristorante del Porto | *Italian*
Sal & Judy's | *Creole/Italian*
Bistro Daisy | *American*
Crabby Jack's | *Po' Boys*
MiLa | *Contemp. Louisiana*
Ruth's Chris | *Steak*
La Petite Grocery |
   Contemp. LA/French
Martinique Bistro | *French*
Irene's Cuisine | *Italian*
RioMar | *Seafood*
Cuvée | *Continental/Creole*
La Divina Gelateria | *Italian*
Emeril's Delmonico | *Creole*
Domilise's | *Cajun/Creole*
Mosca's | *Italian*
Pelican Club | *American*
NOLA | *Contemp. Louisiana*
Bistro Maison de Ville |
   Creole/French
Le Parvenu | *Amer./Creole*

BY CUISINE

AMERICAN (NEW)

28	Stella!
	Bayona
	Dakota
	Gautreau's
26	Herbsaint

AMERICAN (TRAD.)

25	Surrey's Juice
24	Parasol's
	Port of Call
23	Camellia Grill
22	Mother's

BARBECUE

25	Joint
23	Hillbilly BBQ
20	Ugly Dog Saloon
	Voodoo BBQ
19	Corky's BBQ

BURGERS

24	Port of Call
21	Beachcorner
	Clover Grill
20	Lee's Hamburgers
	Bud's Broiler

CAJUN

27	K-Paul's
25	Cochon
24	Bon Ton Café
22	Petunia's
	Mother's

CHINESE

24	Royal China
23	Trey Yuen
22	Five Happiness
	Café East
	China Doll

COFFEEHOUSES

25	Morning Call
24	Café Du Monde
22	Caffe! Caffe!
19	Chateau Coffee
	CC's Community Coffee

COFFEE SHOPS/DINERS

24	Elizabeth's
23	Coffee Rani
22	Bluebird Cafe
21	Clover Grill
	Slim Goodies

CONTEMP. LOUISIANA

28] Brigtsen's
Dakota
26] Vizard's
Upperline
MiLa

CREOLE

27] Clancy's
Commander's Palace
La Provence
Cypress
Galatoire's

DESSERT

28] Hansen's Sno-Bliz
Angelo Brocato
26] La Divina Gelateria
25] Sucré
Morning Call

FRENCH

28] Gautreau's
August
27] La Provence
Galatoire's
26] Herbsaint

FRENCH (BISTRO)

26] Lilette
Martinique Bistro
25] Chateau du Lac
24] Meauxbar
Café Degas

ITALIAN

26] Ristorante del Porto
Sal & Judy's
Irene's Cuisine
La Divina Gelateria
Mosca's

JAPANESE

25] Sushi Brothers
24] Little Tokyo
Horinoya
Kyoto
NINJA

MEDITERRANEAN

24] Acropolis
Vega Tapas
Jamila's Cafe
22] Byblos
Maple St. Cafe

MEXICAN

21] Juan's Flying Burrito
El Gato Negro
Taqueria Corona
20] Casa Garcia
Superior Grill

PIZZA

24] Theo's
23] Slice
22] Venezia
Mark Twain's Pizza
Louisiana Pizza

PO' BOYS

26] Crabby Jack's
Domilise's
25] Parkway Bakery
24] Parasol's
Galley

SANDWICHES

26] St. James Cheese Co.
25] Central Grocery
23] Martin Wine Cellar
Stein's Market
Whole Foods

SEAFOOD

26] GW Fins
Martinique Bistro
RioMar
25] Casamento's
Drago's

SOUL FOOD/SOUTHERN

26] Jacques-Imo's
25] Willie Mae's
24] Dooky Chase
Eat
22] Praline Connection

THAI

22] La Thai
Singha∇
21] Basil Leaf
20] Bangkok Thai

VIETNAMESE

25] Café Minh
Pho Tau Bay
24] Nine Roses
Kim Son
23] Dong Phuong∇

BY SPECIAL FEATURE

BREAKFAST
25 Rib Room
Surrey's Juice
24 Brennan's
Croissant d'Or
Begue's

BRUNCH
27 Commander's Palace
La Provence
25 Ralph's on Park
Arnaud's
Patois

BUSINESS DINING
28 August
27 Commander's Palace
Galatoire's
26 Herbsaint
Emeril's Delmonico

CHILD-FRIENDLY
26 Domilise's
25 Drago's
Crescent City Steak
Dante's Kitchen
24 Acropolis

DINING ALONE
26 Upperline
Domilise's
Pelican Club
NOLA
25 Mr. B's Bistro

FAMILY-STYLE
26 Mosca's
24 Kim Son
Shogun
Jamila's Cafe
Royal China

HOTEL DINING
28 Stella!
(Hotel Provincial)
26 MiLa
(Renaissance/Marquette)

Ruth's Chris
(Harrah's)
Cuvée
(St. James Hotel)
Bistro Maison de Ville
(Maison de Ville)

LATE DINING
24 Little Tokyo
Port of Call
22 Delachaise
Coop's Place
21 Beachcorner

OFFBEAT
26 Dick & Jenny's
Jacques-Imo's
25 Eleven 79
Central Grocery
24 Parasol's

PEOPLE-WATCHING
28 Bayona
Gautreau's
27 Clancy's
K-Paul's
26 Upperline

POWER SCENES
28 Gautreau's
27 Commander's Palace
Galatoire's
26 Lilette
Ruth's Chris

QUIET CONVERSATION
27 La Provence
26 Cuvée
Le Parvenu
25 Broussard's
24 Horinoya

WINNING WINE LISTS
28 Brigtsen's
Bayona
27 Clancy's
Commander's Palace
26 Cuvée

BY LOCATION

CARROLLTON/ RIVERBEND

28 Brigtsen's
26 Jacques-Imo's
25 One Rest. & Lounge
   Dante's Kitchen
24 NINJA

CENTRAL BUS. DISTRICT

28 August
26 MiLa
   Ruth's Chris
   Cuvée
25 Drago's

COVINGTON

28 Dakota
26 Ristorante del Porto
23 Coffee Rani
22 Acme Oyster
   Etoile

FAUBOURG MARIGNY

24 Adolfo's
   Wasabi
22 Marigny Brasserie
   Praline Connection
21 Feelings Cafe

FRENCH QUARTER

28 Stella!
   Bayona
27 K-Paul's
   Galatoire's
26 GW Fins

GARDEN DISTRICT

27 Commander's Palace
26 La Divina Gelateria
25 Sucré
21 Reginelli's
   Slim Goodies*

GRETNA

25 Pho Tau Bay
24 Nine Roses
   Kim Son
22 Tony Mandina's
21 Sun Ray Grill

HARAHAN

23 Zea
21 Reginelli's

   Taqueria Corona
20 La Madeleine
17 Smilie's

KENNER

26 Le Parvenu
24 Harbor Seafood
23 Sake Cafe
   Zea
21 Reginelli's

LOWER GARDEN DISTRICT

26 Emeril's Delmonico
25 Sushi Brothers
   Eleven 79
   Surrey's Juice
24 Mr. John's

MANDEVILLE

24 Little Tokyo
   Nuvolari's
23 Coffee Rani
   Trey Yuen
22 Caffe! Caffe!

METAIRIE

27 Cypress
26 Ruth's Chris
25 Drago's
   Morning Call
24 Little Tokyo

MID-CITY

28 Angelo Brocato
25 Parkway Bakery
   Ralph's on Park
   Café Minh
   Crescent City Steak

UPTOWN

28 Gautreau's
27 Clancy's
26 Dick & Jenny's
   Vizard's
   St. James Cheese Co.

WAREHOUSE DISTRICT

27 La Boca
26 Herbsaint
   RioMar
25 Emeril's
   Tommy's Cuisine

---

* Indicates a tie with restaurant above

Top Decor Ratings

<u>28</u> Commander's Palace

<u>27</u> August
La Provence

<u>26</u> Ralph's on Park
Sucré
Muriel's Jackson Sq.
Bayona
Café East
Cuvée
Emeril's Delmonico
Stella!
Arnaud's

<u>25</u> Antoine's
MiLa
Galatoire's
New Orleans Grill
Rib Room
Café Amelie
Brennan's
Dickie Brennan's

Napoleon House
GW Fins
Bacco
Café Adelaide
Emeril's

<u>24</u> Court of Two Sisters
Nuvolari's
Bistro Maison de Ville
Gautreau's
Broussard's
Begue's
Upperline
Mr. B's Bistro
Pelican Club
NOLA
Etoile
Tommy's Cuisine
Dakota
Ristorante del Porto
Audubon Park

OUTDOORS

Bayona
Broussard's
Café Amelie
Cafe Rani
Commander's Palace

Dante's Kitchen
Feelings Cafe
Martinique Bistro
Mat & Naddie's
Napoleon House

ROMANCE

Arnaud's
August
Bistro Maison de Ville
Café Degas
Cafe Giovanni

Feelings Cafe
Irene's Cuisine
La Crêpe Nanou
La Provence
Stella!

ROOMS

Antoine's
Arnaud's
Brennan's
Broussard's
Café Adelaide

Commander's Palace
Emeril's
Gautreau's
New Orleans Grill
Rib Room

VIEWS

Audubon Park
Begue's
Café Du Monde
Cafe Pontalba
Commander's Palace

Landry's Seafood
Muriel's Jackson Sq.
Ralph's on Park
Restaurant des Familles
Superior Grill

Top Service Ratings

27
Brigtsen's
Commander's Palace
Galatoire's
August
Stella!

26
Bayona
Dakota
Gautreau's
Arnaud's
La Provence

25
Jamila's Cafe
Rib Room
Clancy's
Emeril's Delmonico
Ralph's on Park
Dickie Brennan's
Ruth's Chris
Brennan's
Tommy's Cuisine
Mr. B's Bistro

Emeril's
Dick & Jenny's
NOLA
GW Fins
Cypress
Antoine's
Bistro Daisy
Upperline

24
Cuvée
Ristorante del Porto
Broussard's
Bistro Maison de Ville
K-Paul's
Morton's
Vizard's
Besh Steak
Bacco
Camellia Grill
Pelican Club
Herbsaint

Best Buys

In order of Bang for the Buck rating.

1. Hansen's Sno-Bliz
2. Angelo Brocato
3. Morning Call
4. CC's Community Coffee
5. La Divina Gelateria
6. PJ's Coffee
7. rue de la course
8. La Boulangerie
9. Croissant d'Or
10. Café Du Monde
11. Sucré
12. Crêpes à la Cart
13. Raising Cane's
14. Betsy's Pancake
15. Bud's Broiler
16. Roly Poly
17. Parkway Bakery
18. Caffe! Caffe!
19. Café Reconcile
20. Lee's Hamburgers
21. Central Grocery
22. Camellia Grill
23. Domilise's
24. Popeyes
25. Joint
26. Bluebird Cafe
27. Slim Goodies
28. Clover Grill
29. Coffee Rani
30. Chateau Coffee
31. Russell's Short Stop
32. Cafe Beignet
33. Surrey's Juice
34. DiMartino's
35. Come Back Inn
36. St. James Cheese Co.
37. Mike Serio's
38. Whole Foods
39. Blue Plate Cafe
40. Slice

OTHER GOOD VALUES

Acropolis
Adolfo's
Apple Seed
Audubon Park
Babylon Café
Ba Mien
Bennachin
Boswell's Jamaican
Byblos
Cafe Rani
Casamento's
Ciro's Côté Sud
Crabby Jack's
Dong Phuong
Doson's Noodle
Easy Dogs
Eat
El Gato Negro
Elizabeth's
Felipe's Taqueria
Fellini's
Five Happiness
Frosty's Caffe
Gelato Pazzo
Grocery
Il Posto Café
Imperial Garden
Islas Roatan
Italian Pie
J'anita's
Jazmine Café
Johnny's Po-Boy
Kim Son
Lakeview Brew
Lebanon's Café
Li'l Dizzy's Cafe
Louisiana Pizza
Mahony's
Martin Wine Cellar
New Orleans Cake Café
Nine Roses
Oak Street Cafe
P&G
Pho Bang
Reginelli's
Stein's Market
Superior Grill
Taqueria Sanchez
Voodoo BBQ
Vucinovich

40,000 places to eat, drink, stay & play – free at ZAGAT.com

DINING
DIRECTORY

Dining

	FOOD	DECOR	SERVICE	COST

Abita Brew Pub Ⓜ *Creole/Eclectic*   19 | 19 | 18 | $22

Abita Springs | 72011 Holly St. (bet. Hwys. 36 & 59) | 985-892-5837 |
www.abitabrewpub.com

"So it's not highbrow", but this "lively", "touristy" "country brewpub" in
"rural Abita Springs" is a "destination" for its "ever-changing selection"
of the "freshest beer around" – including "limited" seasonal editions –
"made just down the road"; while the "hearty" Creole-Eclectic food
gets mixed marks and the service "could be quicker", connoisseurs
call it an "awesome jaunt" when you want to "sample the suds."

Acme Oyster House *Seafood*   22 | 14 | 19 | $24

French Quarter | 724 Iberville St. (bet. Bourbon & Royal Sts.) | 504-522-5973
Metairie | 3000 Veterans Memorial Blvd. (N. Causeway Blvd.) |
504-309-4056
Covington | 1202 N. Hwy. 190 (bet. Crestwood Blvd. & 17th Ave.) |
985-246-6155
www.acmeoyster.com

"There's a wait out the door for a reason" at this French Quarter "old
faithful" (with less historic outposts in the 'burbs) whose "phenomenal" oysters ("raw, char-grilled and fried") as well as other "inexpensive", "off-the-boat" seafood is the stuff "you write about in
postcards"; tourists "sit elbow-to-elbow with natives" in the "merry",
"faux-divey" digs, while those in-the-know head to the bar's "marble
counter" for a close-up of the shuckers' "floor show."

Acropolis Ⓜ *Mediterranean*   24 | 16 | 24 | $22

Metairie | 3841 Veterans Memorial Blvd. (Taft Park) | 504-888-9046
A "surprise in a shopping center", this Metairie Med "doesn't look like
much from the outside" and the interior could be "better", but it serves
some of the "finest" Greek food in town (as well as some Italian dishes)
and the "specials are always special"; brightened up by a staff that
"makes you feel like you're in someone's kitchen swapping stories", most
agree it's a real "value" for lunch or an early dinner (closes at 9 PM).

Adolfo's ⊄ *Italian*   24 | 17 | 20 | $26

Faubourg Marigny | 611 Frenchmen St. (Chartres St.) | 504-948-3800
It's "worth the climb" to find this second-floor Frenchmen Street
"scene" of "eclectic customers" dining on "fabulous", "affordable"
Southern Italian fare prepared with "superlative sauces" and a "man-
datory New Orleans twist"; the combo of a "dark, dated" dining room
that could have been a "one-bedroom apartment" and a "kitchen the
size of an SUV" means waits can last over an hour, but that's enough
time to "catch a hot new band" at the bar below; N.B. cash only.

NEW Alligator Pear *Contemp. Louisiana*   - | - | - | I

Harvey | 1901 Manhattan Blvd. (7th St.) | 504-342-2640
Faux Florida lands on the West Bank at this Harvey newcomer whose
large, glass-enclosed room and sidewalk cafe overlook a man-made
lagoon complete with fountains and fake floating fowl; it casually
serves a Contemporary Louisiana menu extending from rotisserie
chicken and ribs to a few wok dishes, while the owner's adjoining
Parrot Pete's opens earlier for breakfast and homebaked goods.

	FOOD	DECOR	SERVICE	COST

Alpine, The *Cajun/Creole* — 18 | 15 | 18 | $25

French Quarter | 620 Chartres St. (bet. St. Peter & Toulouse Sts.) | 504-523-3005 | www.thealpinebistro.com

Its location a block from Jackson Square and a "hawker" outside help lure tourists (while "putting off" many locals) to this "old-time" eatery serving "simply prepared" Cajun-Creole food ranging from "mediocre" to "better than expected"; the service "varies" too, but the "decent" atmosphere is livened up by a "nice courtyard."

Andrea's *Italian/Seafood* — 21 | 20 | 22 | $42

Metairie | 3100 19th St. (N. Causeway Blvd.) | 504-834-8583 | www.andreasrestaurant.com

Chef-owner Andrea Apuzzo "always makes a stop at your table" at this Metairie "standby" known for its "excellent" seafood among other "upscale", "flavorful" Northern Italian cuisine, as well as the big "personality" of its proprietor; while "regulars" appreciate the "gracious" treatment and "elegant" dining room, less enthused eaters find it a bit "stuffy" and lacking in service "if they don't already know you."

Angeli on Decatur ● *Mediterranean/Pizza* — 20 | 15 | 16 | $17

French Quarter | 1141 Decatur St. (bet. Governor Nicholls St. & Ursuline Ave.) | 504-566-0077

On the "edge of the French Quarter", this "offbeat", "divey" Mediterranean is the place to go when that "late-night" "craving" hits for pizzas, pastas and other "inexpensive", "quality" eats with plenty of "veggie variety"; a "somewhat snarky", "tattooed" staff takes care of the "cool" clientele of "young hipsters" (and a recent "influx of tourists" lured by "Brangelina's house" nearby) who linger at their tables well past dessert to watch free nightly "classic flicks."

❷ Angelo Brocato Ⓜ *Dessert* — 28 | 21 | 23 | $8

Mid-City | 214 N. Carrollton Ave. (bet. Bienville Ave. & Iberville Sts.) | 504-486-0078 | www.angelobrocatoicecream.com

"No other can compare" to this century-old "cornerstone of Mid-City" for "unbelievable" gelato and ices made with "in-season fruits", "fresh", "fantastic" cannoli and other Sicilian sweets served by "handsome, jovial teens" in a "retro ice cream parlor" setting that brings back lots of "memories"; you'll always find a "line no matter what time", and the after-dinner crowd makes it "standing-room-only" on the weekends.

Anselmo's Ⓢ *Italian* — 19 | 15 | 20 | $25

Metairie | 3401 N. Hullen St. (15th St.) | 504-889-1212

In suburban Metairie, this "down-home" Southern Italian keeps an older crowd happy with "delicious", "filling fare" like the signature osso buco and Italian shrimp for "value" prices; despite a renovated dining room that critics call "too sterile", many are won over by the "genuine family feel" provided by the owners and staff; N.B. lunch-only on Monday–Tuesday.

❷ Antoine's *Creole/French* — 24 | 25 | 25 | $59

French Quarter | 713 St. Louis St. (bet. Bourbon & Royal Sts.) | 504-581-4422 | www.antoines.com

This Vieux Carré "shrine" to "golden-age" Creole-French cooking "still delivers" the "essence of old New Orleans" in its "rich" signature dishes and desserts like the baked Alaska ("order in advance"); the "beautiful", "antiques-filled rooms" are overseen by a "black-tie-attired" "lifelong staff" that "would bring you the Eiffel Tower if you asked", but to get the full experience "make sure you have the name of a waiter" and "follow his advice"; N.B. closed Tuesday–Wednesday, brunch-only on Sundays.

Apple Seed Shoppe 🗷🍴 *Vegetarian*   ▽ 22 | 12 | 20 | $10

Central Business Dist. | Place St. Charles | 201 St. Charles Ave., 2nd fl. (Common St.) | 504-529-3442

"Eating healthfully is a treat" at this "inexpensive" CBD lunch "alternative" for "huge portions" of largely veggie fare such as "housemade salads, sandwiches" and "delicious soups"; the "cramped" space "on the edge of a food court" means "most take orders to go", but the "charming Southern gent" proprietor makes anyone who stays "feel welcome."

🆕 Arabesque 🗷Ⓜ *Eclectic*   23 | 22 | 23 | $31

Mid-City | 127 N. Carrollton Ave. (Canal St.) | 504-486-7233 | www.cafearabesque.com

"Pleasurable meals" await at this "exciting" new Mid-City Eclectic that whips up a "wild mixture" of midpriced Middle Eastern, Latin American and New Orleans fare, including plenty of "fabulous" small plates, served by a "charming", "professional" staff; while the shotgun setting is "sexy and exotic", it's so "cozy" that patrons plead "stay away so that we can have it all to ourselves."

🆉 Arnaud's *Creole*   25 | 26 | 26 | $56

French Quarter | 813 Bienville St. (bet. Bourbon & Dauphine Sts.) | 504-523-5433 | www.arnauds.com

An "iconic, well-weathered establishment", this "gorgeous grande dame" featuring a "crisp" "collection of intimate dining areas and open rooms" provides a "glorious" atmosphere for supping on "true Creole cuisine", such as "amazing" shrimp Arnaud, and savoring a "fantastic" Sunday jazz brunch; since the staff provides "spectacular" service too (including "proper" tableside preparations), most feel the "top-heavy" bill is justified; P.S. "don't miss the Mardi Gras display upstairs."

Audubon Park Clubhouse Ⓜ *Sandwiches*   15 | 24 | 17 | $22

Uptown | Audubon Pk. | 6500 Magazine St. (East Dr.) | 504-212-5285 | www.auduboninstitute.org

"Relax after a round of golf" at this Uptown clubhouse where the "wonderful" wraparound porch is surrounded by the "great oaks" and "well-manicured greens of the Audubon Park fairway"; it's "nothing fancy" – serving "standard" sandwiches, breakfast items and a Sunday brunch buffet – but "reasonable" and "very pleasant" when it's "not too hot."

🆉 August *Continental/French*   28 | 27 | 27 | $68

Central Business Dist. | 301 Tchoupitoulas St. (Gravier St.) | 504-299-9777 | www.rest-august.com

"Exceptionally creative" celebrity chef/co-owner John Besh "impresses" guests with "attention to detail that's something to behold" at his CBD flagship, crafting an "exciting and satisfying" menu of Continental–New French cuisine that's "filled with fresh, local surprises"; both the "lovely" interior of "exposed brick and shimmering chandeliers" and "terrific" service by a "well-versed" staff complete the "sublime" meal, so "if you can stomach the prices", you'll make your stomach very "happy."

August Moon Ⓢ *Chinese/Vietnamese* | 17 | 13 | 18 | $18

Uptown | 3635 Prytania St. (Louisiana Ave.) | 504-899-5129 |
www.augustmoonneworleans.com

At lunchtime, "doctors and other staff" from the nearby hospital "pack" this "affordable" Uptown Asian that "shines" when it comes to Vietnamese dishes, even if the Chinese is merely "adequate"; the scene calms down at dinner, when many fans opt for "fast delivery."

Austin's Ⓢ *Creole/Seafood* | - | - | - | M

Metairie | 5101 W. Esplanade (Chastant St.) | 504-888-5533

This slightly upscale, white-tablecloth Creole sibling of Mr. Ed's in Metairie is a magnet for locals looking for affordable N'Awlins trad dishes without having to leave the 'hood or go to a chain; focusing on seafood and steaks, it also pleases with plentiful wines by the glass and a piano player on the weekends.

Babylon Café *Mideastern* | 21 | 11 | 16 | $17

Uptown | 7724 Maple St. (Adams St.) | 504-314-0010

"Tasty" Middle Eastern fare (bolstered by "delish" bread) for a "bargain" attracts both Uptown "families" and a "younger" Tulane crowd to this "laid-back", somewhat "divey" BYO "attached to a Laundromat"; while frequenters say the "owner is amazingly nice", some advise "just don't go here if you're in a hurry."

Bacco *Italian* | 24 | 25 | 24 | $44

French Quarter | W French Quarter | 310 Chartres St. (bet. Bienville & Conti Sts.) | 504-522-2426 | www.bacco.com

"Casual but chic", this "Brennan-family winner" in the Quarter offers "inventive turns on Italian" cuisine with "regional influences", served by a "well-trained" staff in a "festive" setting with vaulted ceilings and "big open windows" onto Chartres Street; while the wine list is "impressive", some daytime diners go for the drink specials instead, saying "at 10 cents a pop you can't afford not to enjoy a three-martini lunch."

Ba Mien Ⓜ *Vietnamese* | - | - | - | I

New Orleans East | 13235 Chef Menteur Hwy. (bet. Alcee Fortier & Michoud Blvds.) | 504-255-0500

Don't drive too fast, or you'll miss this New Orleans East Vietnamese tucked way in the back of a strip mall on 'the Chef', furnished in utilitarian style with big granite-topped tables for families feasting on pho, vermicelli bowls and roasted quail; since it closes by 7 PM nightly, some day-trippers seek it out for weekend brunch.

Bangkok Thai *Thai* | 20 | 11 | 18 | $19

Riverbend | 513 S. Carrollton Ave. (St. Charles Ave.) |
504-861-3932

Pad Thai "to dhai for" and other "nearly authentic" Thai dishes are the draw at this Riverbend "find" whose "cheap" tabs keep it popular with students and other budget-conscious customers; sure, it "lacks ambiance", but the "bare-bones" service is "prompt" and the location is convenient "before a bender at Cooter Brown's next door."

	FOOD	DECOR	SERVICE	COST

Barú Bistro & Tapas 🖼️Ⓜ️ *Nuevo Latino* | 23 | 20 | 20 | $30

Uptown | 3700 Magazine St. (Amelia St.) | 504-895-2225

Admirers are "addicted" to the "pleasing" Nuevo Latino nibbles at this "little corner" tapas place where the Colombian-influenced cooking has an "exotic" "Caribbean flair"; while some call it "pricey" for the portions, most agree the "affable" staff and "attractive" digs decked out with custom artwork, plants and "sidewalk seating" make it a "tropical oasis" on Uptown's "see-and-be-seen Magazine Street"; N.B. it's currently BYO, with a liquor license pending.

Basil Leaf *Thai* | 21 | 16 | 20 | $28

Carrollton | 1438 S. Carrollton Ave. (Jeannette St.) | 504-862-9001

You can have it "spicy if you want it" at this "consistent" Carrollton Thai whose "artfully presented" dishes include "many vegetarian options" and "curiously delicious desserts"; the servers are "always on top of their game" and the "candelit" atmosphere is "relaxed", so most don't mind that it costs more than some of the competition.

🅉 Bayona 🖼️ *American* | 28 | 26 | 26 | $58

French Quarter | 430 Dauphine St. (bet. Conti & St. Louis Sts.) | 504-525-4455 | www.bayona.com

"Culinary genius" Susan Spicer creates "imaginative", "delectable" New American dishes with "local flavor", which are delivered by her "crackerjack" staff at this "shining star" in a Creole cottage "tucked away from the craziness of the French Quarter"; its "picturesque" patio and "multiple, intimate" dining areas ("request the first floor") are equally "attractive", adding up to a "slice of heaven" that's "well worth the price"; P.S. "go for lunch" – it's a "bargain" and the "duck PB&J will make you glad you're an adult now."

Beachcorner Bar & Grill ● *Pub Food* | 21 | 11 | 17 | $14

Mid-City | 4905 Canal St. (City Park Ave.) | 504-488-7357

"No beach and no corner", but "wow, one of the best burgers in town" along with a roster of less stellar but well-priced "typical bar grub" can be found at this "dingy", "late-night" Mid-City pub surrounded by cemeteries; so "if you can tolerate the cigarette smoke", then "chill with friends" and let the "quick, smart-witted" staff keep your pint glass replenished; N.B. no one under 21 admitted.

🆕 Beebe's Ⓜ️ *Contemp. Louisiana/Seafood* | ▽ 25 | 21 | 21 | $47

Lakefront | 7224 Pontchartrain Blvd. (Robert E. Lee Blvd.) | 504-302-9657

The "excellent young chef" at this new Lakefront Contemporary Louisianian specializes in savory seafood like Gulf shrimp tempura served amid "nicely decorated" surroundings of Asian red walls and faux marble columns; though the room is "small", it opens onto a porch and patio, and ups the "fun quotient" by doubling as a "music club" with regular jazz shows, including sets by owner Brenda Mac's band.

Begue's *Creole/French* | 24 | 24 | 23 | $43

French Quarter | Royal Sonesta Hotel | 300 Bourbon St. (bet. Bienville & Conti Sts.) | 504-553-2278 | www.royalsonestano.com

They "pull out all the stops for Sunday brunch" with "flowing champagne", a "panoply of hot and cold" dishes and "unending tables of desserts" at this Creole–New French inside the Quarter's Royal

Sonesta Hotel; with "attentive" service, "lovely traditional decor" and a "beautiful view of a lush courtyard", it delivers an "elegant" meal that "doesn't break the bank"; N.B. dinner served Friday–Saturday only.

Bennachin ⊘ African/Vegetarian

▽ 23 | 14 | 15 | $17

French Quarter | 1212 Royal St. (bet. Barracks & Governor Nicholls Sts.) | 504-522-1230

"Enticing aromas" lead eaters to this "funky" "joint" "on the edge of the Quarter" for "sensational" West African cooking, including "numerous well-prepared vegetarian choices"; a mere "$20 will cover your desires" (it's BYO-only with no corkage fee), and "any failings in service are more than made up for with the food."

Besh Steak Seafood/Steak

25 | 22 | 24 | $59

Central Business Dist. | Harrah's Casino | 4 Canal St. (S. Peters St.) | 504-533-6111 | www.harrahsneworleans.com

"If you're in the mood for an entire side of beef" with a "top-notch" helping of surf, bet on chef John Besh's "fabulous" steakhouse off the floor of Harrah's CBD casino; many complain about the "clang of slot machines and smoke" drifting in (and some "gasp" at the cost), but the original Rodrigue "blue dog paintings" and the "wonderful" staff make even high rollers who had a bad night "feel like they're lucky."

Betsy's Pancake House American

22 | 13 | 21 | $12

Mid-City | 2542 Canal St. (bet. Dorgenois & Rocheblave Sts.) | 504-822-0213

"Step back in time to when beehives were all the rage" at this all-American "classic" in Mid-City filled with a "real cross-section of New Orleans people" chowing down on "homestyle" breakfast and lunch eats; the "price is always right", the "staff makes you feel like family" and "you're likely to be called dahlin'", though many lament that after the tragic murder of owner Betsy McDaniel during a home invasion, the place "won't be the same" ("God rest Ms. Betsy").

Big Al's Seafood Cajun/Seafood

19 | 18 | 18 | $26

NEW **Lower Garden Dist.** | 1377 Annunciation St. (bet. Melpomene Ave. & Terpsichore St.) | 504-265-0324 Ⓜ

Houma | 1226 Grand Caillou Rd. (Evelyn Ave.) | 985-876-7942

Houma | 1377 W. Tunnel Blvd. (Hollywood Rd.) | 985-876-4030

www.bigalsseafood.net

"The mudbugs are up to par" at this Lower Garden District newcomer (part of a Houma-based mini-chain) serving "well-seasoned" "boiled and fried" morsels from the sea, lake and swamp; though some cite "tourist prices", many appreciate the "open space" of the "redone fire station" (with a "dog-friendly patio") and "hope they stick around."

Bistro at Maison de Ville Ⓜ Creole/French

26 | 24 | 24 | $50

French Quarter | Hotel Maison de Ville | 733 Toulouse St. (bet. Bourbon & Royal Sts.) | 504-528-9206 | www.hotelmaisondeville.com

"Good things come in small packages" at this "romantic" French Quarter bistro where chef Greg Picolo crafts "fresh, local ingredients" into "terrific", "imaginative" and "lovingly prepared" French-Creole food served by a "generously accommodating" staff; while the "lush" yet "relaxed" setting feels "like Paris", guests appreciate that they can "pay the bill without wincing."

	FOOD	DECOR	SERVICE	COST

Bistro Daisy 🖈Ⓜ *American/Southern* | 26 | 23 | 25 | $50

Uptown | 5831 Magazine St. (bet. Eleonore St. & Nashville Ave.) | 504-899-6987

A "tiny place for a big dining experience", this "up-and-comer" by the "charming" couple of chef Anton and Diane Schulte (ex La Petite Grocery) offers a "small" but "sophisticated" menu of "market-driven" New American–Southern fare with a "Louisiana" touch; boasting a "cozy" Creole cottage setting and a "staff that offers intelligent suggestions", it's already "popular" with the "Uptown crowd."

Bluebird Cafe Ⓜ⇌ *Diner* | 22 | 14 | 20 | $13

Uptown | 3625 Prytania St. (bet. Antonine & Foucher Sts.) | 504-895-7166

"Eat here and feel like a local" affirm fans of this "bohemian" Uptown "greasy spoon" known for huevos rancheros ("a big favorite"), "awesome" corned beef hash and other "satisfying" daytime staples set down by "eclectic characters" who "call you baby"; there's "always a line on weekend mornings", but the "cheeky, offbeat artwork will put you in a good mood" while you wait; N.B. closed Monday–Tuesday.

Blue Plate Cafe 🖈 *American* | 22 | 17 | 20 | $17

Lower Garden Dist. | 1330 Prytania St. (Thalia St.) | 504-309-9500

"Thank heavens they finally reopened" gush grateful guests of this Lower Garden District cafe that "thinks outside the box" with "inventive" twists on American "regional classics" for breakfast and lunch, including "unique, tasty" sandwiches; despite the "healthy wait" for a table, the "whimsical", "window-wrapped" dining room and "affordable" tabs keep customers smiling.

Bon Ton Café 🖈 *Cajun* | 24 | 19 | 23 | $35

Central Business Dist. | 401 Magazine St. (bet. Natchez & Poydras Sts.) | 504-524-3386

"Popular with the local bench and bar", this weekday-only "gold standard for a business lunch" in the CBD provides "fastidious family recipes" of "refined Cajun cuisine" served with "*beaucoup* butter" and plenty of "Southern hospitality" in a "historic", brick-walled dining room that "hovers between casual and more formal"; vets advise "dress up a little" and be sure to leave space for the "second-to-none" whiskey bread pudding that "should be dished out to the pious at the pearly gates."

Boswell's Jamaican Grill 🖈 *Jamaican* | - | - | - | I

🆕 **Mid-City** | 3521 Tulane Ave. (bet. Clark & S. Genois Sts.) | 504-482-6600

Jazz Fest favorite Boswell Atkinson whips up Jamaican favorites like oxtails with broad beans, jerk chicken and veggie patties at this relocated Mid-City joint with an island vibe; despite daunting surroundings of bail bondsmen's offices and cheap motels, it's worth a visit for the $8.50 lunch buffet on weekdays; N.B. closes at 6 PM Mondays, 9 PM other nights.

Bourbon House Seafood & Oyster Bar *Seafood* | 21 | 23 | 22 | $42

French Quarter | Astor Crowne Plaza Hotel | 144 Bourbon St. (bet. Canal & Iberville Sts.) | 504-522-0111 | www.bourbonhouse.com

"Dickie Brennan has done it again" at this "lively" "white-tablecloth" seafooder featuring "knowledgeable" service, "retro decor" (accented with "gold globe lights") and a "wonderful" oyster bar where the "entertaining shuckers" "will flirt with your date if you turn your back"; its "steady" dishes are complemented by an extensive list of Southern elixirs that might make it "the best place for bourbon on Bourbon."

Bozo's ⊠M Seafood
22 | 12 | 18 | $23

Metairie | 3117 21st St. (bet. N. Causeway Blvd. & Ridgelake Dr.) | 504-831-8666

"On Fridays during Lent, it can be tough to get a table" at this "family" place in suburban Metairie that "cooks to order" "simple", "scrumptious" fried seafood and shucks some of the "plumpest oysters in town"; though detractors dis the "depressing decor", fans overlook its flaws since it's a "good value" and "one of the few remaining restaurants where you can still enjoy the superb taste of wild catfish."

Bravo! Cucina Italiana Italian
20 | 21 | 20 | $27

Metairie | Lakeside Shopping Ctr. | 3413 Veterans Memorial Blvd. (Severn Ave.) | 504-828-8828 | www.bestitalianusa.com

Setting down "colorful, light" dishes amid "sophisticated" "Roman" surroundings, this Metairie Italian works well "before the movies or after church with the family", even if some call it "a bit commercial for New Orleans"; still, with an "affable" staff and "prices at the right level", it's "not bad for a chain restaurant."

☑ Brennan's Creole
24 | 25 | 25 | $57

French Quarter | 417 Royal St. (bet. Conti & St. Louis Sts.) | 504-525-9711 | www.brennansneworleans.com

"Breakfast is truly an event" with "a touch of class and a touch of sass" at this "handsomely priced" French Quarter Creole – an "indispensable pillar" of New Orleans cuisine – that's "great for dinner too", but "don't check your cholesterol level for weeks after eating here"; the staff is "motivated to please" and the dining rooms are "ritzy", though some long for the days before tourists in "shorts and fanny packs" outnumbered the "gents wearing jackets."

Brick Oven Cafe Italian
21 | 19 | 20 | $26

Kenner | 2805 Williams Blvd. (Veterans Memorial Blvd.) | 504-466-2097

"Near the airport", this "solid suburban" Italian in Kenner "exceeds expectations" for a "quick meal out" with "consistent" pizza and pasta at an attractive price; some find it "dated" and merely "ordinary" all around, but regulars feel they can "always count on it."

☑ Brigtsen's ⊠M Contemp. Louisiana
28 | 23 | 27 | $53

Riverbend | 723 Dante St. (Maple St.) | 504-861-7610 | www.brigtsens.com

"Believe everything you've heard" about chef/co-owner Frank Brigtsen's "marvelous", "innovative" Contemporary Louisiana "comfort food with flair" presented at a "perfect pace" by a "delightful", "down-to-earth" staff (helmed by wife and manager Marna Brigtsen) at this Riverbend "winner", rated No. 1 in New Orleans for Food and Service; many "love the atmosphere" in a "quaint" cottage too (though critics call it "cramped"), finding the whole experience "New Orleans through and through" and a "great value" to boot.

	FOOD	DECOR	SERVICE	COST

☑ Broussard's Ⓢ *Creole/French*   25 | 24 | 24 | $56

French Quarter | 819 Conti St. (Bourbon St.) | 504-581-3866 | www.broussards.com

It's "not as well-known to tourists as some other longtime establishments", but many consider this Vieux Carré "marvel" in a historic house the city's "ultimate white-linen restaurant" where chef-owner Gunter Preuss "maintains the tradition" of preparing "exquisite" Creole-French dishes matched with a "superb wine list"; "exceptional" rooms, a "gorgeous" courtyard and a "talented" staff that "caters to you from the time you enter" all make it a "grand experience."

Bubba Gump Shrimp Co. *American/Seafood*   13 | 15 | 15 | $27

French Quarter | 429 Decatur St. (Conti St.) | 504-522-5800 | www.bubbagump.com

"If you eat here while in this town, then you are not reading this book" (or else you were caught in a "severe thunderstorm" or "caved into the kids") conclude surveyors baffled by the appeal of this "commercial to the nth degree" American seafood chain link "overly committed to a 1990s movie"; the "staff has fun" stumping tourists with *Forrest Gump* trivia, and the shrimp is "alright", but "if this is your idea of NOLA cuisine, there's also a McDonald's you should try."

Bud's Broiler *Burgers*   20 | 7 | 13 | $9

Jefferson | 4101 Jefferson Hwy. (Monticello Ave.) | 504-837-9419 ☒⑃
Jefferson | 9327 Jefferson Hwy. (Orchard Rd.) | 504-738-2452 ⑃
Kenner | 2800 Veterans Memorial Blvd. (Roosevelt Blvd.) | 504-466-0026 ☒
Metairie | 2008 Clearview Pkwy. (W. Napoleon Ave.) | 504-889-2837 ◑⑃
Metairie | 2929 Causeway Blvd. (Veterans Blvd.) | 504-833-3770
Uptown | 3151 Calhoun St. (S. Claiborne Ave.) | 504-861-0906 ⑃
Marrero | 5100 Lapalco Blvd. (Barataria Blvd.) | 504-348-0492 ☒⑃
www.budsbroiler.com

Charbroiled "burgers at their best" (topped with "killer" sauce), "first-class fries" and "great milkshakes" make this "run-down" local chain the "secret indulgence" of many; "don't expect decent service" (or "graffiti"-free tables), but it's a "real dump with character" that "natives love."

Byblos *Mideastern*   22 | 20 | 20 | $25

Metairie | 2020 Veterans Memorial Blvd. (Beverly Garden Dr.) | 504-837-9777
Old Metairie | Metairie Shopping Ctr. | 1501 Metairie Rd. (bet. Bonnabel & Codifer Blvds.) | Metairie | 504-834-9773
Uptown | Tulane University | 29 McAlister Dr. (bet. Drill Rd. & Freret St.) | 504-835-8332
Uptown | 3218 Magazine St. (bet. Harmony & Pleasant Sts.) | 504-894-1233
www.byblosrestaurants.com

This area mini-chain "keeps kebab-in' along", turning out "generous portions" of "affordable" Mediterranean and Middle Eastern "standards" "executed with care" and served by an "accommodating" staff; the atmosphere is generally "relaxed", but every Thursday the "chic" Uptown branch heats up with "fun" live belly dancing.

Bywater Bar-B-Que *American/BBQ*   16 | 13 | 16 | $17

Bywater | 3162 Dauphine St. (Louisa St.) | 504-944-4445

"Ample servings" beef up the appeal of this "earthy", "dark" Bywater hangout delivering "plain-Jane BBQ", "better-than-average pizza" and other American eats to a "varied clientele (from debutantes to leather boys)"; the "often slow service" offers time to "catch up on the local happenings" and kick back on the patio; N.B. closed Wednesdays.

Café Adelaide *Creole* — 24 | 25 | 24 | $49

Central Business Dist. | Loews | 300 Poydras St. (S. Peters St.) | 504-595-3305 | www.cafeadelaide.com

"Every visit is a pleasant experience" at this "more casual" "cousin to Commander's Palace" in the CBD's Loews hotel, offering "refined" "contemporary Creole" cuisine with the expected "crisp service" of a Brennan family establishment; both "politicos" and posh "dates" frequent the "sophisticated", "inviting" space and often head to the "hoppin'" adjoining Swizzle Stick Bar for "fabulous" postprandial cocktails; N.B. the recent arrival of chef Chris Lusk may not be reflected in the Food score.

Café Amelie Ⓜ *Contemp. Louisiana* — 23 | 25 | 21 | $34

French Quarter | Princess of Monaco | 912 Royal St. (bet. Dumaine & St. Philip Sts.) | 504-412-8965 | www.princessofmonaco.com

French Quarter neighbors adore the "gorgeous carriage-house setting" and "luscious patio" "complete with burbling fountains" and night-blooming jasmine at this Royal Street hideaway cooking up "fresh", "light" and seasonal Contemporary Louisiana dishes; a "prompt", "knowledgeable" staff and "fair" tabs make it an even more tempting "treat"; N.B. closed Monday-Tuesday.

Cafe Atchafalaya Ⓜ *Creole/Southern* — 19 | 20 | 18 | $30

Irish Channel | 901 Louisiana Ave. (Laurel St.) | 504-891-9626 | www.cafeatchafalaya.com

"A bit out of the way but oh-so-worth-it", this long-running Creole-Southern in the Irish Channel serves "traditional but inventive" fare "without all the fuss" of some other New Orleans eateries; it's a "touch on the pricey side" and can have a tough time "handling peak crowds", but its "upgraded" shotgun digs and "unique flair" (especially during the "lively" Sunday brunch) keep customers "coming back for more."

Cafe Beignet *Cajun* — 20 | 16 | 16 | $13

French Quarter | Musical Legends Park | 311 Bourbon St. (Bienville St.) | 504-525-2611
French Quarter | 334B Royal St. (Conti St.) | 504-524-5530
French Quarter | 819 Decatur St. (St. Ann St.) | 504-522-9929
www.cafebeignet.com

"Piping-hot" beignets that "bridge the divide between breakfast and dessert" along with Cajun omelets and sandwiches served all day keep this mini-chain "heavily trafficked" with "out-of-towners and funky French Quarter types" morning to night; though "destined to always be a bridesmaid" to Café Du Monde, many consider it a "quicker", "calmer" alternative and appreciate the "nice courtyard with live music" on weekend nights at the Bourbon Street branch.

Café Degas Ⓜ *French* — 24 | 22 | 21 | $35

Faubourg St. John | 3127 Esplanade Ave. (Ponce de Leon St.) | 504-945-5635 | www.cafedegas.com

At this "popular" Faubourg St. John bistro, the "excellent", "unassuming" Gallic fare showcases "simple flavors done correctly", "taking you

	FOOD	DECOR	SERVICE	COST

back to Paris" as you dine nearly "alfresco" on the "covered porch" that has a "tree growing right through" the roof; staffed by "eclectic", "accommodating" servers (some of whom are "French natives"), it's a "chameleon in dining" that can be "funky" by day and *"très romantique"* at night; N.B. closed Monday–Tuesday.

Cafe DiBlasi ⑤Ⓜ *Italian*   ▽ 21 | 16 | 20 | $27
Terrytown | 1801-4 Stumpf Blvd. (Wright Ave.) | 504-361-3106
"Comforting" Italian food that only makes a "small hit on the wallet" is the main draw of this Terrytown eatery; though the space "could use some work", "personable service" adds to its "family-friendly" feel.

☒ Café Du Monde ●Ⓓ⇌ *Coffeehouse/Dessert*   24 | 16 | 16 | $10
French Quarter | French Mkt. | 800 Decatur St. (St. Ann St.) | 504-525-4544 | www.cafedumonde.com
"You have to be baptized with powdered sugar falling off the beignets to truly have visited NOLA" assert lovers of this 24/7 "landmark" purveyor of "amazing" "crispy puffs of fried dough" paired with chicory coffee that'll "put hair on your chest"; its "open-air" setting across from Jackson Square allows for "wonderful" people-watching, so despite the "surly waiters" and the "stickiest tables in the city", it's a "must for tourists, a tradition for locals and a rendezvous for revelers" – "shame on you if you miss it."

☒ Café East *Chinese*   22 | 26 | 21 | $26
Metairie | 4628 Rye St. (Clearview Pkwy.) | 504-888-0078 | www.cafeeastnola.com
Standing out amid Metairie's "suburban sprawl", this "upscale" Chinese boasts a "beautifully decorated" "modern setting" for dining on "contemporary", "imaginative" Asian cuisine with a number of "light" and "hot" options; since the "attentive" staff delivers "lots for the cost" (especially during the "bargain lunch"), guests call it a "good value" too.

Cafe Giovanni *Italian*   24 | 23 | 24 | $46
French Quarter | 117 Decatur St. (bet. Canal & Iberville Sts.) | 504-529-2154 | www.cafegiovanni.com
"Let chef Duke feed you" say diners delighted by the "inspired" Italian tasting menu offered at this "secret" French Quarter trattoria whose "elegant" space with a "fabulous" bar hosts a live opera singer several nights a week; since the talent is "marvelous", most find the meal "entertaining", even if it's "pricey when you get past the pasta."

Café Granada *Spanish*   ▽ 22 | 18 | 19 | $28
(fka Fiesta Bistro)
Carrollton | 1506 S. Carrollton Ave. (Jeannette St.) | 504-865-1612
"Glad I found it" affirm amigos who've stumbled on this Carrollton tapas bar providing a "nice array" of "enjoyable" Spanish small plates for a "reasonable" bill; pictures of flamenco dancers and matadors adorn the room, which features a live guitarist Tuesdays, Thursdays and Fridays.

Cafe Maspero ⇌ *Po' Boys*   19 | 15 | 16 | $17
French Quarter | 601 Decatur St. (Toulouse St.) | 504-523-6250
"If you can brave" the "long line of tourists", aren't bothered by the "brusque" but brisk service and ignore the "mess-hall atmosphere",

then this cash-only po' boy and sandwich shop offers a "respite" in the French Quarter for "your tired bones"; though many consider it "middle-quality", the plates are "heaped" with "more food than you'll know what to do with", including "loaded" hot muffalettas and "crispy" fried seafood, and the drinks are sold at "Depression-era prices."

Café Minh 🅼 🅼 *French/Vietnamese* | 25 | 20 | 24 | $38 |

Mid-City | 4139 Canal St. (S. Carrollton Ave.) | 504-482-6266

Chef-owner Minh Bui's "clever", "haute takes" on French-Vietnamese dishes and "housemade" desserts "never disappoint" at this Mid-City "gourmet", a "worthy addition to the post-Katrina restaurant scene" decked out in "simple", "minimalist" decor; it's "quiet and comfortable", and at midday the quick, "witty waiters" ensure that lunch is "feasible even for working patrons with time limits."

Cafe Pontalba *Cajun/Creole* | ▽ 18 | 18 | 17 | $24 |

French Quarter | 546 St. Peter St. (Chartres St.) | 504-522-1180

Guests "grab lunch while watching the constant entertainment in Jackson Square" from this Cajun-Creole that "caters to the out-of-towner" with its "prime" location and big windows to "take in the scenery"; the food ranges between "satisfying" ("if you order carefully") and "a bit bland", but wags warn "they want to get you in and out, so don't expect the red-carpet treatment."

Café Rani *Eclectic/Vegetarian* | 20 | 18 | 16 | $22 |

Garden District | 2917 Magazine St. (bet. 6th & 7th Sts.) | 504-895-2500

"Healthy-minded eaters" with a "hankering" for "huge", "amazing" salads among other "different and delectable" Eclectic dishes flock to this "fairly priced" cafe in the Garden District; while the staff can be "slow" and "surly" and the interior is "plain", on "non-humid days" it's "wonderful" to dine on the tree-shaded patio – even if the "fearless" pigeons are a "bit of a nuisance"; N.B. closes at 4 PM Sunday–Monday.

Café Reconcile 🅼 *Southern* | 22 | 14 | 20 | $13 |

Central City | 1631 Oretha Castle Haley Blvd. (Euterpe St.) | 504-568-1157 | www.cafereconcile.com

"Politicians", "Uptown matrons" and "civic activists" are just some of the customers who seek out this lunch-only, "cafeteria-style" Central City cafe where the "earnest", "well-trained" young staff is part of a "splendid" program to "help at-risk youth"; but "don't just eat here because it's good for the soul, it's also good for the belly", serving "ample portions" of "hearty, tasty" Southern cooking that make it one of the "best bargains in the city"; N.B. closed weekends.

Cafe Roma *Pizza* | 20 | 15 | 18 | $17 |

Chalmette | Park Plaza | 3358 Paris Rd. (Josephine St.) | 504-270-0999

Lower Garden Dist. | 1901 Sophie Wright Pl. (St. Mary St.) | 504-524-2419 | www.caferomauptown.com ☕

The pizzas "rarely disappoint" and the other dishes are "basic" but "delish" at these "reliable", separately owned Italians in the Lower Garden District (open till midnight every day) and Chalmette; though the service can be "hit-and-miss", many appreciate the "convenience" and "value."

	FOOD	DECOR	SERVICE	COST

Café Sbisa ⓜ Creole — | — | — | E

French Quarter | 1011 Decatur St. (bet. St. Philip St. & Ursuline Ave.) |
504-522-5565 | www.cafe-sbisa.com

New chef-owner Glen Hogh (Vega Tapas Cafe) takes a welcome big
step with the relaunch of this historic French Quarter landmark
(opened in 1899) whose exposed beams, brick walls, antique mirrors
and grand mahogany bar with artist George Dureau's mural above it
are just as locals remember; taking a playful approach to the past, the
menu offers Hogh's twists on classic Creole dishes augmented by a
number of daily dinner specials; N.B. closed Monday–Tuesday.

Caffe! Caffe! ⓩ Coffeehouse 22 | 16 | 19 | $13

Metairie | 4301 Clearview Pkwy. (W. Esplanade Ave.) |
504-885-4845
Mandeville | 3900 Hwy. 22 (Hwy. 190) | 985-727-4222
www.caffecaffe.com

"Always bustling", these "go-to" coffeehouses on both sides of the lake
in Metairie and Mandeville deliver "terrific" salads and sandwiches as
well as "outstanding" desserts to go with the "great" java; staffed by
"pleasant young" servers, they play host to many a "mother-daughter
meet-up" for "light lunches" that "won't break the wallet."

Camellia Grill American 23 | 17 | 24 | $15

Riverbend | 626 S. Carrollton Ave. (St. Charles Ave.) |
504-309-2679

"Bump knuckles" with the "hip", "bantering" "cast of characters" that
"makes sure orders come out quickly" at this "landmark" Riverbend
diner where "locals rule the roost" (and "stand in line" for a seat); under a new owner who spiffed it up and "brought back the cloth nap-
kins" post-Katrina, it remains a "time warp to 1955", turning out
"classic" American breakfasts ("long live pecan waffles") and a
"cheeseburger and mocha freeze" that some surveyors would "choose
for a death row meal"; P.S. "plastic is now accepted."

Cannon's American/Seafood 16 | 18 | 18 | $28

Uptown | 4141 St. Charles Ave. (Milan St.) | 504-891-3200 |
www.cannonsrestaurants.com

Some visitors admire the "view of St. Charles Avenue and the streetcars rumbling past" from the windows of this "spacious", fairly "inexpensive" Uptown venue that's a sought-out stop "during Carnival"; for
most, however, it's "completely forgettable", serving "nondescript"
American dishes and seafood selections that "don't live up" to the surroundings ("how can you miss with this location? somehow they do"),
leading critics to conclude that dining here is like "coming to New
Orleans and eating at Applebee's."

Carmine's Italian Seafood Grill ⓜ Italian 20 | 17 | 19 | $31

Metairie | 4101 Veterans Memorial Blvd. (Lake Villa Dr.) |
504-455-7904

"Tasty" seafood and "traditional" Italian dishes "topped with that
wonderful red sauce" are prepared at this "neighborhood joint" in
Metairie that's "moderately priced" (even if the specials can get "expensive"); while the room's nautical features lend a "hokey" touch, the
"family-friendly" service helps "make up for the decor."

	FOOD	DECOR	SERVICE	COST

Carreta's Grill *Mexican*

| 19 | 16 | 20 | $18 |

Metairie | 2320 Veterans Memorial Blvd. (I-10) | 504-837-6696 Ⓜ
Slidell | 1340 Lindberg Dr. (Gause Blvd.) | 985-847-0020

At this "reasonable" Metairie Mex (with a Slidell sib) the "typical" fare gets a boost from "top-shelf", *"muy sabrosas"* margaritas that really "make the place"; even if the seating is "close together", it's "bright and colorful" and the "vibe varies nightly", with a somewhat "rowdy young crowd" coming for live music Wednesdays and Fridays, and a wave of "wee ones" in tow for Thursday night magic shows.

Casablanca *Moroccan*

| ▽ 21 | 18 | 20 | $23 |

Metairie | 3030 Severn Ave. (21st St.) | 504-888-2209 | www.koshernola.com

"Take a leap of faith and try" the signature chicken b'steeya pie (accented with saffron and cinnamon) among other "well-prepared" dishes at this kosher Metairie Moroccan with "kitschy" North African decor; it's "slightly expensive", but observant eaters feel "lucky" to have it around; N.B. closed Friday night and Saturday.

Casa Garcia *Mexican*

| 20 | 18 | 20 | $19 |

Metairie | 8814 Veterans Memorial Blvd. (David Dr.) | 504-464-0354

"Free" "fantastic bean dip" ("score!") is just one of the perks at this family-owned Mexican "standby" in Metairie serving "fresh", "relatively authentic" cuisine for a "cost-effective" meal; though the "strip-mall" setting is unremarkable, after-work regulars say it has a "nice ambiance" and "great margaritas" that "make hump day seem like a day to celebrate."

Casamento's Ⓧ Ⓜ ⇄ *Seafood*

| 25 | 17 | 19 | $22 |

Uptown | 4330 Magazine St. (Napoleon Ave.) | 504-895-9761 | www.casamentosrestaurant.com

"Locals" pack this "legendary" Uptown "oyster-rama" because the raw ones are "big, fat and juicy" and the fried ones filling the po' boys are "life-changing"; "dig in your heels and prepare for a long wait", but the "service is a hoot" with "great guys shucking" away in the "squeaky-clean" rooms with glazed "white tile everywhere"; P.S. it closes at 2 PM Tuesday–Wednesday, and sticks loosely to the "'R' month rule", closing every June–September.

CC's Community Coffee House *Coffeehouse*

| 19 | 18 | 20 | $7 |

Central Business Dist. | 228 St. Charles Ave. (Common St.) | 504-566-1859 Ⓢ
Central Business Dist. | 650 Poydras St. (bet. Camp St. & St. Charles Ave.) | 504-586-0278
French Quarter | 505 Decatur St. (St. Louis St.) | 504-962-5603
French Quarter | 941 Royal St. (St. Philip St.) | 504-581-6996
Garden District | Commons Shopping Ctr. | 2917 Magazine St. (bet. 6th & 7th Sts.) | 504-891-2115
Metairie | 3647 Veterans Memorial Blvd. (bet. Division St. & Hessmer Ave.) | 504-454-1200
Metairie | Old Metairie Village Shopping Ctr. | 701 Metairie Rd. (Focis St.) | 504-831-1449
Mid-City | 2800 Esplanade Ave. (N. White St.) | 504-482-9865
NEW Uptown | Loyola University | 6363 St. Charles Ave. (Calhoun St.) | 504-861-3265

(continued)

(continued)

CC's Community Coffee House

Uptown | 900 Jefferson Ave. (Magazine St.) | 504-891-4969
www.ccscoffee.com

It's easy to "support the local market" when the "deluxe joe" is "rich, strong" and "much better quality than Starsomething" say advocates of this Baton Rouge–based chain that also offers "frosty" drinks and "yummy" baked goods, even if a few lament "they don't make muffins like they used to"; staffed by "laid-back baristas who seem to enjoy their work", the branches often "teem with students, which gives them a lively feel."

☑ Central Grocery Company ☒Ⓜ *Sandwiches* | 25 | 14 | 16 | $13

French Quarter | 923 Decatur St. (bet. Dumaine & St. Philip Sts.) | 504-523-1620

The "masterpiece" muffaletta at this "landmark" Italian grocery in the French Quarter "will easily fill two New Orleans residents or four tourists", though the "must-eat" meaty sandwiches (dressed with "incomparable" cracked olive salad) still come with a "huge side of attitude" from the "terse" but "efficient" staff; "don't expect more than a stool at the counter" for comfort, but "on a sunny day" you can take the "wax paper–wrapped treasure" "down to the riverbank and catch a cool breeze."

Chad's Bistro *American* | ▽ 18 | 18 | 20 | $27

Metairie | 3216 W. Esplanade Ave. (N. Causeway Blvd.) | 504-838-9935 | www.chadsbistro.com

Considering its "reasonable prices" for "solid" American fare, some surveyors find this "little-known" white-tablecloth bistro in Metairie a "pleasant surprise"; others, however, claim that it's "not always on target pairing traditional with modern flavors", turning out "mediocre", "inconsistent" meals in a room that's just "not happening."

Charlie's Steak House ☒Ⓜ *Steak* | – | – | – | M

Uptown | 4510 Dryades St. (bet. Cadiz & Jena Sts.) | 504-895-9323 | www.charliessteakhousenola.com

It's back, and locals are thrilled and flocking to this elemental Uptown steakhouse with no menu, just two kinds of steak in different sizes (T-bones are 20, 24 and 28 ounces, filets are 10) with potatoes au gratin, a vegetable or two and the iconic wedge of iceberg salad covered in blue cheese dressing; under new owner Matthew Dwyer (once the restaurant's unofficial bartender), it's still the ticket for hungry folk who know exactly what they want when they walk in.

Chateau Coffee Café *Coffeehouse* | 19 | 14 | 17 | $12

Kenner | 3501 Chateau Blvd. (W. Esplanade Ave.) | 504-465-9444
Lakeview | 139 Robert E. Lee Blvd. (bet. West End Blvd. & Wuerpel St.) | 504-286-1777
Metairie | East Bank Regional Library | 4747 W. Napoleon Ave. (Clearview Pkwy.) | 504-888-0601

This coffeehouse trio balances the caffeine with a "nice variety" of "light", "dependable" breakfast items, sandwiches and pastries that are a "notch above your average cafe" fare; it's "convenient if you're in the 'burbs", though service is often "lacking", and the setting is "rather generic."

	FOOD	DECOR	SERVICE	COST

Chateau du Lac 🅱️Ⓜ️ *French* | 25 | 20 | 22 | $53

Old Metairie | 2037 Metairie Rd. (Atherton Dr.) | Metairie | 504-831-3773 | www.chateaudulacbistro.com

"Genuine French chef" and owner Jacques Saleun offers an "escape" to Paris with his "thoughtfully prepared and presented" bistro dishes ("best escargots in town") at this "treat for Old Metairie", recently relocated from Kenner; with its new, larger digs that are "lovely" for "date night", its "popularity is growing", so it's often "tightly packed" despite the "high" cost.

China Doll 🅱️ *Chinese* | 22 | 16 | 19 | $19

Harvey | 830 Manhattan Blvd. (Westbank Expwy.) | 504-366-1700

A "steady clientele" gets its "Chinese fix" at this Harvey "tradition" for "generous portions" of "consistently good" Cantonese "staples"; while the "worn-out decor" is a downside, the low tabs keep it a neighborhood "favorite."

Churros Café 🅱️ *Coffeehouse/Cuban* | - | - | - | I

Metairie | 3100 Kingman St. (Veterans Memorial Blvd.) | 504-885-6516

This "fun little outpost" in Metairie for "reasonably priced" "Cuban sandwiches, lunch plates" and coffee is also one of the only places in New Orleans for Spanish beignets – its namesake sweets; though humbly decorated, it nonetheless makes you "feel like you've walked into a private club"; N.B. closes at 4 PM Monday–Tuesday.

Ciro's Côté Sud ⬆️ *French* | - | - | - | M

Uptown | 7918 Maple St. (S. Carrollton Ave.) | 504-866-9551 | www.cotesudrestaurant.com

Cozy and welcoming with its stenciled mustard-yellow walls, this 36-seat Uptowner turns out Provençal-inspired bistro fare at moderate prices, along with champagne cocktails and more than a dozen wines by the glass; idle chitchat with French owners Sophie and Ollivier Guiot adds to its charm, and those with offspring can even skip the babysitter – there's brick-oven pizza for the kids; N.B. closed Tuesdays.

🆉 Clancy's 🅱️ *Creole* | 27 | 22 | 25 | $51

Uptown | 6100 Annunciation St. (Webster St.) | 504-895-1111

"You can get lost finding" this "clubby" Uptown "institution" that's "among the last of the haute Creole houses", where "traditional waiters" serve "outstanding" dishes like oysters with Brie and smoked soft-shell crab at upscale but "fair" prices; boasting a "high-octane atmosphere", it plays host to plenty of "back-slapping" among the "old-guard" crowd, and is still the "place where you're most likely to see someone in seersucker."

Clémentine 🅱️Ⓜ️ *Belgian* | ▽ 24 | 20 | 22 | $33

Gretna | 2505 Whitney Ave. (Fredericks St.) | 504-366-3995 | www.bistrogallerie.com

Seekers of "authentic *moules et frites*" and Flemish beer ("watch it, these aren't watered-down domestics") "discover" a piece of "Belgium in their own backyard" at this midrange Gretna "gem"; the "elegant", "mod-Euro" space doubles as an art gallery and the management is "friendly", leading many to label it a "sleeper" that deserves more *amour*.

	FOOD	DECOR	SERVICE	COST

Clover Grill ● *Diner*   21 | 14 | 16 | $13

French Quarter | 900 Bourbon St. (Dumaine St.) | 504-598-1010 | www.clovergrill.com

"Homophobes, head for the hills" because this "gay in a great way" Bourbon Street "greasy spoon" dishing up "cheap", "satisfying" diner grub (such as a "mouthwatering burger" grilled "under a hubcap") always includes a free side of "sass"; if the "flamboyant" staff is "somewhat slow", that's only because they're occupied with an "impromptu floor show" for the "around-the-clock" clientele.

Cochon ⧉ *Cajun*   25 | 22 | 23 | $41

Warehouse District | 930 Tchoupitoulas St. (bet. Andrew Higgins Dr. & S. Diamond St.) | 504-588-2123 | www.cochonrestaurant.com

"The pig has now been perfected!" applaud patrons of this "hot, hot, hot" Warehouse District Cajun where chef/co-owners Donald Link (Herbsaint) and Stephen Stryjewski present "brilliantly prepared", "outrageously flavorful" large and small plates (many out of the wood-burning oven) that are "easy on the wallet"; a "smart", "jovial" staff can tip off curious customers about the "don't-miss moonshine list", while occasional "celebrity sightings" add a "New York vibe" to the "modern", "pseudo-farmhouse" digs.

Coffea Cafe *Coffeehouse*   - | - | - | I

Bywater | 3218 Dauphine St. (bet. Louisa & Piety Sts.) | 504-342-2484

"Cool" and "eclectic", this Bywater coffeehouse with a "pleasant" patio dishes up "fresh, innovative" breakfasts and "tasty" lunches to a "hipster" crowd; though the "tattooed and pierced" staff can be "surly" and "you might have to sit around a little while", since the space hosts "revolving shows by local artists", "there's plenty to look at while you wait."

Coffee Pot *American/Creole*   21 | 19 | 21 | $20

French Quarter | 714 St. Peter St. (bet. Bourbon & Royal Sts.) | 504-524-3500

"Jammin' jambalaya" and other "scrumptious", "fat-drenched" dishes like calas (rice fritters) make it "worth the wait even when the line is around the block" at this "very local" "jewel in the Quarter" for Creole-American eats; not only is it "inexpensive", but you'll walk out with a "smile on your face" after getting the "warmest welcome" from an "honest", "colorful" staff that calls everyone "baby."

Coffee Rani *Diner*   23 | 19 | 19 | $15

Covington | 234A Lee Ln. (Boston St.) | 985-893-6158
Mandeville | 3517 Hwy. 190 (Causeway Blvd.) | 985-674-0560

For a "simple, relaxing" repast, North Shore regulars go for the "wonderful" salads that are "full of toppings", "fresh" sandwiches and "dreamy" desserts at these Covington and Mandeville coffee shops; they're "casual" and "inexpensive", and the counter service is "quick"; N.B. they close at 3 PM on Sundays.

Come Back Inn *American*   19 | 9 | 15 | $12

Kenner | 3826 Williams Blvd. (bet. 38th & 39th Sts.) | 504-443-1623 ⧉
Metairie | 8016 W. Metairie Ave. (David Dr.) | 504-467-9316

"Grandma will think they stole her recipes" at this Metairie "joint" (with a Kenner cousin) plating up American "hometown foods" like "po' boy standards" and "cooked-to-order" fried chicken; it's not much to look at and the service is "just fair", but "low prices" help compensate.

DINING

	FOOD	DECOR	SERVICE	COST

Z Commander's Palace *Creole*   **27 | 28 | 27 | $62**

Garden District | 1403 Washington Ave. (Coliseum St.) | 504-899-8221 |
www.commanderspalace.com

"To be the king", go to this Garden District "palace" for "culinary
masterpieces" that "honor Creole tradition while being creative" at
the same time; once again voted the city's Most Popular restaurant (a
title it held for 17 consecutive years prior to an extended post-Katrina
closure), it's also rated No. 1 for Decor following a "gorgeous" renovation by owners Lally Brennan and Ti Martin; the "old-style" service is
"top-notch" too, and "Sunday jazz brunch in the garden room is a
must"; P.S. try the "quarter-martini lunch if you're on a budget."

Coop's Place ⊘ *Cajun/Southern*   **22 | 11 | 16 | $19**

French Quarter | 1109 Decatur St. (Ursulines Ave.) | 504-525-9053 |
www.coopsplace.net

The "huge chalkboard that graces the old brick wall" lists a full range
of "knockout" Cajun-Southern food like "earthy" rabbit and sausage
jambalaya and fried chicken that "should be world-famous" at this
"funky" French Quarter destination for a "late-night" bite and brew;
sure, it looks like a "dive" and the staff can be "snarky", but it's the
place "where the not-so-elite meet to eat."

Copeland's *Cajun/Creole*   **19 | 18 | 18 | $28**

NEW Jefferson | 1319 W. Esplanade Ave. (bet. Arizona Ave. &
Chateau Blvd.) | 504-617-9146
Harvey | 1700 Lapalco Blvd. (Manhattan Blvd.) | 504-364-1575
Covington | 680 N. Hwy. 190 (I-12) | 985-809-9659
Houma | 1534 Martin Luther King Jr. Blvd. (bet. Enterprise Dr. &
Hollywood Blvd.) | 985-873-9600
www.copelandsofneworleans.com

"Flashy" founder Al Copeland (who also gave the world Popeyes) died
last year, but his eponymous Cajun-Creole "answer to Applebee's"
lives on with a "crazy huge menu" of "formulaic" but "flavorful" platters of "artery-clogging fried food"; samplers say the "service varies"
across the chain and the feel ranges from "overbearing" to "upscale
steakhouse" depending on the location.

Copeland's Cheesecake Bistro *American*   **19 | 18 | 17 | $28**

Lower Garden Dist. | 2001 St. Charles Ave. (St. Andrew St.) |
504-593-9955
Metairie | 4517 Veterans Memorial Blvd. (Clearview Pkwy.) | 504-454-7620
www.copelandscheesecakebistro.com

Some call the American eats "better than anticipated" at these "imitations of the Cheesecake Factory" in Metairie and the Lower Garden
District that "look like cheap Vegas buffets" and sport "menus so long
it takes 45 minutes to decide" which of the "plentiful" plates to order;
others are turned off by the "bland" cooking and "inconsistent" service, but still "pop in" for the "enticing" signature desserts.

NEW Copeland's Social City *American*   **- | - | - | M**
(fka Sweet Fire & Ice)

Metairie | 701 Veterans Memorial Blvd. (Focis St.) | 504-831-3437 |
www.copelandssocialcity.com

Al Copeland, Jr. – son and heir of the Popeyes creator – has recon-
ceived the former home of Sweet Fire & Ice to launch at press time

with a completely different menu of New American dishes crafted into small and large plates served till midnight; with live bands on weekends and a jazz brunch on Sundays, it promises a red hot and social time.

Corky's Ribs & BBQ *BBQ*   19 | 13 | 16 | $18

Metairie | 4243 Veterans Memorial Blvd. (Houma Blvd.) | 504-887-5000 | www.corkysbarbq.com

Gorge on the "foods your cardiologist warned you to go easy on" at this Metairie link of the Memphis-based chain that smokes "sliced and chopped pieces of heaven" hailed by many as the "best BBQ in a non-BBQ town"; though some critics call it merely "decent", with a "worn", "uninviting" look, the "fair price" means it's "always packed with families."

NEW Country Club *American*   ∇ 22 | 23 | 22 | $29

Bywater | 634 Louisa St. (bet. Chartres & Royal Sts.) | 504-945-0742 | www.thecountryclubneworleans.com

Smitten surveyors ask "what's not to love?" about this "tropical"-feeling Bywater newcomer in a pristine "historic" mansion, serving "well-executed" New American dishes for modest tabs; the "breezy front porch makes you feel like a pampered plantation guest" and the "super-sweet and inviting staff makes the meal memorable", though the option of a postprandial "clothing-optional dip" in the club's pool (nightly membership passes are available) is something else that few forget; N.B. the Food score does not reflect a post-Survey chef change.

Country Flame *Cuban/Mexican*   18 | 8 | 14 | $14

French Quarter | 620 Iberville St. (Exchange Pl.) | 504-522-1138

While "most people walk right past" it, this "bare-bones" French Quarter fixture turns out "tasty", "authentic" Cuban food (including "top-notch" sandwiches) supplemented by "ok" Mexican eats that "won't break the bank" or even require a withdrawal; the "working-man" crowd "speaks more Spanish than English", and the "service is quick, though not necessarily with smiles."

Court of Two Sisters *Creole*   20 | 24 | 21 | $44

French Quarter | 613 Royal St. (bet. St. Peter & Toulouse Sts.) | 504-522-7261 | www.courtoftwosisters.com

The daily jazz buffet brunch, abundant with "seafood and salads", is festively "filled with culinary sins" covering the "classic Big Easy style" at this vintage French Quarter Creole whose "picturesque" courtyard continues to draw "loads" of "out-of-towners"; foes consider it "over-priced" "factory food", however, and warn that "locals will mock you for falling for the hype."

☒ Crabby Jack's ☒ *Po' Boys*   26 | 10 | 16 | $15

Jefferson | 428 Jefferson Hwy. (bet. Dakin St. & Knox Rd.) | 504-833-2722

Jefferson's "lunchtime alter-ego" to sib Jacques-Imo's, this "shack" may "look abandoned from the outside" and "spartan" on the inside, but what matters are its "fantastic", "unique" po' boys ("especially the duck") and the "entree specials that would be a steal at twice the price"; expect "counter service and communal tables loaded with New Orleans characters", and if you arrive too late to claim a seat "it's worth eating standing up in the parking lot."

Crazy Johnnie's Steakhouse *Steak*

21	12	19	$24

Metairie | 3520 18th St. (Arnoult Rd.) | 504-887-6641 |
www.crazyjohnnies.net

Beef eaters come to Fat City for the "best cheap steaks in town" ("try the filet mignon po' boy") along with "piled-high potatoes" and "flowing drinks" at this Metairie chophouse; it has a "sports-grill" vibe with "no attempt at decor" and the "utilitarian staff" is "somewhat unrefined", but for many it's "200% improved since the smokers moved outside."

NEW Creole Skillet ⓜ *Contemp. Louisiana*

-	-	-	E

Warehouse District | 200 Julia St. (Fulton St.) | 504-304-6318 |
www.thecreoleskillet.com

A space that once housed a coffeehouse and alternative theater is now this spiffed-up, white-tablecloth Contemporary Louisianian serving up crabmeat cheesecake, redfish Pontchartrain and other homegrown indulgences for Warehouse District neighbors and nearby Convention Center conferees; a mural of a French Quarter balcony scene by artist Federico Salas adds a jazzy touch.

Crêpes à la Cart ⊘ *French*

25	9	17	$9

Uptown | 1039 Broadway St. (bet. Freret & Zimpel Sts.) | 504-866-2362 |
www.crepesalacarts.com

"Luxurious" lunches and "midnight snacks" can be found at this takeout stand "on the edge of Tulane" that prepares "spectacular" "savory and sweet" crêpes the "proper French way"; "meager" seating is a drawback, but the "friendly" service helps "make up for it."

Crescent City Brewhouse *Contemp. Louisiana*

17	19	17	$27

French Quarter | 527 Decatur St. (bet. St. Louis & Toulouse Sts.) |
504-522-0571 | www.crescentcitybrewhouse.com

"Typical New Orleans fare with a flourish", rather than an "earth-shattering dining experience", can be found at this Contemporary Louisiana "riverfront brewpub" whose highlight is the "very good homemade beer"; location is another plus, as the "attractive" "old building" plays host to "locals and tourists" who "sit on the upper porch and watch the action" down on Decatur Street.

Crescent City Steak House ⓜ *Steak*

25	18	22	$42

Mid-City | 1001 N. Broad St. (St. Philip St.) | 504-821-3271 |
www.crescentcitysteaks.com

This "unapologetic carnivore's castle" in a "dicey" section of Mid-City "turns out steaks full of love" and "swimming in butter" that meat mavens say match the quality of competitors "charging a lot more"; an "old-school" staff tends to the "genteel" room and its "private wood-paneled booths", where since the 1930s "many a backroom deal has been made" by the "loyal clientele"; N.B. closed Monday–Tuesday.

Croissant d'Or Patisserie ⊘ *Bakery*

24	17	18	$10

French Quarter | 617 Ursulines Ave. (bet. Chartres & Royal Sts.) |
504-524-4663

"Give me a croissant, a café au lait and a Sunday paper, and I am happy" affirm fans who while away "peaceful mornings" over "amazing" pastries and "savory" bites at this "charming" French Quarter bakery with a "European" feel; set "away from the tourist hubbub", it's a "popular" stop for those in-the-know.

DINING

	FOOD	DECOR	SERVICE	COST

Crystal Room *Creole/French*   `- | - | - | E`
Central Business Dist. | Le Pavillon Hotel | 833 Poydras St. (Baronne St.) |
504-581-3111 | www.lepavillon.com
"The service reminds me of Paris without the condescension" says one
surveyor about this CBD hotel restaurant that serves "delicious" if
"somewhat unimaginative" Creole–New French fare in a "romantic",
century-old room featuring marble floors, a fireplace and high ceilings; its weekday lunch buffet is a signature, and it's also sought out
for "brunch before a Saints game."

Z Cuvée Ⓢ *Continental/Creole*   `26 | 26 | 24 | $61`
Central Business Dist. | St. James Hotel | 322 Magazine St. (bet. Gravier &
Natchez Sts.) | 504-587-9001 | www.restaurantcuvee.com
"Luscious", low-lit decor in a historic building with "exposed-brick
walls" complements chef Bob Iacovone's "exquisite" Continental-
Creole cuisine that "surprises the palate" at this CBD cousin of The
Dakota, making for a "memorable" experience that merits "melting
some plastic"; both the "fantastic" tasting menu (with wine pairings)
and an "elaborate" list of bottles that reads "more like a short novel"
seduce serious sippers, and though a few diners detect a "pretentious" air, many feel "pampered" by the "fine" staff; N.B. lunch served
Wednesday–Thursday only.

Z Cypress Ⓢ Ⓜ *Creole*   `27 | 21 | 25 | $37`
Metairie | 4426 Transcontinental Dr. (W. Esplanade Ave.) | 504-885-6885 |
www.restaurantcypress.com
"A bit out of the way", this "unexpected" sleeper in a Metairie strip mall
boasts the talents of chef/co-owner Stephen Huth, who "really knows
his flavors" and uses "fresh, local ingredients" to craft "fabulous" contemporary Creole food; fans also appreciate the moderate prices,
"funny" staff and "family-friendly" atmosphere, judging it a "jewel"
that could "rival just about any establishment in the city"; P.S. "seating
is limited" and reservations aren't taken, so "get there early."

Z Dakota, The Ⓢ *American/Contemp. Louisiana*   `28 | 24 | 26 | $57`
Covington | 629 N. Hwy. 190 (¼ mi. north of I-12) | 985-892-3712 |
www.thedakotarestaurant.com
From "crab and Brie soup to die for" to game, seafood and some of the
"best steaks on the North Shore", this "long-standing" Covington destination dazzles diners with chef Kim Kringlie's "outstanding" New
American–Contemporary Louisiana fare set off by an "excellent" 600-
bottle wine list and "fabulous" service; despite its "suburban" highway
location, most find the richly toned, flower-filled interior a "sophisticated" setting to indulge in an "expensive", "one-of-a-kind" meal.

NEW Daniel's on the Bayou Ⓢ *Creole/Italian*   `- | - | - | M`
Faubourg St. John | Esplanade at City Pk. | 3443 Esplanade Ave.
(Bayou St. John) | 504-940-5939
Guarded by an imposing apartment building across from the New
Orleans Museum of Art, this new midrange arrival offers an unexpectedly cheerful setting for Creole, Italian and Pan-Latin dishes by
Ecuadorean chef/co-owner Daniel Tobar; the colorful space is a bit of
a squeeze, but customers can wait for a table next door at the even
smaller Bayou Bar.

Dante's Kitchen *Contemp. Louisiana/Creole* | 25 | 21 | 23 | $38 |

Riverbend | 736 Dante St. (River Rd.) | 504-861-3121 |
www.danteskitchen.com

Natives "in-the-know" "love" this "unpretentious" little cottage in the
Riverbend where chef-owner Emanuel Loubier's frequently "changing"
menu of "stellar" Contemporary Louisiana cooking offers "surprising
twists on traditional Creole preparations", matched by "neat specialty
drinks"; "excellent" brunches, a "personable" staff and a "welcoming"
setting with patio dining add to the "festive" feel; N.B. closed Tuesdays.

Deanie's Seafood *Seafood* | 22 | 14 | 20 | $25 |

Bucktown | 1713 Lake Ave. (Plaquemine Ave.) | Metairie | 504-831-4141 | Ⓜ
French Quarter | 841 Iberville St. (bet. Bourbon & Dauphine Sts.) |
504-581-1316
www.deanies.com

It takes about "three hungry adults" to "tackle the seafood platter" at
this "consistent" duo in Bucktown and the French Quarter that provides lots of fried and boiled shellfish "for the money" to "price-
conscious" families and tourists; service is "attentive" despite the
"chainlike" atmosphere, though critics calls the grub "nothing spectacular", with too much that "tastes the same" out of the fryer.

Delachaise, The ⦿ *French* | 22 | 20 | 15 | $28 |

Uptown | 3442 St. Charles Ave. (bet. Delachaise St. & Louisiana Ave.) |
504-895-0858 | www.thedelachaise.com

"Innovative", "delectable small plates" make for "civilized pub grub"
at this Uptown "it bar" where the "late-night" French bistro fare complements a "fantastic" wine list; though some reviewers report "too
much attitude" from the staff and complain about "smoky" surroundings and a "paucity of comfortable dinner seating", many are fond of
the "dark, moody" setting for a "romantic" nightcap; N.B. the Food
score may not reflect the recent departure of chef Chris DeBarr, who
has been replaced by former sous-chef RJ Tsarov.

☒ Dick & Jenny's ☒Ⓜ *Creole/Eclectic* | 26 | 22 | 25 | $41 |

Uptown | 4501 Tchoupitoulas St. (Jena St.) | 504-894-9880 |
www.dickandjennys.com

As irresistible as a "Southern woman's open arms", this "charming",
no-reservations Uptowner offers a "modern take on Crescent City flavors" with its "out-of-this-world" "haute" Creole-Eclectic fare served
by an "engaging", "efficient" staff in a "funky" clapboard cottage; factor in prices that don't "break the bank", and diners "don't mind having
a bottle of wine on the porch" while waiting for a table – a speed bump
many view as part of the "wonderfully New Orleans" experience.

☒ Dickie Brennan's Steakhouse *Steak* | 25 | 25 | 25 | $58 |

French Quarter | 716 Iberville St. (bet. Bourbon & Royal Sts.) | 504-522-2467 |
www.dickiebrennanssteakhouse.com

"Excellent" prime beef paired with "delicious" housemade sauces draw
carnivores to this "upscale" French Quarter steakhouse, "another
Brennan success" where "spectacular" servers "treat you like a VIP";
mavens say the "masculine", "mahogany-and-leather feel" makes you
want to "order a bourbon and talk about the stock market", but steak-
loving "ladies" "enjoy" it too.

DINING

	FOOD	DECOR	SERVICE	COST

DiMartino's Muffulettas *Sandwiches*   `22` `11` `16` `$13`

Algiers | 3900 General de Gaulle Dr. (Holiday Dr.) | 504-367-0227
Marrero | 6641 Westbank Expwy. (Michael St.) | 504-341-4096
Terrytown | 1788 Carol Sue Ave. (Wright Ave.) | 504-392-7589 ⬛
www.dimartinos.com

"Warm", "fantastic muffs" and "sloppy" roast beef po' boys "worth the pounds you put on" are the stars of this suburban "sammich" trio offering a children's menu too ("you'll probably want to steal a few" of your small fry's chicken fingers); despite "fast-food digs" it's a "much better choice than Burger King", so customers with a craving are willing to "make the drive" across the river.

⚡ Domilise's Po-Boys ⬛⊘ *Cajun/Creole*   `26` `11` `18` `$13`

Uptown | 5240 Annunciation St. (Bellecastle St.) | 504-899-9126
"Any shrimp or oyster should be honored to give its life for the best seafood po' boy in town" – though the "dripping" dressed roast beef is equally "renowned" – at this "Uptown shanty" where the "nice ladies" behind the counter have been making these sandwiches "since forever"; it's "pure New Orleans" and utterly "beloved", but some warn you should "bring a good book to read" while you wait in line, or "call ahead for takeout"; N.B. closed Sundays and Thursdays.

Dominique's ⬛Ⓜ *French*   ▽ `25` `24` `23` `$55`

French Quarter | Maison Dupuy | 1001 Toulouse St. (bet. Burgundy & N. Rampart Sts.) | 504-586-8000 | www.dominiquesrestaurant.com
Those who venture to this high-end "secret rendezvous spot" on the "outer edge of the French Quarter" in the Maison Dupuy hotel find "superior", "beautifully presented" New French dishes with a tropical touch by chef Dominique Macquet; the atmosphere is a bit "staid and quiet" for some, but many commend the "good" service and light up at the cotton candy given as "lagniappe" for dessert.

Dong Phuong *Vietnamese*   ▽ `23` `9` `20` `$17`

New Orleans East | 14207 Chef Menteur Hwy. (bet. Alcee Fortier & Michoud Blvds.) | 504-254-0296
"True" Vietnamese cuisine, including phos, cold noodles and sandwiches, as well as Korean BBQ can be had at this "wonderful" New Orleans East eatery that caters to a mainly Asian clientele; don't miss a visit to the attached bakery where the bread and pastries made "all day long" are themselves "worth the trip"; N.B. open till 4 PM, closed Tuesdays.

Don's Seafood Hut *Seafood*   `19` `17` `19` `$25`

Metairie | 4801 Veterans Memorial Blvd. (Harvard Ave.) | 504-889-1550
"Nothing fancy here", just an "old-school" Metairie seafooder (kin to the Lafayette original) with "great fried food", "scrumptious" crabmeat au gratin and "good gumbo" dished up in "chain-type" surroundings; though some sniff it's "run-of-the-mill", the "reasonable" menu, "family atmosphere" and "friendly service" make it a "decent" option for the "'burbs."

Dooky Chase ⬛Ⓜ *Creole/Soul Food*   `24` `19` `22` `$32`

Treme | 2301 Orleans Ave. (Miro St.) | 504-821-0600
After a storied "comeback from Katrina's ravages", this "national treasure" in Treme is once again dispensing chef Leah Chase's "legendary"

FOOD · DECOR · SERVICE · COST

Creole and soul food, including "fine gumbo and fried chicken", to diners who "inhale" it and achieve "nirvana"; the service is "sweet as sweet tea" but a bit "slow", and after 2:30 PM only takeout is available; N.B. closed Saturday–Monday.

Doson's Noodle House ☒ *Chinese/Vietnamese* | 19 | 12 | 16 | $19 |

Mid-City | 135 N. Carrollton Ave. (Iberville St.) | 504-309-7283

"Huge" steaming bowls of "comforting" pho and "addicting" pan-fried noodles scent the air at this Mid-City go-to for "flavorful" Vietnamese and Chinese food that's "better than most" (though some argue it's "more authentic on the West Bank"); it's fairly "cheap", and the room is "basic" but has a "relaxed neighborhood feel."

☒ Drago's ☒ *Seafood* | 25 | 18 | 21 | $35 |

Central Business Dist. | Hilton New Orleans Riverside | 2 Poydras St. (Convention Center Blvd.) | 504-584-3911
Metairie | 3232 N. Arnoult Rd. (bet. 17th & 18th Sts.) | 504-888-9254
www.dragosrestaurant.com

Get the "incredible" "charbroiled ersters" and "don't let them take the plate away" until you've "soaked up every ounce of buttery sauce" scream legions of locals who "line up" for the "destination dish" at this "priced-right", "family-run" seafood house (serving an otherwise "ho-hum" menu); most declare the older Metairie location "tops" and the larger new branch in the CBD's Hilton Riverside "convenient" but "plain vanilla" by comparison.

Dunbar's Creole Cooking ☒ *Creole* | ▽ 25 | 13 | 22 | $14 |

Uptown | Loyola University Broadway Activities Ctr. | 501 Pine St. (Dominican St.) | 504-861-5451

"What a deal!" exclaim diners of the "delicious" fried chicken, greens and other Creole delights at chef Celestine Dunbar's Uptown "labor of love", which relocated to the Loyola campus after Katrina; while the institutional, cafeteria-style setup (open weekdays till 2 PM) is open to both students and drop-ins, many "miss" the dear old digs on Freret Street and "wish she would move back."

Easy Dogs ☒M *Hot Dogs* | ▽ 19 | 18 | 21 | $11 |

Gretna | 307 Huey P. Long Ave. (3rd St.) | 504-367-1001 |
www.neworleanseasydogs.com

An "adorable place to grab a dog" (all-beef dressed with "inventive" toppings), a "cold beer" and a "Hubig's pie à la mode", this Gretna joint brightened with Louisiana folk art is "a hoot", especially on "bingo night"; if you're not a frank fan, there are burgers and "veggie options" too, plus it's "such a fun place that the food doesn't even matter."

Eat M *Southern* | 24 | 21 | 22 | $23 |

French Quarter | 900 Dumaine St. (Dauphine St.) | 504-522-7222 |
www.eatnola.com

"In a quiet corner of the Quarter", this "secret" Southern BYO draws a "hip" crowd of "regulars" with its "contemporary twists on Louisiana favorites" and other "unexpected pairings" (including a "craveable" blue cheese and fig torte) at a "price practically anyone can afford"; the "solid" staff, "tasteful" setting and "see-and-be-seen" brunch complete the "stylish" picture, so "other than the price" (and, say, the crawfish pie) it feels "more NY than NO."

	FOOD	DECOR	SERVICE	COST

Eleven 79 🖪 *Creole/Italian* — 25 | 22 | 23 | $49

Lower Garden Dist. | 1179 Annunciation St. (Calliope St.) |
504-299-1179

It's "like stepping into a scene in *Goodfellas*" at this "sexy little hide-away" with a "happening bar" in the Lower Garden District that lends a real "Rat Pack" mystique to meals of "outstanding" Creole-Italian cuisine, big on garlicky pastas and "veal, veal and more veal"; it's staffed by "people who know what they're doing" and "go the extra mile", adding to the "old-world charm"; N.B. the Food score may not reflect a recent chef change.

El Gato Negro *Mexican* — 21 | 14 | 18 | $19

French Quarter | 81 French Market Pl. (Barracks St.) | 504-525-9752 |
www.elgatonegronola.com

A "welcome newcomer" that's part of the "changing social landscape post-Katrina", this "standout" "right across from the French Market" provides "authentic" Mexican food made with "upscale ingredients" and "unique" drinks boasting "fresh-squeezed juices"; it's "simple" and "cute" in a small converted warehouse space, and the "hands-on owner really sells" it, ensuring "friendly" service and "reasonable" prices.

Elizabeth's 🖾 *Diner* — 24 | 14 | 19 | $20

Bywater | 601 Gallier St. (Chartres St.) | 504-944-9272 |
www.elizabeths-restaurant.com

Guests "get out of bed on Sundays" for the "divine" praline bacon and other "expertly prepared" Southern diner eats dished up in "gargantuan portions" at this "cheap" "Bywater baby" set in a "funky" "old house" within spitting distance of the Mississippi River; though a few find the service "lacking", many say the "quirky" "tattooed staff" makes them feel right "at home."

🖪 Emeril's *Contemp. Louisiana* — 25 | 25 | 25 | $62

Warehouse District | 800 Tchoupitoulas St. (Julia St.) | 504-528-9393 |
www.emerils.com

"Mega-star" Emeril Lagasse "demonstrates why he's a household name" at this Warehouse District "culinary flagship" that still makes die-hard fans shout "solid gold bam, baby!" when they fork up "magnificent", "spicy" New Orleans–style dishes and signature "banana cream pie that screams Mardi Gras every night"; "upscale" comfort and "decadent" service ("a waiter on each side of you") thrill most, but some say "bring your earplugs" and prepare for "expense-account" prices; P.S. sit at the chef's bar to watch the "kitchen in action."

🖪 Emeril's Delmonico *Creole* — 26 | 26 | 25 | $64

Lower Garden Dist. | 1300 St. Charles Ave. (Erato St.) | 504-525-4937 |
www.emerils.com

"More intimate" and "elegant" than Emeril Lagasse's original venue, but still "over-the-top", this richly appointed Lower Garden District locale (first opened as Delmonico in 1895) showcases "tantalizing" contemporary Creole cuisine and "can't-miss" steaks matched by "superior" wines from the 8,500-bottle cellar; commending the "superb" staff, most call it a "fine place" to "celebrate", especially if "someone else is paying."

	FOOD	DECOR	SERVICE	COST

Ernst Cafe ◐ *American*
16 | 16 | 18 | $20

Warehouse District | 600 S. Peters St. (Lafayette St.) | 504-525-8544 | www.ernstcafe.net

"When you need something to soak up the alcohol", this "decent bar" in the Warehouse District hits the spot with its "not-bad" burger and other American grub served till 4 AM most nights; it's "festive and charming" with "friendly" service and some of the original 1902 decor intact, but many feel "you can do better" for food.

Etoile *American/French*
22 | 24 | 21 | $35

Covington | 407 N. Columbia St. (E. Gibson St.) | 985-892-4578

"People with an arty side on the North Shore" appreciate this "feast for the eyes and the stomach" owned by painter James Michalopoulos, whose colorful work decorates the "sparkling" space in Downtown Covington; with "creative", "semi-high-priced" French–New American bistro fare complemented by an "outstanding" wine list, it makes for a "nice night out"; N.B. closes at 3 PM Sunday–Monday.

Fausto's Bistro ⊠ *Italian*
22 | 15 | 19 | $28

(aka Fausto's Kitchen)

Metairie | 530 Veterans Memorial Blvd. (bet. Aris & Nursery Aves.) | 504-833-7121 | www.faustosbistro.com

"Always full of happy patrons", this "bustling" Metairie trattoria gets lots of "love" for its "garlicky" Sicilian and Northern Italian dishes that "soothe" the soul; though it's a bit of a "dive" inside, regulars appreciate the "low" cost and a staff that's "there for life", serving up "no surprises", just "consistent" cuisine.

Fazzio's ⊠ *Italian*
▽ 20 | 15 | 17 | $24

Mandeville | 1841 N. Causeway Blvd. (Rte. 109) | 985-624-9704

Big plates of "very good" steaks, seafood and pastas for "bargain" prices make this "old-fashioned" Mandeville Italian a lunchtime "hot spot" and a big hit with the North Shore "happy-hour" crowd; though some find it just "ho-hum", many feel it "holds its own" against the competition.

Feelings Cafe Ⓜ *American/Creole*
21 | 24 | 22 | $37

Faubourg Marigny | 2600 Chartres St. (Franklin Ave.) | 504-945-2222 | www.feelingscafe.com

The "cheesy name" mystifies, but the "gorgeous" courtyard and "real-deal" piano bar answer the question "how romantic can it get?" at this "delightful" "secret" "tucked away" in a historic Marigny house; most consider the Creole-American food "delicious" if somewhat "uneven" and the service "fabulous", making it a natural when you want to "stay late" and "woo someone"; N.B. closed Monday–Wednesday.

Felipe's Taqueria *Mexican*
- | - | - | I

NEW French Quarter | 301 N. Peters St. (Bienville St.) | 504-267-4406

Uptown | 6215 S. Miro St. (Calhoun St.) | 504-309-2776 www.felipesneworleans.com

Uptown university students and now budget-minded French Quarter fans dig into the burritos, quesadillas and tacos at this vibrant fast-food twosome; touches like fresh salsas and mix-free margaritas lend it more zing than the typical Mex chain.

	FOOD	DECOR	SERVICE	COST

Felix's Oyster Bar *Creole/Seafood*

-	-	-	I

French Quarter | 739 Iberville St. (Bourbon St.) | 504-522-4440 |
www.felixs.com

The French Quarter's famous oyster bar is back up and running for
mollusk mavens looking for the freshest, briniest raws, along with
other Creole seafood, served in a brightly lit, crowded room; for the
full experience, belly up to the marble counter and down a dozen while
gabbing with the sure-handed shuckers.

Fellini's *Italian/Mediterranean*

20	14	17	$18

Mid-City | 900 N. Carrollton Ave. (Dumaine St.) | 504-488-2147

"Sit outside and watch the streetcars" at this "easygoing" Mid-City
Med-Italian offering an "eclectic" menu of "pleasantly surprising"
gourmet pizzas, salads and lavosh wraps to a "casual" crowd; while
it's "not as adventurous as its namesake" and a bit "sparse" in appearance, the affordable, "filling" dishes keep it "popular."

Fiesta Latina *Pan-Latin*

-	-	-	I

Kenner | 1924 Airline Dr. (bet. Daniel & Minor Sts.) | 504-469-5792 |
www.fiestalatinarestaurant.com

"Everything is great" at this "authentic" Kenner eatery "near the air-
port" serving morning-to-night Pan-Latin food – mainly Mexican and
Central American – to "Katrina construction workers" among a strong
Hispanic clientele; it's easy on the "budget", but it does help to "know
Spanish", at least if you want to follow what's on TV.

Fiorella's Café *Creole/Soul Food*

21	11	15	$16

French Quarter | 1136 Decatur St. (bet. Governor Nicholls St. &
Ursuline Ave.) | 504-528-9566

"Claim-to-fame" fried chicken, "to-die-for" banana pudding and other
"local foodstuffs" make this "laid-back" Creole soul food kitchen a
"French Quarter classic that must be experienced" even if it's a
"dump"; though a few feel "Katrina has taken its toll" on the quality
and service, most declare it's still one of the "best deals" around when
you're in the mood for "mama's cooking."

Fire of Brazil *Brazilian/Steak*

21	21	23	$45

French Quarter | 725 Iberville St. (bet. Bourbon & Royal Sts.) | 504-552-4446 |
www.fireofbrazil.com

"Carnivores unite" at this all-you-can-eat Brazilian steakhouse in
the French Quarter dishing up a "phenomenal" feast of sirloin, ribs
and other red meat "of sufficient grade to warrant gluttony", supplemented by a "noteworthy" salad bar; with "accommodating"
service (signaled by flipping a red/green card) and a "sizzling" atmosphere, it makes for a "memorable evening out."

Five Happiness *Chinese*

22	21	21	$22

Carrollton | 3605 S. Carrollton Ave. (Palm St.) | 504-482-3935 |
www.fivehappiness.com

In a town "not overly blessed with Chinese restaurants", this "quality"
Carrollton Sichuan is "always a favorite", presenting a "huge" selection of "flavorful" "traditional Americanized" dishes "done right";
many commend its "chic", "high-end" remodel and service that suits a
"nice evening out" – while stay-at-home types add that "if you're too
lazy to go they'll bring it to your door in record time."

	FOOD	DECOR	SERVICE	COST

Flaming Torch, The *Continental/French*
23 | 21 | 23 | $41

Uptown | 737 Octavia St. (bet. Constance & Magazine Sts.) | 504-895-0900 | www.flamingtorchnola.com

"Sublime" onion soup, "fragrant" coq au vin and other French-Continental specialties star on the "well-honed" menu at this "upscale" bistro "nestled near Magazine Street", whose "charming" dining room is lit by "fabulous" faux torches; with its "intimate" ambiance and "excellent" service, it attracts "Uptown couples young and old" for "romantic" tête-à-têtes.

Franky & Johnny's ⊠ *Cajun*
20 | 10 | 17 | $21

Uptown | 321 Arabella St. (bet. Annunciation & Tchoupitoulas Sts.) | 504-899-9146 | www.frankyandjohnnys.com

"There's no denying it's a dive", but this Uptown Cajun proffers "quintessential New Orleans fried goodness" in the form of "terrific po' boys and "crave"-worthy green pepper rings along with boiled seafood washed down with "cold Abitas"; sure, its red-and-white checked-tablecloth decor "could be improved", but the old-time jukebox and "real *y'at* service" make up for the fact that the "five-second rule" on eating food that's fallen on the floor "definitely will not work here"; N.B. open Sundays during Saints games, Jazz Fest and Mardi Gras.

Fresco Cafe *Mediterranean/Pizza*
▽ 19 | 15 | 17 | $17

Uptown | 7625 Maple St. (Adams St.) | 504-862-6363 | www.frescocafe.us

"Better-than-average" pizzas, lavosh rolls and other Mediterranean eats swell the "eclectic" menu at this "cute little" Uptown cafe frequented by the "campus" crowd and others in need of "cheap" sustenance and $3 pitchers of beer (served Monday–Wednesday); it's convenient for a "late-night" bite (till midnight on the weekends), though some say the quality of service "depends on your luck."

Frosty's Caffe ⊠ *Vietnamese*
▽ 25 | 10 | 19 | $11

Metairie | 3400 Cleary Ave. (bet. Marion St. & Veterans Blvd.) | 504-888-9600
Harvey | 2800 Manhattan Blvd. (Lapalco Blvd.) | 504-361-9099

"Fresh" Vietnamese food and the "best bubble tea ever" in "unusual flavors" are a "steal for lunch" at this Metairie coffee shop (with a Harvey sib) housed in "claustrophobic" digs; fans only wish that it had "more space" and stayed open later at night.

Fury's ⊠ *Creole/Italian*
23 | 12 | 20 | $24

Metairie | 724 Martin Behrman Ave. (Veterans Memorial Blvd.) | 504-834-5646

"Down-home" Creole-Italian dishes, including "cooked-to-order seafood and fried chicken", make up the "simple, straightforward" meals at this "dependable" Metairie mainstay; "old-style service" and "value" keep it "popular" with the "65-plus" set, so go early as "tables are tight."

☑ Galatoire's Ⓜ *Creole/French*
27 | 25 | 27 | $58

French Quarter | 209 Bourbon St. (Iberville St.) | 504-525-2021 | www.galatoires.com

"It's not just a restaurant, it's an experience" effuse fans of this "cherished New Orleans tradition", a French Quarter "temple" of "superlative" Creole-French fare (especially seafood) served by "impeccable" waiters who look like they "stepped out of a painting"; so "dress your best" and "head over early for Friday lunch" – when local blue bloods feast and "get smashed" in the "classy" mirrored dining room downstairs, often carousing "till dinner" – or Sunday brunch among "beautiful ladies" and "gentlemen who looked like they enjoyed putting on a tie"; N.B. jackets required after 5 PM and on Sundays.

Galley ☒Ⓜ Po' Boys/Seafood
24 | 11 | 18 | $24

Old Metairie | 2535 Metairie Rd. (bet. Avalon Way & Labarre Dr.) | Metairie | 504-832-0955

Families of hungry swabbies pour into this "roadside" "joint" in Old Metairie for "deliciously seasoned" "gigantic" boiled shrimp and "awesome fried fare" including the soft-shell crab po' boy that's a Jazz Fest "hit"; "long waits" for "jammed tables" are a drawback, but unfazed fans say the "feisty" staff "makes a party out of every outing."

☒ Gautreau's ☒ American/French
28 | 24 | 26 | $54

Uptown | 1728 Soniat St. (Danneel St.) | 504-899-7397 | www.gautreausrestaurant.com

"Exquisite", "adventuresome" New American–New French dishes created by "up-and-coming" chef Sue Zemanick and served by an "outstanding" staff keep natives returning to this "old Uptown favorite", a "rarified" retreat "hidden" in a residential neighborhood with "no sign" out front; post-K, proprietor Patrick Singley gave the "civilized" converted-drugstore setting a face-lift by re-creating the "original hammered tin ceiling" and adding trompe l'oeil walls with a draping effect, so it feels as if you're dining "inside a very decadent tent."

GB's Patio Bar & Grill American
17 | 13 | 17 | $17

Riverbend | 8117 Maple St. (bet. Dublin St. & S. Carrollton Ave.) | 504-861-0067

"Tasty" burgers, "loaded baked potatoes" and "alfresco" seating "steps away from the streetcar route" make this Riverbend "standby" a "comfy" "college hangout"; "homemade" desserts are tempting too, and though it's "not perfect", it always "pleases the pocketbook."

Gelato Pazzo Caffè Ⓜ Italian
▽ 25 | 17 | 18 | $14

Carrollton | 8115 Oak St. (S. Carrollton Ave.) | 504-304-6908 | www.gelatopazzo.com

"The gelato is great but the panini are the bomb" at this family-owned Carrollton cafe that's a prime place to "sample Italy's best"; while some enthusiasts simply drop in for their espresso fix, "interesting, colorful" decor and a private room in back add to its appeal for parties.

NEW Gimchi Japanese/Korean
▽ 19 | 21 | 21 | $29

Metairie | 3322 N. Turnbull Dr. (Veterans Memorial Blvd.) | 504-454-6426

"Killer" Korean cuisine, including "grill-it-yourself" BBQ that "kids over the age of five will love", heads up the menu at this Metairie newcomer from the owners of Mikimoto that also satisfies with "good" sushi; some samplers find the offerings a bit "average", but agree that it "fills a void" in a city short on bulgogi.

Gordon Biersch ● American
16 | 17 | 16 | $25

Central Business Dist. | 200 Poydras St. (Convention Center Blvd.) | 504-552-2739 | www.gordonbiersch.com

"Beer is the star" of this "upbeat" brewpub chain link in the CBD where the "standard" American grub plays second fiddle to the suds (though aficionados say the "to-die-for garlic fries" are the thing to order); the "loud" volume doesn't seem to faze its "rollicking" "frat-boy" following.

NEW Gott Gourmet Café *Contemp. Louisiana*
‒ | ‒ | ‒ | I

Garden District | 3100 Magazine St. (bet. Louisiana & Washington Aves.) | 504-373-6579 | www.gottgourmetcafe.com

At this brand-new Garden District corner cafe, former caterer David Gotter brings his high-end ingredients to the public with a Contemporary Louisiana menu of sandwiches, salads and sides; the upbeat, contemporary interior has green leanings – all take-out containers are made from renewable sources – and while no alcohol is served, you can BYO for a $5 corkage fee.

Grand Isle *Creole*
19 | 22 | 19 | $35

Warehouse District | 575 Convention Center Blvd. (bet. Girod & Poydras Sts.) | 504-520-8530 | www.grandislerestaurant.com

The upscale fish-camp decor makes for a "pleasant atmosphere" at this Creole arrival near the Convention Center by co-owner Joel Dondis (La Petite Grocery, Sucré) whose "high-quality" fish with a "real Southern kick" "adds refinement to the seafood boil"; still, some critics complain of being given the "tourist treatment", citing "hit-or-miss" dishes, inconsistent service and slightly "overpriced" tabs.

Great Wall ⊠ *Chinese*
∇ 22 | 16 | 25 | $17

Old Metairie | 2023 Metairie Rd. (bet. Atherton Dr. & Helios Ave.) | Metairie | 504-833-2585

"They treat you like family" at this "off-the-beaten-path" Old Metairie Chinese turning out a "great variety" of "well-prepared" Mandarin and Sichuan staples; everything is "low-cost" and "ready when promised", making it "perfect" for takeout.

Grocery, The ⊠ *Contemp. Louisiana*
‒ | ‒ | ‒ | I

Garden District | 2854 St. Charles Ave. (6th St.) | 504-895-9524 | www.thegroceryneworleans.com

There are racks of chips on the counter next to a blackboard announcing the price of brownies and cookies at this down-home corner sandwich shop, a Garden District go-to for pressed po' boys, muffalettas, gumbo and other Contemporary Louisiana lunchtime goods; set in a former pharmacy, it has high pressed-tin ceilings and a smattering of outdoor tables ideal for watching the streetcar rumble by.

Gumbo Shop *Creole*
21 | 18 | 19 | $25

French Quarter | 630 St. Peter St. (bet. Chartres & Royal Sts.) | 504-525-1486 | www.gumboshop.com

Dubbed the "Baskin Robbins of gumbo", this French Quarter Creole offers "numerous" "gratifying" varieties of its namesake soup along with "authentic" renditions of NOLA staples (including the "best red beans and rice") for a "good value"; though its central location "near St. Louis Cathedral" means "long lines" of "tourists", even "proud" locals like feasting on the "comforting" grub in the "lovely" courtyard.

⊠ GW Fins *Seafood*
26 | 25 | 25 | $53

French Quarter | 808 Bienville St. (bet. Bourbon & Dauphine Sts.) | 504-581-3467 | www.gwfins.com

From "lobster dumplings you'll remember the rest of your days" to "fin-tastic", "fanatically" "fresh" fish of many sorts, this "suave", "top-flight" French Quarter seafood house has diners praising its "dyna-mite" cooking that's "nontraditional" for New Orleans but "always in-teresting" (and accompanied by "delicious" biscuits "right out of the oven"); though many find the "relaxed" setting "romantic", a few de-tect a "fern-bar feel" and complain that though it's "a stone's through from Bourbon Street", "it could be anywhere."

Hana Japanese *Japanese*   21 | 14 | 19 | $25
Riverbend | 8116 Hampson St. (bet. Dublin St. & S. Carrollton Ave.) | 504-865-1634
Fin fans praise the "artistic" sushi and give a "low bow" to the shrimp tempura at this "easy" Riverbend Japanese where a "friendly", "calm" atmosphere prevails; even if some call it "just ok", with "little" in the way of "frills", the "inexpensive" menu nevertheless ensures a "great crowd."

☑ Hansen's Sno-Bliz Ⓜ🖝 *Dessert*   28 | 14 | 22 | $5
Uptown | 4801 Tchoupitoulas St. (Bordeaux St.) | 504-891-9788 | www.snobliz.com
"The legend continues" in third-generation Hansen hands at this Uptown "marvel" (voted the city's top Bang for the Buck) where the "fluffy shaved ice", "lovingly poured" "not-too-sweet" "homemade" syrups ("try the nectar cream") and other toppings combine to make "a miracle of taste and texture", aka "the best sno-balls in the known universe"; so don't be afraid to "stand in line", dawlin', and wait for your "little slice of true New Orleans culcha"; N.B. hours are seasonal, so call ahead.

Harbor Seafood & Oyster Bar *Seafood*   24 | 12 | 18 | $21
Kenner | 3203 Williams Blvd. (32nd St.) | 504-443-6454
Bivalve buffs swoon over this "classic" Kenner "hole-in-the-wall" with its "tremendous oyster po' boys", "excellent gumbo" and other "sim-ple", market-fresh boiled and fried fare that's "cooked consistently well"; other pluses are the "good value" and proximity to the airport, making it tempting for a seafood fix "one last time" before winging it out of the Big Easy.

Hard Rock Cafe *American*   13 | 21 | 16 | $28
French Quarter | 418 N. Peters St. (St. Louis St.) | 504-529-5617 | www.hardrock.com
It's "just like any other Hard Rock Cafe, but the T-shirts say 'New Orleans'" at this French Quarter link in the rock 'n' roll-themed American chain, turning out "mundane" grub, "haphazard" service and "way too loud" acoustics; still, defenders give it a nod for "surprisingly decent burgers", "chatty" bartenders and all that "fun music memorabilia."

☑ Herbsaint ⊠ *American/French*   26 | 22 | 24 | $50
Warehouse District | 701 St. Charles Ave. (Girod St.) | 504-524-4114 | www.herbsaint.com
"Love it!" is still the word on this "brilliant" New American–New French bistro in the Warehouse District where "big-time" chef/co-owner Donald Link continues to coax "amazing flavors" from "local" ingredients in his "sophisticated" take on Big Easy cuisine; among the highlights are "wonderful", "well-priced" small plates and cocktails (including the "best" Sazerac), "courteous" service and a "clean, refreshing" setting with a "wall of windows" where you "see the streetcar go by", all add-ing up to a "real winner."

	FOOD	DECOR	SERVICE	COST

Hillbilly BBQ 🈂️Ⓜ️ *BBQ*   `23` `7` `15` `$15`

River Ridge | 208 Tullulah Ave. (Jefferson Hwy.) | 504-738-1508 | www.hillbillybbq.com

Smokaholics keep this "out-of-the-way" River Ridge "joint" "crowded" thanks to the skills of pit masters Kelly Moskaw and Larry Wyatt, who turn out "juicy", "Kentucky-style", hickory-smoked BBQ with "homemade" sauces and "spicy" sides; though the "family"-run service lends it extra "charm", it's "not much to look at", so lots of customers opt for "takeout."

Hipstix 🈂️ *Asian Fusion*   `21` `18` `19` `$25`

Warehouse District | 870 Tchoupitoulas St. (St. Joseph St.) | 504-581-2858

"Scrumptious" Pan-Asian offerings with a "street"-food bent and a touch of Louisiana fusion lure a "young crowd" to this "cool" Warehouse District hangout with an "upscale" look; though some think the "Top 40 music gets old", the "fantastic" drinks fuel a "fun" scene.

Horinoya 🈂️ *Japanese*   `24` `18` `21` `$35`

Central Business Dist. | 920 Poydras St. (bet. Baronne St. & O'Keefe Ave.) | 504-561-8914

A menu of "inventive" sushi and other dishes "you won't find anywhere else" make this "attentively" tended CBD Japanese an "oasis in a city of fried food"; its location within walking distance of "most of the city's skyscrapers" draws a big "lunch crowd", though some critics complain it's a bit "cramped" and on the "expensive" side for what it delivers.

🆕 Hoshun ⬤ *Chinese/Japanese*   `▽` `23` `23` `20` `$29`

Lower Garden Dist. | 1601 St. Charles Ave. (Terpsichore St.) | 504-302-9716

"Fresh" sushi and Chinese and Thai plates that "you can eat before or after you go out" make this late-night, two-floor newcomer a "creative" midrange addition to the Lower Garden District; though some think it's "still finding its way", with "too many cuisines" and "mixed" service, most are impressed by its "beautiful" art deco look and "knock-your-socks-off" flavor combos.

🆕 Hostel New Orleans 🈂️Ⓜ️ *French*   `-` `-` `-` `E`

French Quarter | 329 Decatur St. (Bienville Ave.) | 504-587-0036 | www.hostelnola.com

This is no place for backpackers since chef Richard Richardson (ex Arnaud's and Dakota) prepares French fare for a price at this French Quarter yearling where housemade pâtés and desserts, along with delicacies delivered daily from St. James Cheese Company, add a savvy touch; the rustic, high-ceilinged surroundings are decked out with couches and a columned antique bar, inviting guests to stop in for drinks as well as full Gallic feasts.

Houston's *American*   `22` `20` `21` `$32`
(fka Gulfstream St. Charles)

Lower Garden Dist. | 1755 St. Charles Ave. (Felicity St.) | 504-524-1578
Metairie | 4241 Veterans Memorial Blvd. (Clearview Pkwy.) | 504-889-2301
www.hillstone.com

"Popular" and "reliable", this national franchise with branches in the Lower Garden District and Metairie "clicks" thanks to its menu of "all-American comfort" items (including a notoriously "addicting spinach dip") and a "modern metropolitan" ambiance that brings in "mingling singles" after work; despite debate on the cost – "inexpensive" vs. "overpriced" – most report "solid quality" here.

Ignatius Eatery Creole/Po' Boys

21 | 17 | 19 | $18

Uptown | 4200 Magazine St. (Milan St.) | 504-896-2225

From "excellent" crawfish étouffée to an "incredible" roast beef po' boy on the "correct bread" to the bottle of "Abita in a brown paper bag", this "clever" Uptowner takes you on a "culinary tour of all New Orleans in a nutshell" inside a replicated "old-time grocery" that already "feels as if it's been here forever"; some gripe it's "trying too hard to be quaint", but it's still a "nice spot to grab a bite" when you're shopping on Magazine; N.B. closed Tuesdays.

NEW Il Posto Café ⓜ Italian

▽ 24 | 21 | 23 | $16

Uptown | 4607 Dryades St. (Cadiz St.) | 504-895-2620

The "freshest ingredients" go into chef-owner Madison Curry's "delicious" panini and other "lovely", "upscale" Italian bites at this "super-cute" new cafe on a "quiet" Uptown block; "excellent coffee" and "H&H bagels for breakfast" plus "hard-to-find-wines at fair prices" are extra perks.

Impastato's ⓢⓜ Creole/Italian

23 | 20 | 22 | $38

Metairie | 3400 16th St. (bet. N. Hullen St. & Severn Ave.) | 504-455-1545 | www.impastatos.com

"Loosen your belt" for "ginormous portions" of Creole-Italian dishes at this "well-priced" Metairie "throwback" known for "fabulous" pecan-smoked filet mignon and "addictive" pastas; chef-owner Joe Impastato and his "great" staff keep it hopping while a nightly singer adds retro "'50s-style ambiance", and though it's closed most Sundays, it stays open during Saints games ("Mr. Joe is a huge fan").

Imperial Garden ⓢ Chinese

- | - | - | M

Kenner | 3331 Williams Blvd. (bet. 33rd & 34th Sts.) | 504-443-5691

Yes, it's in one of the endless strip malls along a dreary stretch out in the 'burbs near the airport, but if the quest for authentic Sino specialties is your thing, this Kenner Chinese is the place to treat your palate to dishes of meat-filled dumplings and shrimp and pecans; a friendly staff and swift service make up for a distinct lack of ambiance.

Irene's Cuisine ⓢ Italian

26 | 22 | 24 | $44

French Quarter | 539 St. Philip St. (bet. Chartres & Decatur Sts.) | 504-529-8811

"Unsurpassed" Southern Italian food awaits at this "intimate", "convivial" French Quarter "standout" where "overwhelmingly fabulous", "garlicky" smells cause a line to start forming "at 4 PM" (reservations are limited); "tremendous", "hospitable" service and fairly "moderate" tabs clinch the deal, so add your name to the list and be prepared to "have a drink or 12" while you steep in the "funky" ambiance at the "rockin' piano bar."

Iris ⓢ American

25 | - | 22 | $46

French Quarter | Bienville House | 321 N. Peters St. (bet. Bienville & Conti Sts.) | 504-299-3944 | www.irisneworleans.com

Having moved in fall 2008 from its former Carrollton digs to a larger space in the French Quarter's Bienville House, this "splendid" New

	FOOD	DECOR	SERVICE	COST

American "marvel" is a "sleeper hit" thanks to dishes by chef Ian Schnoebelen (ex Lilette) that are both "pristine" and "cutting-edge", and matched by "creative" cocktails and "well-selected" wines; a "full-of-personality" staff rounds out the "coolly" "upscale" meal.

Islas Roatan Bar & Grill Ⓜ *Honduran*

–	–	–	I

Mid-City | 2501 Canal St. (Carrollton Ave.) | 504-826-5690

What previously housed a simple Brazilian churrascaria is now an equally affordable Honduran corner bar and grill in Mid-City, serving both familiar and unusual Latin dishes for hungry working folk at lunch and neighborhood families in the evening; weekends bring out those who like to dine and dance under the rotating glitter ball, as live bands play and the adjacent bar stays open till the wee hours of the morning.

NEW Italian Barrel Ⓜ *Italian*

–	–	–	M

French Quarter | 430 Barracks St. (bet. Decatur St. & French Market Pl.) | 504-569-0198

Verona native Samantha Castagnetti returned to her mother's hometown to open her own *piccola* trattoria near the French Market, cooking up pastas, panini and crostini with ingredients overnighted from Italy; it's small, simple and candlelit inside, with a few sidewalk tables as well, and plans are afoot to create a private room for two.

Italian Pie *Pizza*

17	10	14	$14

Central Business Dist. | 417 S. Rampart St. (Perdido St.) | 504-522-7552 🖾
Jefferson | 5650 Jefferson Hwy. (Edwards Ave.) | 504-734-3333
Kenner | 3600 Williams Blvd. (W. Esplanade Ave.) | 504-469-4999
Metairie | 5406 Veterans Memorial Blvd. (Green Acres Rd.) | 504-887-9977
Metairie | 901 Veterans Memorial Blvd. (Oaklawn Dr.) | 504-832-1121
Mid-City | 4840 Bienville Ave. (N. Anthony St.) | 504-483-9949
Harvey | 1530 Lapalco Blvd. (Manhattan Blvd.) | 504-362-3657
Mandeville | 4350 Hwy. 22 (N. Causeway Blvd.) | 985-626-5252
Slidell | 1319 Gause Blvd. (Eastridge Dr.) | 985-661-0240
www.italianpierestaurants.com

"Cheap", "reliable" pizzas and other "filling" Italian eats "get the job done" even if there's "nothing spectacular" about this Southern chain; due to "subpar" service and some branches with "dingy" digs, it's "not necessarily a pleasant in-house experience", but delivery devotees say "they can bring it to my house anytime."

Jack Dempsey's 🖾Ⓜ *Seafood*

19	13	19	$26

Bywater | 738 Poland Ave. (bet. Dauphine & Royal Sts.) | 504-943-9914

"Soak up" the deep-fried "culcha" at this "treasured" Bywater anachronism, a humble little "hideaway" where the "most generous seafood platter to be found" pleases plenty of loyalists; still, the service is merely "no nonsense", leaving some visitors feeling "ignored", and a few find the food "pretty average" besides.

⧉ Jacques-Imo's Café 🖾 *Creole/Soul Food*

26	21	22	$38

Carrollton | 8324 Oak St. (bet. Cambronne & Dante Sts.) | 504-861-0886 | www.jacquesimoscafe.com

Chef-owner Jack Leonardi may swan around this "always crowded" and "convivial" Carrollton "hole-in-the-wall" in a "chef's coat and fancy boxer shorts", but make no mistake, his "scrumptious" Creole soul food – from "slammin'" alligator cheesecake to "heaven-on-a-plate" fried chicken – is "as good as any in town"; "plenty of food for the price" and "quirky", "backwoods-eclectic" decor help offset the "insane waits", adding up to a "unique" dining experience "you're unlikely to forget"; N.B. reservations accepted for five or more.

NEW Jager Haus German

- | - | - | M

French Quarter | 833 Conti St. (bet. Bourbon & Dauphine Sts.) | 504-525-9200

Local Goths and other late diners have found this humble new German storefront in the middle of the French Quarter serving schnitzels, wurst salad and potato pancakes, and even a goulash or two, until midnight on the weekends; hearty breakfasts and European sweets lend it appeal at 7 AM as well.

Jamila's Cafe Ⓜ Mediterranean/Tunisian

24 | 15 | 25 | $32

Uptown | 7808 Maple St. (Burdette St.) | 504-866-4366

"Hands-on" co-owners, chef Jamila and Moncef Shaa, "take pride" in "deeply flavorful" Tunisian and Mediterranean dishes "you won't find anywhere else" at this Uptown "jewel"; they'll also "remember your name with only one visit", and while the ambiance comes more from the "family" feel than the middling decor, Saturday night belly dancing makes it a "wonderful change from the ordinary."

NEW J'anita's BBQ/Southern

▽ 23 | 17 | 23 | $15

Lower Garden Dist. | 1906 Magazine St. (St. Mary St.) | 504-373-5337 | www.janitas.com

"Creative" and "comfy for blue-collar and white-collar" folks alike, this "cool addition to the lower Magazine dining scene" "carves out a niche" by offering a "unique" selection of Southern fare and BBQ, such as the "utterly delicious" Swamp Reuben (a real "Frankenstein of a sandwich") and daily dessert specials; admirers also appreciate the "unpretentious" staff and "funky" digs, decorated with "mismatched furniture" and local art on 150-year-old brick walls.

Jazmine Café Vietnamese

19 | 12 | 16 | $17

Riverbend | 614 S. Carrollton Ave. (St. Charles Ave.) | 504-866-9301

Though it "feels like an airport bar" to some, this "healthy" Riverbend Vietnamese wins points for serving "bright", "well-executed" cooking with "delicate" sauces and lots of "veggie" choices, and "keeping your tea filled" too; "popular" with college students and others on a "budget", it's "convenient" for Uptowners with a craving.

Jazz Tacos Ⓩ⊄ Central American

▽ 16 | 7 | 15 | $13

French Quarter | 307 Exchange Alley (bet. Chartres & Royal Sts.) | 504-872-0015

"Light-on-the-pocketbook" pupusas and other Honduran specialties provide a "decent" "alternative to po' boys" at this little Quarterite "hidden" in a "quiet alley near St. Louis Cathedral"; it's a "total dive" but the "alfresco option" is a bonus for the "local Spanish community" that frequents it; N.B. closes at 8 PM (earlier in the summer).

Joey K's Ⓩ Creole

19 | 14 | 17 | $21

Garden District | 3001 Magazine St. (7th St.) | 504-891-0997 | www.joeyksrestaurant.com

"As casual as they come", this "home-cooking mecca" in the Garden District delivers "real New Orleans po' boys", "all-you-can-eat crispy" catfish and other "solid" Creole plates "you wish your mother made" in an "easygoing" setting complete with "chilled mugs" of beer; since the "huge" portions are a "bargain", lunch crowds often flow "out the door."

Johnny's Po-Boy ⊘ Po' Boys
| - | - | - | I |

French Quarter | 511 St. Louis St. (bet. Chartres & Decatur Sts.) | 504-524-8129

Special sandwiches are served in not-so-special surroundings at this family-owned French Quarter deli that's always crowded and noisy beyond belief; to avoid the crush, lots of regulars order their po' boy, pay at the counter and then walk over to the river and have a picnic.

Joint, The ☒ BBQ
| 25 | 12 | 19 | $14 |

Bywater | 801 Poland Ave. (Dauphine St.) | 504-949-3232 | www.alwayssmokin.com

"Get your oink on" exclaim 'cue lovers who trek to this "true joint" in Bywater delivering "high-quality" meats that are "heavy on the smoke, in a good way", along with "homemade sauces" and savory sides; it's a "bare-bones" operation with "picnic-table decor", but you can "check out the jukebox" or get a breather in the "small courtyard" in back.

Juan's Flying Burrito Mexican
| 21 | 15 | 16 | $16 |

Mid-City | 4724 S. Carrollton Ave. (Canal St.) | 504-486-9950
Uptown | 2018 Magazine St. (bet. Josephine & St. Andrew Sts.) | 504-569-0000
www.juansflyingburrito.com

"Huge, flavor-filled burritos" and other Mexican grub that doesn't "swallow your wallet" keep these Mid-City and Uptown taquerias "packed" with "frugal" fans; the music ("so loud it's like they're asking you to leave"), the decor and the staff "all scream punk rock and disarray", so either get into the "grungy" vibe ("that second margarita would not be a bad idea") or get your eats to go.

Julie's Little Indian Kitchen at Schiro's ☒ Creole/Indian
| ▽ 18 | 11 | 19 | $15 |

Bywater | 2483 Royal St. (St. Roch Ave.) | 504-945-4425 | www.schiroscafe.com

"Basic" Cajun-Creole staples like gumbo, po' boys and "fried seafood" sit on the Schiro's side of the menu, while subcontinental fare at "reasonable" prices comes from the Julie's Little Indian Kitchen section at this "pretty good" Bywater bohemian; shoppers, lodgers and washers are particularly "glad it's here", since it's also a grocery store, liquor store, guesthouse and Laundromat.

Kanno ☒ⓂJapanese
| ▽ 28 | 12 | 26 | $28 |

Metairie | 3205 Edenborn Ave. (bet. 18th St. & Veterans Memorial Blvd.) | 504-455-5730

Owner–sushi chef Hidetoshi Suzuki is the "king" of this "sleeper" – a "small neighborhood" Japanese in a Metairie strip mall serving "fresh", "creative" rolls to a devoted following; most call it a "bargain" for the "generous" feast, making it "worth the trip to Fat City."

Kim Son ☒ Chinese/Vietnamese
| 24 | 13 | 20 | $22 |

Gretna | 349 Whitney Ave. (Westbank Expwy.) | 504-366-2489

"Messy", "to-die-for" salt-baked crab is a favorite at this "fast", "inexpensive" Gretna Asian offering an "enormous menu" of "flavorful"

Vietnamese fare and some "top-notch" Chinese food too; most fans "forget about" its generic "strip-mall" looks or just opt for takeout – which they "promptly eat in the car."

Korea House *Korean*
▽ 24 | 14 | 21 | $22

Metairie | 3547 18th St. (N. Arnoult Rd.) | 504-888-0654

"Best-in-the-South" bibimbop and "spicy" Korean barbecue cooked at the table are the stars at this low-cost Metairie eatery; though it doesn't have a lot of local competition, it delivers food just "like we had in Korea" for seasoned customers.

Kosher Cajun NY Deli & Grocery *Deli*
21 | 13 | 18 | $15

Metairie | 3519 Severn Ave. (bet. W. Esplanade Ave. & Veterans Memorial Blvd.) | 504-888-2010 | www.koshercajun.com

"The only game in town" for "corned beef on rye with a Cel-Ray (yes)" and "matzo ball soup just like mom makes", this family-run kosher deli offers "a little piece" of Manhattan in Metairie, along with some "surprising" Cajun dishes; customers also commend the "attentive" staff and the selection of "hard-to-obtain" groceries and wines lining the store's shelves; N.B. closed Saturdays and closes at 3 PM Fridays and Sundays.

☒ K-Paul's Louisiana Kitchen ☒ *Cajun*
27 | 21 | 24 | $54

French Quarter | 416 Chartres St. (bet. Conti & St. Louis Sts.) | 504-596-2530 | www.kpauls.com

"Put this one on your A-list" affirm acolytes of "culinary legend" Paul Prudhomme's French Quarter shrine, a "well-oiled establishment" where exec chef Paul Miller continues to mesmerize "tourist" hordes (and a few "locals") with "authentic" Cajun cuisine boasting "incredible flavors" that "live up to the hype"; while it's "expensive", the "cozy", "understated" space and "talented" staff create just the right "laid-back" mood for savoring the "joyful, plentiful" meal.

Kyoto ☒ *Japanese*
24 | 17 | 20 | $27

Uptown | 4920 Prytania St. (bet. Robert & Upperline Sts.) | 504-891-3644

"Creative rolls, beautifully presented sashimi" and "exquisite" Japanese dishes draw a "bustling" crowd to this "small" Uptown "sushi haven" where the "accommodating" staff "remembers every face"; "affordable" tabs are a plus, and the "fabulous" location "next to the Creole Creamery ice cream parlor" gives it an after-dinner edge.

Kyoto II ☒ *Japanese*
▽ 22 | 15 | 20 | $25

Harahan | Citrus Palm Shopping Ctr. | 5608 Citrus Blvd. (Kuebel St.) | 504-818-0228

In the Citrus Palm Shopping Center, this "often overlooked" Harahan Japanese (owned separately from the Uptown Kyoto) provides sushi "so fresh it's still swimming" among other "wow"-worthy dishes; advocates call it a "great place to head after the movies" at the Palace or for a "quick" lunch served by a "nice" staff, and since "you're not paying for the decor", it's easy to "leave full at a fair price."

☒ La Boca ☒ *Argentinean/Steak*
27 | 20 | 24 | $44

Warehouse District | 857 Fulton St. (St. Joseph St.) | 504-525-8205 | www.labocasteaks.com

Lovers of "red meat and red wine" say "run, don't walk" to this "tiny" Warehouse District Argentinean (a sib of RioMar) where the specialty is "superbly cooked" "unusual cuts" of steak escorted by "interesting" "homemade" sauces and "fantastic" sides, as well as "tasteful" vino from the same region; the staff "makes you feel at home", while soccer uniforms and photos of the "Boca Juniors team" lend a spirited touch to the "masculine" setting.

Ⓩ La Boulangerie 🍴 *Bakery*   28 | 17 | 21 | $10

Uptown | 4600 Magazine St. (Cadiz St.) | 504-269-3777

"When airfares and Euros are out of reach", Francophiles get their fix at this always-fragrant Uptown bakery offering "fabulous" breads, "quintessential croissants" and other "delectable delights" (including "amazing" King Cakes during Mardi Gras); its new "expanded" space is a plus, making it an "enjoyable" place to "drink coffee, nibble on pastries and pretend."

La Côte Brasserie *Contemp. Louisiana*   22 | 22 | 21 | $42

Warehouse District | Renaissance Arts Hotel | 700 Tchoupitoulas St. (Girod St.) | 504-613-2350 | www.lacotebrasserie.com

Boasting a "shiny", "airy" interior, this somewhat "undiscovered" Warehouse District venue offers "uncomplicated", seafood-focused Contemporary Louisiana fare that patrons consider a "pleasant surprise" for hotel dining; some opt for the "fantastic lunch specials", but even critics who consider the cuisine "nothing too impressive" say the sweeping bar and "great bartenders" make it a "nice place for an after-dinner drink."

La Crêpe Nanou Ⓩ *French*   24 | 23 | 22 | $34

Uptown | 1410 Robert St. (Prytania St.) | 504-899-2670 | www.lacrepenanou.com

Every night at 6 PM when the doors open, a "bohemian" "local crowd" spills into this "enchanting", no-reservations Uptown "jewel box" and is "transported to Paris for the night" over "divine" French bistro fare, including "savory mussels and "delicate" crêpes; with "plush", "art nouveau" decor, "excellent" service and "outstanding value", it's a "romantic" "winner" that draws "lines around the block on Valentine's Day."

Ⓩ La Divina Gelateria *Italian*   26 | 19 | 22 | $8

NEW **French Quarter** | 621 St. Peter St. (bet. Chartres & Royal Sts.) | 504-302-2692

Garden District | 3005 Magazine St. (7th St.) | 504-342-2634 www.ladivinagelateria.com

Those craving a quick trip to Positano can substitute this "heavenly" Garden District gelateria, home of "transcendent" gelati and sorbetti in "always-changing", "gourmet" flavors ("try the Aztec chocolate" or "crème brûlée with bits of burnt sugar"), along with "amazing" sandwiches and coffee drinks; designed in "chic", "environmentally conscious" style (even the cups are "compostable"), it's "kid-friendly without being a buzzkill for date-goers"; N.B. a new branch recently opened in the French Quarter.

NEW La Famiglia *Creole/Italian*   - | - | - | E

Metairie | 541 Oaklawn Dr. (Veterans Blvd.) | 504-833-8877

The latest iteration in a space that has turned over many times, this softly lit, upscale Creole-Italian has Metairie locals and citywide fans of chef-owner T.J. Quotub (ex Andrea's) following him to chow down on cioppino, bracioloni and other hearty specialties; during the day, affordable soups, salads and pastas bring in the ladies who lunch.

NEW Lago ⓜ American

▽ 24 | 19 | 21 | $39

Lakeview | 900 Harrison Ave. (Marshall Foch St.) | 504-486-8229 | www.lagoneworleans.com

A "refined" addition to beleaguered Lakeview, this ambitious New American proffers "fine" fare like flatiron steaks, double-cut pork chops and a "must-have" oyster and grits appetizer; though a few find it "pricey for a local restaurant", it wins over most with its amiable service and "intimate" blue-hued setting featuring a martini bar shaking up more than 40 different types of cocktails; N.B. hours are seasonal, so call ahead.

NEW Lakeview Brew
Coffee Cafe ⓢ Coffeehouse

- | - | - | I

Lakeview | 5606 Canal Blvd. (bet. Florida Blvd. & Homedale St.) | 504-483-7001

Still-recovering Lakeview locals have an easy daytime option in this new coffeehouse set in a former flower shop; its basic breakfasts and lunches lean toward healthy soups and salads, but the homemade desserts served till 9 PM are the real hook.

Lakeview Harbor Pub Food

20 | 13 | 16 | $18

Lakeview | 911 Harrison Ave. (bet. Argonne Blvd. & Marshall Foch St.) | 504-486-4887

Lakeview customers say they're "happy to have" this "popular" pub back to pre-Katrina form and still serving up "awesome" burgers that come "piled high" with toppings and plated with loaded baked potatoes; so even in spite of a "nothing fancy" setting, it remains "crowded with families" most nights.

La Madeleine Bakery

20 | 17 | 16 | $16

Harahan | Elmwood Shopping Ctr. | 5171 Citrus Blvd. (Clearview Pkwy.) | 504-818-2450
Metairie | 3300 Severn Ave., Ste. 201 (17th St.) | 504-456-1624
Riverbend | 601 S. Carrollton Ave. (St. Charles Ave.) | 504-861-8661
Mandeville | 3434 Hwy. 190 (bet. Asbury Dr. & Hwy. 22) | 985-626-7004
www.lamadeleine.com

"Reasonably priced, somewhat Americanized" French bistro fare turns up at this "dependable" bistro/bakery chain with a big, "something-for-everyone" selection that's ordered "cafeteria-style" and available for breakfast, lunch and dinner; "ersatz" Gallic decor and authentic staff "attitude" to the contrary, it's still "nice within its niche."

Landry's Seafood House Seafood

16 | 19 | 17 | $35

French Quarter | 400 N. Peters St. (Conti St.) | 504-558-0038
Lakefront | 8000 Lakeshore Dr. (Canal Blvd.) | 504-283-1010
www.landrysseafoodhouse.com

Offering a "predictable" seafood experience, these NOLA branches of a Texas-based chain suffice for "competent" Southern-style standards like crab cakes and crawfish étouffée presented in "plentiful portions"; though the French Quarter locale features live music and its sib is set in "prime" digs "overlooking Lake Pontchartrain", critics knock "expensive" tabs and "below par" service, concluding they "don't live up" to the "hype."

☒ La Petite Grocery 🖼️Ⓜ️ *Contemp. Louisiana/French*

26	23	24	$47

Uptown | 4238 Magazine St. (General Pershing St.) | 504-891-3377 | www.lapetitegrocery.com

"They make you feel right at home" at this "sweet little bistro" Uptown that's "very much a locals' hangout" (though still "welcoming" even if you're just visiting) where chef Justin Devillier makes "clever use of local ingredients" in his "expertly crafted" Contemporary Louisiana–French dinners and recently introduced lunch menu; though it's "pricey", the mood is so "warm" that allies agree it's "worth it."

☒ La Provence Ⓜ️ *Creole/French*

27	27	26	$55

Lacombe | 25020 Hwy. 190 (bet. Bremermann & Raymond Rds.) | 985-626-7662 | www.laprovencerestaurant.com

When celebrity chef/co-owner John Besh took over this "beautiful, rustic" Lacombe manor from "his mentor", the late Chris Kerageorgiou, he inherited "charming" premises evocative of a place "you would stumble upon in the French countryside" and made them gleam; in step with the surroundings are "extraordinary" Creole-Provençal dishes with a "home-cooked touch", enhanced by a "well-thought-out" wine list and "gracious" service that justify the 40-mile drive from New Orleans; N.B. post-Survey, executive chef Randy Lewis (ex Mecca in San Francisco) replaced René Bajeux.

La Thai Cuisine Ⓜ️ *Cajun/Thai*

22	18	21	$31

Uptown | 4938 Prytania St. (bet. Lyons & Robert Sts.) | 504-899-8886 | www.lathaiuptown.com

"Creative" Thai plates come together with more "traditional" preparations and "rockin' cocktails" at this Asian-Cajun now housed in "trendy" new Uptown digs; though food and service both "hit the mark", some say the atmosphere misses, with "uncomfortably noisy" acoustics, especially "on weekends."

Laurentino's Ⓜ️ *Spanish*

∇ 22	18	18	$33

Metairie | 4410 Transcontinental Dr. (W. Esplanade Ave.) | 504-779-9393 | www.laurentinos.com

After "one or two" feasts of "outstanding" paella and other "genuine" Catalonian dishes (plus a few Italian specialties) washed down with "great sangria", "you'll be tempted to be a regular" at this "dark", "tiny" Metairie bistro that will make you forget "you're in a strip mall"; the experience wouldn't be complete without a visit from chef-owner Xavier Laurentino, a "fascinating man who will talk your ear off if you let him"; N.B. an Uptown branch is set to open in early 2009.

La Vita *Italian/Mediterranean*

∇ 13	13	13	$23

Faubourg St. John | 3201 Esplanade Ave. (Ponce de Leon St.) | 504-948-0077 | www.lavitapizza.com

Regulars relish "gourmet" pizzas and other "decent" Italian-Med offerings – though critics claim they've "forsaken quality for quantity" – at this "reasonably priced" Faubourg St. John cafe now under new ownership; though its art-adorned interior has a "pleasant" feel, most prefer the "nice" shaded seating area outside for savoring "a glass of red."

	FOOD	DECOR	SERVICE	COST

Lebanon's Café *Lebanese*

23	15	18	$19

Carrollton | 1500 S. Carrollton Ave. (Jeannette St.) | 504-862-6200 | www.lebanonscafe.com

"Fantastic falafel", "delish" hummus and other "excellent" Lebanese specialties comprise the menu at this Carrollton BYO whose "generous portions" and "low prices" offer one of the "best values in the city"; with "fast" informal service and a "cheery" feel, it's the ultimate "college hangout", drawing quite the crowd on "Friday nights."

Le Citron Bistro Ⓜ *Creole/Italian*

▽ 23	23	24	$33

Lower Garden Dist. | 1539 Religious St. (Orange St.) | 504-566-9051 | www.le-citronbistro.com

Housed in a "historic cottage" dating back to 1810, this "reasonable" Creole-Italian in the Lower Garden District has a "rustic", "European" ambiance, providing "fresh, delicious" dishes, including "life-changing" fried chicken, served in appealingly "unrushed" style; some fans "wish more people knew" about it, but recommend "taking a cab", since the surrounding area can be deserted; N.B. open Wednesday–Saturday for dinner, Sunday for brunch.

Lee's Hamburgers *Burgers*

20	8	15	$10

Metairie | 3516 Veterans Memorial Blvd. (Severn Ave.) | 504-885-4291
Metairie | 904 Veterans Memorial Blvd. (Oaklawn Dr.) | 504-836-6804
Old Metairie | 1507 Metairie Rd. (Bonnabel Blvd.) | Metairie | 504-837-8990

"A greasy slice of heaven" is how fans describe the burgers at these "old-time" "joints" where the caramelized onions "grilled into" the patties "really sets them apart from other fast food"; decor is strictly "bare-bones", but "quick", "friendly" counter service does the trick "when you're in a hurry."

Leonardo Trattoria Ⓢ *Italian*
(fka Trinacria)

-	-	-	M

Warehouse District | 709 St. Charles Ave. (bet. Girod & Julia Sts.) | 504-558-8986

Offering "a pleasant surprise" in the Warehouse District, this "reasonably priced" Sicilian earns kudos for its "wonderful" fare, "friendly service" and "quaint" atmosphere with exposed-brick walls and flat-screen TVs tuned to vintage Italian flicks; given its proximity to Le Chat Noir, fans also find it especially "handy for dinner" before a show.

Ⓩ Le Parvenu *American/Creole*

26	22	22	$41

Kenner | 509 Williams Blvd. (bet. Kenner Ave. & Short St.) | 504-471-0534

Those who never thought they'd be eating lobster in cognac sauce in the 'burbs have had to eat their hats at this "best-kept secret" in Kenner where chef Dennis Hutley whips up "luscious" Creole–New American dishes "that will have you swooning"; service is usually "excellent", while the "cozy", "country cottage" setting feels made for "romance", especially if you choose the porch on a starry night.

Liborio Cuban Restaurant Ⓢ *Cuban*

21	14	18	$25

Central Business Dist. | 321 Magazine St. (bet. Canal & Poydras Sts.) | 504-581-9680 | www.liboriocuban.com

"Locals meet for lunch" at this "dependable" Cuban "favorite" in the CBD turning out garlicky ropa vieja, pressed sandwiches and other "solid", "inexpensive" standbys in a "genteel" pale-green setting with

	FOOD	DECOR	SERVICE	COST

paddle fans spinning overhead; wallet-watchers warn that dinner prices can feel "a little steep", particularly if you indulge in a few of the "real-deal" mojitos; N.B. open Monday for lunch only.

Li'l Dizzy's Cafe *Creole* — 22 | 16 | 20 | $19

Central Business Dist. | Whitney, a Wyndham Historic Hotel | 610 Poydras St. (bet. Camp St. & St. Charles Ave.) | 504-212-5656
Mid-City | 1500 Esplanade Ave. (Robertson St.) | 504-569-8997 Ⓢ

Creole soul breakfasts and lunches are "just grand" at this Mid-City "joint" that "on any given day is packed with post-K volunteers, clergy, planners, judges" and "indicted politicos", all there to feast on chef-owner Wayne Baquet's "best-in-town" fried chicken, trout and other specialties; the "Southern hospitality" and "inexpensive" bill both score points, plus the newer CBD offshoot in a former bank is "great for brunch before a Saint's game" since it's just blocks away from the Superdome.

☒ Lilette Ⓢ Ⓜ *French* — 26 | 23 | 24 | $50

Uptown | 3637 Magazine St. (Antonine St.) | 504-895-1636 | www.liletterestaurant.com

"Prove to your date you're a class act" at this "popular" Uptown "jewel box" where "forward-thinking" chef-owner John Harris "wows with every course", from the "superb", "inventive" French bistro dishes to "exquisite" desserts by pastry chef Beth Biundo; though the "gracious" service can be slightly "uneven", most guests leave impressed with the "tight, smart wine list" ("one of the better buys in town") and "lovely" surroundings with "stylish" cream-toned banquettes.

Little Tokyo *Japanese* — 24 | 18 | 21 | $27

Metairie | 1521 N. Causeway Blvd. (bet. 43rd & 44th Sts.) | 504-831-6788 ◖
Mid-City | 310 N. Carrollton Ave. (Bienville Ave.) | 504-485-5658
Mandeville | 590 Asbury Dr. (Desoto St.) | 985-727-1532 | www.littletokyosushi.com

"Amazing sushi" including "intriguing" maki – like the FEMA roll with salmon, snow crab and spicy tuna – draws a devoted following to this "reasonably priced" Japanese trio staffed by a "first-rate" crew; though the "casual" digs aren't memorable, most surveyors leave feeling "tranquil and well-fed"; N.B. the Mandeville branch is separately owned.

Liuzza's by the Track Ⓢ *Creole* — 23 | 11 | 19 | $18

Faubourg St. John | 1518 N. Lopez St. (Grand Route St. John St.) | 504-218-7888

"It doesn't get much more New Orleans" than this eternally "crowded" Faubourg St. John Creole, a revered "dive" serving serious gumbo, "mouthwatering" BBQ shrimp po' boys and Bloody Marys stuffed with "enough veggies to meet your daily requirement"; "you may have to wait", but rest assured a meal here is quite possibly "the best bet you'll make anywhere near a racetrack", and "a must during Jazz Fest" too; N.B. the kitchen closes at 7 PM.

Liuzza's Restaurant & Bar Ⓢ Ⓜ ⊅ *Creole/Italian* — 21 | 13 | 20 | $21

Mid-City | 3636 Bienville Ave. (bet. N. Genois & N. Telemachus Sts.) | 504-482-9120 | www.liuzzas.com

The "quintessential" "corner restaurant", this "beloved" Mid-City "landmark" is famed for its "simple" Creole-Italian fare like "wonderful" po' boys, "crave"-worthy onion rings and "huge frosted mugs of draft beer", all rustled to the table by waitresses "who call you honey"; despite the strictly "no-frills" setting, a motley mix of true-blue customers – from "cops" to "city councilmen" – keeps it "roaring with life."

Lola's ⊅ *Spanish*
25 | 19 | 22 | $31

Faubourg St. John | 3312 Esplanade Ave. (Verna Ct.) | 504-488-6946
"Garlic lovers" flock to this "funky" "bohemian" "haunt" in Faubourg St. John for "tantalizing" paellas, "excellent" rack of lamb and other "unabashedly robust" Spanish dishes; it's a "locals' favorite", but given its "tiny" quarters and no-reservations policy, "go early", or expect to "wait"; N.B. the house offers sangria, beer and wine, but diners can still tote their own bottles for a $5 corkage fee.

Louisiana Pizza Kitchen *Italian*
22 | 16 | 19 | $20

French Quarter | 95 French Market Pl. (Barracks St.) | 504-522-9500 | www.louisianapizzakitchen.com
Riverbend | 615 S. Carrollton Ave. (St. Charles Ave.) | 504-866-5900
"Well-prepared" "wood-fired" pizzas with "paper-thin" crusts and "unique" toppings are the name of the game at these "consistent" Italians that also serve "lovely" salads, pastas and wraps; the Riverbend location has a "cheery" (if chain-y) air and caters to families and students, while the separately owned French Quarter branch has a longer beer and wine list, a slightly more upscale menu and "scenic" outdoor seating across from the French Market.

Lucy's Retired Surfer's
Bar & Restaurant *Californian/Mexican*
14 | 16 | 15 | $19

Warehouse District | 701 Tchoupitoulas St. (Girod St.) | 504-523-8995
Mandeville | 124 Girod St. (Lakeshore Dr.) | 985-624-9331
www.lucysretiredsurfers.com
Scores of "singles" seek out this "quirky" surf-themed twosome in the Warehouse District and Mandeville whose "hopping" bar scenes and "cheap" tabs ensure they're "always crowded"; though gourmets gripe the "cheap" Cal-Mex grub's only "passable", most admit it "tastes better" after a couple of their "strong drinks"; N.B. the Food score may not fully reflect a 2008 chef change at the Tchoupitoulas branch.

Lüke *French*
23 | 23 | 22 | $41

Central Business Dist. | 333 St. Charles Ave. (bet. Gravier & Perdido Sts.) | 504-378-2840 | www.lukeneworleans.com
"John Besh scores again" with this "sophisticated" brasserie in the CBD – a more "casual" alternative to August – where the "top-notch, yet unfussy" cooking showcases "hearty" Alsatian dishes with a NOLA accent as well as "towering" raw bar platters and a burger that's "a work of art"; service can be "uneven", but "surprisingly reasonable" price tags (especially the prix fixe Express Menu at dinner) redeem so most maintain they'd "go back in a heartbeat"; N.B. the Food score does not reflect the post-Survey departure of chef Jared Tees.

NEW Mahony's Po-Boy Shop ⊠ *Po' Boys*
– | – | – | I

Uptown | 3454 Magazine St. (Delachaise St.) | 504-899-3374 | www.mahonyspoboys.com
At this converted Uptown cottage, chef-owner Ben Wicks (ex RioMar) offers a creative take on one of N'Awlins' basic food groups, preparing crunchy French bread po' boys with combos like grilled shrimp, fried

green tomatoes and rémoulade sauce, and fried chicken livers and coleslaw; throw in a huge side of crispy fried shaved onion rings and a soda from the cooler, and it's a cheap, but filling, lunch.

Mandina's Creole

| 23 | 17 | 20 | $27 |

Mid-City | 3800 Canal St. (Cortez St.) | 504-482-9179 ⑰
Mandeville | Azalea Shopping Ctr. | 4240 Hwy. 22, #1 (Dalwill Dr.) | 985-674-9883 Ⓢ
www.mandinasrestaurant.com

"If you leave hungry it's your own fault" because this "quintessential" Creole "joint" in Mid-City (with a Mandeville cousin) tries to "make you happy with generous portions of Louisiana staples", including "terrific" fried seafood and "don't-miss" turtle soup; "most of the local characters are back standing at the bar", and "lawyers and construction workers sit table-to-table" in the "expanded", "freshened-up" dining room, staffed by "familiar", "accommodating" servers.

Maple Street Cafe Italian/Mediterranean

| 22 | 18 | 20 | $29 |

Carrollton | 7623 Maple St. (bet. Adams & Hillary Sts.) | 504-314-9003 | www.maplecafe.net

"Try it, you'll like it" say supporters of this Carrollton "sleeper" where the "capable chef" prepares "excellent" Italian-Med cuisine so modestly priced "you'll think you were only charged for bread and water"; though it's in the middle of a "college shopping street", its "quaint elegance" makes it an appealing "date spot."

Marigny Brasserie Eclectic

| 22 | 23 | 22 | $39 |

Faubourg Marigny | 640 Frenchmen St. (bet. Chartres & Royal Sts.) | 504-945-4472 | www.cafemarigny.com

"More modern and upscale than the typical Frenchmen Street eatery", this Marigny bistro turns out "imaginative", "carefully prepared" Eclectic cooking by new chef Daniel Esses in a "bright, airy" space across from Washington Square Park; the atmosphere is "congenial" with a staff that "aims to please", plus weekly jazz performances by the Pfister Sisters make Sunday brunch "a trip!"

Mark Twain's Pizza Ⓢ Ⓜ Pizza

| 22 | 13 | 17 | $17 |

Old Metairie | 2035 Metairie Rd. (bet. Atherton Dr. & Jefferson Ave.) | Metairie | 504-832-8032 | www.marktwainspizza.com

"Thin-crust pizza" "made the New York way" backs up a bounty of "innovative" topping combos that "will have you scratching your head until you take a bite" at this Old Metairie pie parlor; "limited hours and no delivery" are downsides, but the service is "decent", and despite new ownership, many still consider it the "tastiest in town."

Ⓩ Martinique Bistro Ⓜ French

| 26 | 23 | 23 | $43 |

Uptown | 5908 Magazine St. (Eleonore St.) | 504-891-8495 | www.martiniquebistro.com

A "sweet little surprise" on a "beautiful" stretch of Magazine Street "surrounded by shade trees", this Uptown "treasure" showcases "outstanding" seafood among other "modern", high-end French bistro fare by chef Eric LaBouchere that "makes you want to come back tomorrow to try what you didn't have today"; the servers are "well trained" and the "charming courtyard" "oozes romance", so contented customers only hope it continues to be "untainted by tourists."

Martin Wine Cellar *Sandwiches*

23 | 14 | 17 | $17

Metairie | 714 Elmeer Ave. (Veterans Memorial Blvd.) | 504-896-7350 |
www.martinwine.com

At this Metairie bistro/deli inside a "surprisingly busy wine store",
fans say the "food is always fresh, the salads superb" and the sandwiches can be ordered with an "endless combination of ingredients";
the daily specials often reach "dizzying heights" too, but there's little
in the way of "decor or ambiance", and the "strong following" means
"lunch can be risky if you only have an hour."

Mat & Naddie's ⊠ *Contemp. Louisiana*

23 | 21 | 22 | $34

Riverbend | 937 Leonidas St. (Leake Ave.) | 504-861-9600 |
www.matandnaddies.com

This "charming little" Riverbend cottage with a "fine patio" lures foodies
"off the beaten track" for chef Steven Schwartz's "hearty" Contemporary
Louisiana cuisine "with a touch of funk" and "flashes of genius"; the "$10
lunch buffet" is "one of the best bargains in town", the staff is "professional, informative and just plain nice", and the "chummy patrons" turn
it into a "party", especially during the "live gypsy-style jazz" on Monday
nights; N.B. lunch-only Tuesday–Wednesday, dinner-only Saturday.

Mayas Ⓜ *Pan-Latin*

- | - | - | M

Lower Garden Dist. | 2027 Magazine St. (bet. Josephine & St. Andrew Sts.) |
504-309-3401 | www.mojitoland.com

"The classic mojitos", sangrias and margaritas are "awesome" at this
rustic Pan-Latin arrival in the Lower Garden District, though while
some deem the food "different" and "delicious", others say the "mix of
flavors" "doesn't excite like the exotic menu promises"; despite any
shortcomings, most agree the "service is great"; N.B. it offers a 15%
discount for veterans and members of the military.

Meauxbar ⊠Ⓜ *French*

24 | 22 | 23 | $42

French Quarter | 942 N. Rampart St. (bet. Dumaine & St. Philip Sts.) |
504-569-9979 | www.meauxbar.com

"On the quiet side of the Quarter", this "unassuming", "cute corner"
bistro (whose owners formerly ran a Hamptons restaurant) provides a
"subtly chic", Indochine-accented setting for dining on "inventive",
"brightly flavored" French fare with an "Asian twist"; both "young professional" regulars and "new walk-ins" are "warmly greeted" – part of
the reason its "popularity is on the steep rise."

Mélange *Contemp. Louisiana*

▽ 19 | 24 | 17 | $64

French Quarter | Ritz-Carlton | 921 Canal St. (bet. Burgundy & Dauphine Sts.) |
504-524-1331 | www.ritzcarlton.com

A "stunning" dining room featuring "delightful" weekend jazz by trum-
peter Jeremy Davenport upstages the menu of "New Orleans' signature dishes" (aka "copycat recipes from great restaurants") at this
Contemporary Louisianian in French Quarter; it's a "fun experience",
but many find the service "not up to Ritz standards" or the high tabs.

Melting Pot *Fondue*

19 | 20 | 21 | $43

Lower Garden Dist. | 1820 St. Charles Ave. (bet. Felicity & St. Mary Sts.) |
504-525-3225 | www.meltingpot.com

"Change-of-pace" mavens and "do-it-yourself" types are fond of this
Lower Garden District link in the "novel" fondue franchise for its "in-

teractive" approach, i.e. the chance to "cook your own dinner"; the "long, slow meals" make it appropriate for "first dates" or "large crowds", and although the morsels are "tasty", you'll "end up spending a lot of money" for them.

Middendorf's Seafood ⓜ *Seafood*

| 24 | 14 | 21 | $24 |

Manchac | 30160 Hwy. 51 S. (Mary Reno Ln.) | 985-386-6666 | www.middendorfsrestaurant.com

"Thin fried catfish" as "delicate as butterfly wings" with "just the right amount of seasoned breading" is a "real Louisiana treat" at this "out-of-the-way" but way "popular" "fish shack" "overlooking the swamps" in Manchac; the "rude" but "charming" waitresses are still "straight out of the '50s", and while the main room was seriously damaged by Hurricane Ike, new chef/co-owner Horst Pfeifer (of the much-missed Bella Luna) has moved the "rustic" restaurant into a second building on the same property.

Mike Serio's Po-Boys & Deli ⓩ *Po' Boys*

| 19 | 14 | 17 | $14 |

Central Business Dist. | 133 St. Charles Ave. (bet. Canal & Common Sts.) | 504-523-2668 | www.seriosdeli.com

They "won the muffaletta throwdown with Bobby Flay on the Food Network", but some patrons are more partial to the "great po' boys" at this "handy" CBD deli for sandwiches and low-cost lunch specials; even those who find the fare "second-rate" say it's worth a stop for the "LSU decor alone" – "geaux Tigers!"

Mikimoto *Japanese*

| - | - | - | M |

Carrollton | 3301 S. Carrollton Ave. (Forshey St.) | 504-488-1881 | www.mikimotosushi.com

This small Japanese is popular with nearby university students and Carrollton neighbors for its extensive menu of appetizers, noodle dishes and more than 50 versions of sushi; traditional Asian wall hangings and plastic-topped tables painted with pleasant Japanese scenes make it attractive enough to eat in, or you can call ahead for a pick up at the drive-thru window.

ⓩ MiLa *Contemp. Louisiana*

| 26 | 25 | 24 | $52 |

Central Business Dist. | Renaissance Pere Marquette | 817 Common St. (bet. Baronne & Carondelet Sts.) | 504-412-2580 | www.milaneworleans.com

"A new star on the scene", this "adventurous" CBD arrival by married chefs Allison Vines-Rushing and Slade Rushing provides a "remarkable dining experience" highlighting "innovative" Contemporary Louisiana fare such as "don't-miss" deconstructed oysters Rockefeller; though the "cost can be considerable", coaxed along by the "attentive staff" and "trendy", "contemporary" decor (featuring a "great bar"), "locals are coming around to the cutting edge."

Miyako *Japanese*

| 21 | 17 | 21 | $25 |

Lower Garden Dist. | 1403 St. Charles Ave. (Thalia St.) | 504-410-9997 | www.japanesebistro.com

"Sitting at the hibachi bar" and "catching shrimp in the air" is a "blast" at this "group-friendly" Japanese grill with a "prime" location in the Lower Garden District; it serves "fresh" sushi too, and while some feel neither cuisine "is done all that well", "kids love it" and parents appreciate the "inexpensive" bill, especially for lunch.

DINING

FOOD | DECOR | SERVICE | COST

Mona Lisa *Italian*
23 | **20** | **21** | **$22**

French Quarter | 1212 Royal St. (bet. Barracks & Governor Nicholls Sts.) | 504-522-6746

"It would be a mistake to pass by" this "little" "no-pretense" Italian in the "quieter part" of the Quarter that's refreshingly "non-touristy", serving "inexpensive", "wonderful" food and offering a BYO option with a $10 corkage fee; the service is "caring" and "gay-friendly", and the "eccentric" interior features a "plethora of Mona Lisa lookalikes" "watching" from the walls.

Mona's Cafe *Mideastern*
19 | **12** | **18** | **$17**

Carrollton | 1120 S. Carrollton Ave. (bet. Oak & Zimple Sts.) | 504-861-8175
Faubourg Marigny | 504 Frenchmen St. (Decatur St.) | 504-949-4115
Mid-City | 3901 Banks St. (S. Scott St.) | 504-482-7743
Uptown | 4126 Magazine St. (bet. Marengo & Milan Sts.) | 504-894-9800

"Real" gyros and "homemade pita bread" help keep this Middle Eastern mini-chain a "staple for regulars who don't want Creole all the time" and are happy to BYO; though the decor is "not so hot", the service is "sufficiently attentive" and the price "can't be beat."

Morning Call Coffee Stand ●⊖ *Coffeehouse*
25 | **16** | **19** | **$7**

Metairie | Lakeside Plaza | 3325 Severn Ave. (bet. 16th & 17th Sts.) | 504-885-4068 | www.morningcallcoffeestand.com

"Many remember this place before it moved" out of its "historic home" in the Quarter and into a Metairie strip mall, and still "love" its chicory coffee and "dusty-licious" beignets – "crisp outside and tender inside with a sprinkle of powdered sugar" – calling it "way more authentic" than its "more famous counterpart" in the French Market; with plenty of enduring "charm", it offers "true Southern hospitality" 24 hours a day.

Morton's The Steakhouse *Steak*
25 | **23** | **24** | **$73**

French Quarter | Shops at Canal Pl. | 365 Canal St. (N. Peters St.) | 504-566-0221 | www.mortons.com

"Premium steaks" and a wine list with "real red gems begging to be paired with a béarnaise-topped filet" go for "eye-popping prices" at this French Quarter link in the national steakhouse chain; the "amazing" service is performed with "lots of fanfare", but the "heavyweight" decor is "1980s dark, wannabe impressive", and the whole package is a little "boring for New Orleans."

ⓩ Mosca's � *Italian*
26 | **12** | **19** | **$45**

Avondale | 4137 Hwy. 90 W. (bet. Capitol Dr. & Live Oak Blvd.) | 504-436-9942

Some would willingly "swim across the mighty Mississippi" to Avondale for this "religious foodie experience" of "unbelievable" "Italian done the Louisiana way", "laced with fragrant garlic" and served family-style in a "roadside shack" that's a "throwback to the 1940s"; the "cab ride costs more" than the meal, and "no credit cards" are taken, so experienced eaters "bring lots of cash and allow plenty of time."

Mother's *American/Cajun*
22 | **10** | **14** | **$17**

Central Business Dist. | 401 Poydras St. (Tchoupitoulas St.) | 504-523-9656 | www.mothersrestaurant.net

"You can always come home to Mother's", but this "famous" Cajun-American "cafeteria" in the CBD is "not a place for those concerned about their waistline" with its "messy and marvelous" "stick-to-your-arteries" po' boys and breakfasts; while the service can be "gruff", the "sassy" staff is "part of the experience", and "rain or shine" there's "always a line."

☑ Mr. B's Bistro *Contemp. Louisiana*

25 | 24 | 25 | $46

French Quarter | 201 Royal St. (Iberville St.) | 504-523-2078 | www.mrbsbistro.com

This "Brennans signature" in the French Quarter is "back in the swing", serving "impeccable" Contemporary Louisiana dishes like "sumptuous" gumbo ya-ya and the "buttery heaven" of BBQ shrimp ("put on a bib and dig in"); bolstered by a "phenomenal" staff and "casually gorgeous" dining room with "dark-wood-paneled walls and deep banquettes", it has a "hustle-and-bustle" atmosphere that's "tops" for a "business lunch" or "big party."

Mr. Ed's ☑ *Creole/Italian*

20 | 17 | 20 | $21

Metairie | 1001 Live Oak St. (bet. Bonnabel Blvd. & Lake Ave.) | 504-838-0022

Mr. Ed's Creole Grille ☑ *American/Creole*

NEW **Metairie** | 5241 Veterans Memorial Blvd. (Kent Ave.) | 504-889-7992

Dishing up "traditional" Creole "plate lunches", "great fried chicken" and Italian eats, this "old staple" in Metairie's Bucktown neighborhood caters to "families" and "blue hairs" who appreciate the "reasonable cost"; critics call the cooking just "average", and say the best service is reserved for "recognized regulars"; P.S. a new, more "upscale" branch serving a Creole-American menu opened in 2008.

Mr. Gyros *Greek*

∇ 24 | 14 | 20 | $20

Metairie | 3620 N. Causeway Blvd. (W. Esplanade Ave.) | 504-833-9228 | www.mrgyrosnola.com

An Aegean "alternative to fast food", this Metairie Greek pleases with "delicious gyro plates" ("even my Greek girlfriends love it") among a full roster of salads and meze; though its setting on a "traffic-heavy corner" lacks charm, the owner works hard to ensure "outstanding satisfaction."

Mr. John's Ristorante ☑Ⓜ *Steak*

24 | 18 | 21 | $46

Lower Garden Dist. | 2111 St. Charles Ave. (bet. Jackson Ave. & Josephine St.) | 504-679-7697 | www.mrjohnssteakhouse.com

"Ruth who? Dickie what?" ask fans of this Lower Garden District "well-kept steakhouse secret" that also boasts "superb" Italian fare; it's "cozy" with old-fashioned tile floors and "on-the-spot" service, but a few surveyors sniff that it's "overpriced" for a dining experience that's just "not exciting."

Mulate's of New Orleans *Cajun*

19 | 18 | 18 | $28

Warehouse District | 201 Julia St. (Convention Center Blvd.) | 504-522-1492 | www.mulates.com

"Conventioneers" and other "hungry customers" dig into "tasty", "down and dirty" Cajun cooking and kick up their heels on the "full dance floor" at this Warehouse District destination where the live bayou bands "make the meal"; though critics call the dishes "dumbed down" and the service "haphazard", more maintain it's a strong "value for the buck" and "perfect for large groups and loud parties."

	FOOD	DECOR	SERVICE	COST

☑ Muriel's Jackson Square *Creole* — 23 | 26 | 23 | $45

French Quarter | Jackson Sq. | 801 Chartres St. (St. Ann St.) | 504-568-1885 | www.muriels.com

"Every dish is lovingly prepared and served as though it were a gift" at this French Quarter Creole housed in a "fabulous", "historic" setting boasting "uniquely decorated" rooms and a "divine" balcony overlooking Jackson Square; a few find it "overpriced", but others deem the dinner prix fixe a "bargain" and the Sunday jazz brunch "a treat."

Nacho Mama's *Mexican* — 15 | 15 | 17 | $19

Metairie | 1000 S. Clearview Pkwy. (Mounes St.) | 504-736-1188
Uptown | 3242 Magazine St. (Pleasant St.) | 504-899-0031
www.nachomamasmexicangrill.com

"Young patrons keep the energy up" at this Uptown and Metairie Mexican duo known more for its "kick-ass margaritas" and "people-watching" at happy hour than for its "fast and (gr)easy", "less than impressive" grub ("you're right, this is not your mama's"); service is "indifferent" too, but defenders say it "works in a fix."

Napoleon House *Creole/Mediterranean* — 19 | 25 | 18 | $25

French Quarter | 500 Chartres St. (St. Louis St.) | 504-524-9752 | www.napoleonhouse.com

"Pair a Pimm's Cup with a po' boy" (or an "absolutely delicious" hot muffaletta) and "you have a winning lunch" at this "sacred" "French Quarter anachronism" that's "part of New Orleans history"; with a "serious" staff shuttling Creole-Med dishes, a "picturesque" court-yard and a "casual" yet "incomparable" atmosphere infused with the "ghosts of 200 years", it's the kind of place that "makes some stay in the Crescent forever"; N.B. closes at 5:30 PM.

New City Grille ☑ *Contemp. Louisiana* — 22 | 22 | 22 | $37

Metairie | 2700 Metairie Rd. (N. Labarre Rd.) | 504-828-8484 | www.newcitygrille.net

A "top" newcomer in Old Metairie, this "elegant little place" provides a "well-done" Contemporary Louisiana menu for "reasonable" tabs; both the kitchen and the "courteous", "unpretentious" servers show "attention to detail", adding up to a "pleasant" experience for both "families" and "dates."

🆕 New Orleans Cake Café & Bakery Ⓜ *American* — - | - | - | I

Faubourg Marigny | 2440 Chartres St. (bet. Mandeville & Spain Sts.) | 504-943-0100 | www.nolacakes.com

Cakes created by owner-baker Steve Himelfarb, as well as a selection of breakfast and lunch items, draw Marigny mavens to this simple cafe on the corner of a historic block; plump fresh crabmeat brought in by fishers from Lafitte show up in omelets, sandwiches and salads in season, while 'cupcakes for a buck with your meal' make for a sweet ending.

New Orleans Food & Spirits ☑ *Cajun/Seafood* — 22 | 13 | 19 | $23

Harvey | 2330 Lapalco Blvd. (Brooklyn Ave.) | 504-362-0800
Covington | 208 Lee Ln. (bet. E. Boston & Rutland Sts.) | 985-875-0432 | www.neworleansfoodandspirits.com

"You won't leave hungry" after attacking the "unbelievable portions" of "artery-clogging seafood" "spiced just right" at these Cajuns in

Covington and Harvey; they're "dumps" that are often "louder than a Saints playoff game", but the service is "prompt" and "friendly" following the "long wait" for a table; N.B. closed for dinner Monday–Tuesday in Covington, Monday–Thursday in Harvey.

New Orleans Grill *Contemp. Louisiana*   24 | 25 | 21 | $70

Central Business Dist. | Windsor Court Hotel | 300 Gravier St. (bet. S. Peters & Tchoupitoulas Sts.) | 504-522-1992 | www.windsorcourthotel.com

"Gorgeous rooms" filled with "over-the-top flowers" set the stage for "opulent" evenings at this "special-occasion" Contemporary Louisianian in the CBD's Windsor Court Hotel; service wavers from "attentive" to "pretentious", however, and some feel the managers have "frittered away its excellent reputation" with numerous chef changes (the latest is not reflected in the Food score).

New Orleans Hamburger &   17 | 13 | 15 | $15
Seafood Co. *Burgers/Seafood*

Jefferson | 1005 S. Clearview Pkwy. (Mounes St.) | 504-734-1122
Metairie | 6920 Veterans Memorial Blvd. (David Dr.) | 504-455-1272
Metairie | 817 Veterans Memorial Blvd. (Martin Berhman Ave.) | 504-837-8580
NEW Houma | 6131 W. Park Ave. (Douglas Dr.) | 985-872-5965
NEW Mandeville | 3900 Hwy. 22 (N Causeway Blvd.) | 985-624-8035
www.nohsc.com

A somewhat "ambitious answer to fast food in a serious food city", this chainlet is an "easy" choice for "step-above" burgers, fried seafood and other "affordable" eats with a "local twist"; even if it's "nothing to rave about", the order-at-the-counter setup keeps it "quick" and "casual."

New York Pizza *Pizza*   21 | 8 | 16 | $15

Uptown | 5201 Magazine St. (Dufossat St.) | 504-891-2376

"Fantastic thin-crust pizza" offers a "taste of the Big Apple in the Big Easy" at this "garlic-intensive" Uptown pie shop; it's on the "small" side and "not good for dining in", so order to-go and "eat on the street."

Nine Roses *Chinese/Vietnamese*   24 | 15 | 18 | $22

Gretna | 1100 Stephens St. (Westbank Expwy.) | 504-366-7665

Reviewers find the "real deal" at this Gretna "favorite" with a "gigantic menu" ("ask for help") of "incredible", "delicate" Vietnamese dishes that are "meant to be shared", supplemented by less memorable Chinese fare; though the interior is not as "elegant" as the cooking, most don't mind in light of the "inexpensive" bill.

NINJA Ⓜ *Japanese*   24 | 13 | 19 | $26

Carrollton | 8433 Oak St. (S. Carrollton Ave.) | 504-866-1119

"Don't be alarmed" by the "terrible shape" of the downstairs bar and the "institutional atmosphere" advise admirers of this "go-to" Carrollton Japanese that prepares "excellent box sushi"; others are put off by the "greeters wearing Janet Jackson wireless mikes" and the service gets mixed marks, but it's still an "affordable, hidden find."

Nirvana Indian Cuisine Ⓜ *Indian*   21 | 16 | 16 | $23

Uptown | 4308 Magazine St. (Napoleon Ave.) | 504-894-9797 | www.insidenirvana.com

"Varied tastes" of the subcontinent are "well-sampled" at this Uptown Indian offering a dinner menu "loaded with classics and dishes you may have never seen before" as well as a "great-deal" lunch buffet; just "don't go in a hurry" since the "surly" staff can be "hard to catch."

ⓩ NOLA Contemp. Louisiana   26 | 24 | 25 | $54

French Quarter | 534 St. Louis St. (bet. Chartres & Decatur Sts.) | 504-522-6652 | www.emerils.com

"Emeril may be hokey" but his Contemporary Louisiana cuisine is "delectable" and "inventive" at this "upscale bistro" in the Quarter offering "less hype" at a slightly "lower cost" than Lagasse's other venues; the room is "happening" with "high ceilings, high energy and high noise", as well as a "stellar" staff that "bends over backwards to accommodate" tourists, New Orleanians and "single diners."

Nuvolari's Italian   24 | 24 | 23 | $39

Mandeville | 246 Girod St. (Jefferson St.) | 985-626-5619 | www.nuvolaris.com

Mandeville *mangiatori* put this Italian "mainstay" "on the top of the list" when they're in the mood for "awesome pasta", seafood and wine; with a "romantic", mahogany-accented room boasting a "nice side bar" and "attentive" service, it's often sought out for "special occasions."

Oak Alley Restaurant Cajun/Creole   ▽ 19 | 21 | 19 | $30

Vacherie | Oak Alley Plantation | 3645 Hwy. 18 (3 mi. west of Hwy. 20) | 225-265-2151 | www.oakalleyplantation.com

"The view from the road down the oak-lined drive is stunning" at this 300-year-old plantation in Vacherie, where you can have a "delicious Southern breakfast" or lunch of Cajun-Creole food in a 19th-century cottage before "wandering the grounds"; some feel the decor and menu need an "update", while others say it's worth a stop "if you're visiting."

Oak Street Cafe ⊅ Southern   - | - | - | I

Carrollton | 8140 Oak St. (bet. Dublin St. & S. Carrollton Ave.) | 504-866-8710 | www.oakstreetcafe.com

Early-risers and nearby starving University students head to this cluttered, old-fashioned cafe one block off the Carrollton streetcar line for fresh doughnuts along with Southern-accented breakfasts and lunches; come as early as 6 AM, but finish your blue-plate lunch special by 2 PM 'cos that's when they close.

O'Henry's Food & Spirits ◐ American   13 | 11 | 15 | $18

Gretna | 710 Terry Pkwy. (Carol Sue Ave.) | 504-433-4111
Kenner | 8859 Veterans Memorial Blvd. (bet. Massachusetts & Mississippi Aves.) | 504-461-9840
Riverbend | 634 S. Carrollton Ave. (Hampson St.) | 504-866-9741
www.ohenrys.com

Most find the food "mediocre" (except for the "good burgers") at this American chain that lets you "drop peanut shells on the floor", but the Riverbend branch gets reliably "flooded by Tulane and Loyola students" who like the "balcony overlooking the streetcar line"; expect "fair to poor service" at what one surveyor dubs an "Irish Chili's."

Olivier's Creole   21 | 21 | 23 | $41

French Quarter | 204 Decatur St. (bet. Bienville & Iberville Sts.) | 504-525-7734 | www.olivierscreole.com

Passed-down "family recipes" ("ask for the eggplant Olivier") "convey the flavors of old New Orleans" at this "classic" Creole with a "winsome" spirit in the French Quarter; a few find it "inconsistent", but "comfortable" quarters and a staff that "makes you feel at home" have devotees declaring it the "real deal."

One Restaurant & Lounge 🛃 American | 25 | 21 | 23 | $41 |

Riverbend | 8132 Hampson St. (bet. Carrollton Ave. & Dublin St.) | 504-301-9061 | www.one-sl.com

From an "entertaining" open kitchen, chef/co-owner Scott Snodgrass (ex Clancy's) and his "perfectly orchestrated" crew cook "some of the sexiest" seasonal New American dishes around at this "reasonable", "off-the-radar" "neighborhood bistro" in Riverbend; while the room is a bit "spare" and "crowded", its clientele of young "locals and repeat visitors" tends to "focus on the food" as well as the "gracious" service by an "attractive", "professional" staff.

Orleans Grapevine | 22 | 23 | 22 | $33 |
Wine Bar & Bistro French

French Quarter | 720 Orleans Ave. (bet. Bourbon & Royal Sts.) | 504-523-1930 | www.orleansgrapevine.com

"Hidden in plain sight", this French Quarter "find" behind St. Louis Cathedral is a grown-up "oasis" offering a "wide selection" of vintages to match "innovative" French bistro fare that's "surprisingly good for a wine bar"; though the entrees can get "pricey", the "cozy" candlelit interior and "romantic" courtyard have some musing that while it's "not crowded, it should be."

Oscar's ◐ American | ▽ 19 | 13 | 17 | $18 |

Old Metairie | 2027 Metairie Rd. (Jefferson Ave.) | Metairie | 504-831-9540

"Sure, it's a hole-in-the-wall", but this Old Metairie bar makes some of the area's "best" burgers and baked potatoes among other American eats; it's also a fine place to "watch the fights or the LSU game", or take a gander at the "delicious" collection of Marilyn Monroe memorabilia.

Outback Steakhouse Steak | 17 | 14 | 17 | $30 |

Metairie | 2746 Severn Ave. (Veterans Blvd.) | 504-455-6850 | www.outback.com

"Meat lovers on a budget" report that this "midtier", Aussie-themed chain chophouse in Metairie provides terrific "bang for the buck", not to mention "basic" steaks and "hefty sides" (the famed bloomin' onion supplies "a weeks' worth of calories" in a single serving); it's "not known for subtlety" – starting with the "overly friendly, chat 'n' squat" service – but when you "don't want to splurge", it's a "decent" enough option.

Palace Café Creole | 24 | 24 | 23 | $42 |

French Quarter | 605 Canal St. (Chartres St.) | 504-523-1661 | www.palacecafe.com

"Creole concoctions to stimulate the taste buds" stand out on the menu mixing "standards and a few surprises" at this "touristy" Brennan-family option on Canal Street overseen by a "professional" staff; with a "sweeping stairwell and musical murals", it's "playful during the day, sophisticated at night" and "usually easy to get into without a reservation."

	FOOD	DECOR	SERVICE	COST

P&G Ⓢ *American* ▽ 17 | 10 | 14 | $10

Central Business Dist. | 345 Baronne St. (Union St.) | 504-525-9678

"Whoever blurts out their order first" gets served at this "yell place" in the CBD dishing up fried seafood, po' boys and other "economical" American eats; it's "bare-bones" and the system is a little "strange", but the "fast" staff is "friendly, honey."

Parasol's *American/Irish* 24 | 10 | 17 | $16

Irish Channel | 2533 Constance St. (3rd St.) | 504-899-2054 | www.parasols.com

"Don't wear anything nice" to this Irish Channel "watering hole" – the site of the city's "most famous St. Paddy's Day celebration" – "known far and wide" for its "big, sloppy" roast beef po' boys that will send "gravy running down your arm"; the "bartenders are friendly" and if you "tip the cooks, they will be too", so gung-ho guests say "go even if you have to sit on a three-legged chair with gum on it" and prepare to walk away with a "belly full of deliciousness and a head full of stories."

Parkway Bakery *Po' Boys* 25 | 15 | 18 | $13

Mid-City | 538 Hagan Ave. (Moss St.) | 504-482-3047 | www.parkwaybakeryandtavernnola.com

Reviewers roar the "roast beef rocks" at this "crazy popular" "house of gravied meat" in Mid-City turning out "piled-high po' boys like your aunts and uncles remember"; the "super-nice" staff provides only counter service, but folks waiting in line get a chance to study the "pop culture museum" of "New Orleans memorabilia on the walls" before taking their sandwiches outside to "enjoy the Bayou St. John breeze"; N.B. closed Tuesdays.

Pascal's Manale Ⓢ *Italian* 23 | 18 | 22 | $40

Uptown | 1838 Napoleon Ave. (Barrone St.) | 504-895-4877

"You can feel your arteries filling up" when you indulge in a plate of the original BBQ shrimp "swimming" in "glorious butter" at this Uptown New Orleans–style Italian that boasts an "excellent selection of fresh seafood" and a "classic" oyster bar; "disregard the seemingly seedy exterior, because inside you'll find white tablecloths", an "absolutely delightful" staff and a vibe that "evokes your grandparents' time."

Patois Ⓜ *American/French* 25 | 22 | 22 | $49

Uptown | 6078 Laurel St. (Webster St.) | 504-895-9441 | www.patoisnola.com

At this "real up-and-comer" hidden on an Uptown "neighborhood corner", chef/co-owner Aaron Burgau offers "unexpected" takes on "delicate" French–New American dishes highlighting "fresh, locally procured ingredients"; the room is "airy" and "totally transformed" from the former Nardo's space, and though it's "hard to get a table" (as well as the staff's "attention" at times), the "bar is a great place to wait" while sampling "some of the most original signature drinks in town."

Ⓩ Pelican Club *American* 26 | 24 | 24 | $54

French Quarter | 312 Exchange Pl. (Bienville St.) | 504-523-1504 | www.pelicanclub.com

"The only real secret left in the Quarter" enthuse epicures who have discovered chef-owner Richard Hughes' "imaginative" cooking with "unique flair" (the seafood martini is "exceptional") at this

	FOOD	DECOR	SERVICE	COST

"swank", "jovial" New American; a "well-trained" staff and "chic but still soulful", art-adorned surroundings add to its appeal for "special occasions."

🆕 Pellicano Ristorante Ⓜ *American*

-	-	-	E

Kenner | 4224 Williams Blvd. (42nd St.) | 504-467-2930 | www.pellicanoristorante.com

Kennerites looking for a special night on the town dress up for this fancy yearling in the 'burbs showcasing chef Chris Cody's New American cuisine with its Italian, French, Asian and Caribbean influences; the upscale, Tuscan-style room comes complete with a pricey wine list and attentive servers.

Petunia's *Cajun/Creole*

22	18	19	$24

French Quarter | 817 St. Louis St. (Bourbon St.) | 504-522-6440 | www.petuniasrestaurant.com

"Gigantic delicious crêpes" that deserve to be "shared" are stars of the "over-the-top" Cajun-Creole menu at this "charismatic" brunch "favorite" in a "vintage" French Quarter house; "long lines" and a bit of "attitude" can put off some surveyors, but most call the staff of "off-duty actors/comedians" "delightful."

P.F. Chang's China Bistro *Chinese*

20	21	19	$28

Metairie | Lakeside Mall | 3301 Veterans Memorial Blvd. (N. Causeway Blvd.) | 504-828-5288 | www.pfchangs.com

Expect "major hustle-bustle" at this "crowded" Metairie branch of the Chinese chain where the "mass-produced" menus "aren't really authentic" yet do "appeal to most palates" (when in doubt, the "lettuce wraps rule"); service is "cheerful" and the decor "pleasant", though critics call it "boring" and "commercialized", adding that "in New Orleans, you can do better."

Pho Bang *Vietnamese*

▽ 21	9	16	$13

Metairie | 8814 Veterans Memorial Blvd. (Powder Blvd.) | 504-466-8742
New Orleans East | 14367 Chef Menteur Hwy. (Alcee Fortier Blvd.) | 504-254-3929
Harvey | 1028 Manhattan Blvd. (Westbank Expwy.) | 504-365-0339 🏴

"Soothing", "flavorful" pho and other "excellent" dishes offer boffo "bang for the buck" at these far-flung sibs delivering Vietnamese food "without any gimmicks"; service is "quick", but there's "absolutely no atmosphere" and they close pretty "early."

Pho Danh 4 🏴 *Vietnamese*

-	-	-	I

Gretna | 925 Behrman Hwy. (S. Monterey Ct.) | 504-393-8883

In this bright, modern dining room "next to the fascinating Hong Kong Market" in Gretna, customers can feast on "good pho", "terrific" spring rolls and other "authentic", easy-on-the-wallet Vietnamese eats.

Pho Tau Bay Ⓢ *Vietnamese*

25	11	19	$17

Gretna | Expressway Bowling Lanes Shopping Ctr. | 113C Westbank Expwy. (Lafayette St.) | 504-368-9846

Diners take a "daring excursion to the other side of local dining" at this Gretna Vietnamese serving up "addictive" pho and other "fresh", "affordable" dishes with some appealing "veggie" options; set in a "run-down shopping center", it's a "dive", but the "quick", "friendly" staff is "always helpful" with newcomers.

	FOOD	DECOR	SERVICE	COST

PJ's Coffee & Tea Co. *Coffeehouse* — 19 | 16 | 18 | $7

Central Business Dist. | Tulane Medical Ctr. | 134 Elks Pl. (Cleveland Ave.) | 504-585-1775
Central Business Dist. | 644 Camp St. (Girod St.) | 504-529-3658
Central Business Dist. | D-Day Museum | 945 Magazine St. (bet. Andrew Higgins Dr. & St. Joseph St.) | 504-525-0522
Garden District | Riverside Shopping Ctr. | 5300 Tchoupitoulas St. (Valmont St.) | 504-895-2007
Metairie | 800 Metairie Rd. (Focis St.) | 504-828-1460
Mid-City | 3700 Orleans Ave. (N. Jefferson Davis Pkwy.) | 504-281-4343
Uptown | Tulane University | 24 McAlister Dr. (Freret St.) | 504-865-5705
Uptown | 7624 Maple St. (Adams St.) | 504-866-7031
Algiers | Village Aurora Shopping Ctr. | 4100 General DeGaulle Dr. (Holiday Dr.) | 504-392-4280
Mandeville | 4480 Hwy. 22 (Moores Rd.) | 985-624-9015
www.pjscoffee.com

Caffeinated customers are "hooked" on the "iced coffee done right" accompanied by a "nice selection of pastries" at this Southern coffee chain with "local flair"; "students furiously working or chatting with friends" add to the energy at most branches, though some feel they're "tired" places that "haven't kept up with the spiffier competition."

Popeyes *American* — 22 | 7 | 9 | $9

Gretna | 1401 Lafayette St. (Westbank Expwy.) | 504-366-1898
Gretna | 2148 Belle Chasse Hwy. (Wall Blvd.) | 504-392-4361
Lower Garden Dist. | 1243 St. Charles Ave. (bet. Clio & Erato Sts.) | 504-522-1362
Metairie | 1301 Veterans Memorial Blvd. (Bonnabel Blvd.) | 504-833-6732
Metairie | 4701 Veterans Memorial Blvd. (Clearview Pkwy.) | 504-888-1655
Mid-City | 2000 Gentilly Blvd. (Paris Ave.) | 504-943-5072
Mid-City | 3100 S. Carrollton Ave. (Earhart Blvd.) | 504-486-6521
Mid-City | 4238 S. Claiborne Ave. (Napoleon Ave.) | 504-269-8171
Uptown | 4041 Magazine St. (Marengo St.) | 504-895-8608
Algiers | 3825 General de Gaulle Dr. (Holiday Dr.) | 504-362-6033
www.popeyes.com

"Al Copeland's gift to mankind" is still this city's "guilty pleasure" and "classic hangover cure" with "fried chicken like mother made", "flaky biscuits" and "some of the best red beans and rice"; "service and cleanliness vary by location", but despite an "attitudinal" staff it still gets raves even from folks who "rarely eat at fast-food places."

Port of Call ● *American* — 24 | 13 | 15 | $19

French Quarter | 838 Esplanade Ave. (Dauphine St.) | 504-523-0120 | www.portofcallneworleans.com

"Everyone from the mayor to Mardi Gras Indians rubs elbows" at this French Quarter bar "famous" for "out-of-this-world" "colossal burgers and gigantic loaded potatoes", both "piled high" with toppings; "decorated like an uncle's family room with wood paneling and fishnets", it's "dim", "decrepit" and "cramped", but the "dreadfully long waits are even enjoyable" with a "Big Gulp–style", rum-laced Monsoon.

Praline Connection *Soul Food* — 22 | 13 | 18 | $20

Faubourg Marigny | 542 Frenchmen St. (Chartres St.) | 504-943-3934 | www.pralineconnection.com

"Bring your appetite and forget about the calories" at this Marigny soul food "staple" that dishes up "large portions" of "first-rate" fried chicken, collard greens and other Southern "square meals" along with sweets; it's a little "rough on the edges" and service can be "slow when it's crowded", but the "staff dressed in ties and fedoras adds a touch of class" to the "laid-back atmosphere."

Pupuseria Divino

∇ 21 | 13 | 18 | $19

Corazon 🖫 *Central American/Mexican*

Gretna | 2300 Belle Chasse Hwy. (23rd St.) | 504-368-5724

"Here's another reason to go to West Bank" say supporters of this "authentic" Gretna eatery whose Central American–Mexican menu features "tasty" pupusas, "meat pies" and "fabulous refried beans"; the space is humble, but everything is "inexpensive" and delivered by a "proud", "friendly" staff.

Pupuseria La Macarena 🅼 *Pan-Latin*

- | - | - | I

Metairie | 8016 W. Metairie Ave. (N. Howard Ave.) | 504-464-4525

Pan-Latin dishes, such as pupusas and garlic shrimp, are "served with care" amid "simple surroundings" at this colorful Metairie locale with a Salavadoran bent; still, some say "since the post-Katrina explosion of Latin eateries, there are better deals available."

Raising Cane's *American/Chicken*

18 | 12 | 15 | $9

Metairie | 4036 Veterans Memorial Blvd. (bet. Lake Villa Dr. & Richland Ave.) | 504-297-1632 | www.raisingcanes.com

Your choice of mains are chicken fingers, chicken fingers or chicken fingers at this Louisiana-based chain in Metairie, and if some Cajun-weaned customers deem them "bland" (though "awesomely fried" and "moist"), they just "spice" them up with the "so-good-I-could-drink-it" dipping sauce; "addictive lemonade, iced tea" and Texas toast are "worth a stop" unto themselves, and though the ambiance is strictly "fast food", there's nothing wrong with "cheap eats" now and then.

🆉 Ralph's on the Park *Contemp. Louisiana*

25 | 26 | 25 | $48

Mid-City | 900 City Park Ave. (N. Alexander St.) | 504-488-1000 | www.ralphsonthepark.com

"Ask for a table by a window" or "on the balcony" for "splendid views of City Park" and its "magnificent oaks" at this "charming vintage building" in Mid-City serving "rich, flavorful" ("if slightly pricey") French-tinged Contemporary Louisiana cuisine alongside an "extensive wine list"; the "superb", "professional" service and "romantic" atmosphere further help to "burnish the Brennan family's already illustrious reputation."

NEW Rambla *French/Spanish*

- | - | - | M

Central Business Dist. | International House Hotel | 221 Camp St. (Common St.) | 504-587-7720 | www.ihhotel.com

A vibrant new venue by co-owners Bob Iacovone, Kim Kringlie and Kenny LaCour (Cuvée, The Dakota), this CBD arrival in the International House Hotel celebrates the city's European culinary influences with a menu bringing together Spanish tapas and French *petits plats*, prepared with largely local ingredients; both thoughtful wine pairings and the option of communal seating at bar-high tables make it extra festive for both groups and mingling amigos.

	FOOD	DECOR	SERVICE	COST

R & O's *Italian*
| | 21 | 10 | 18 | $18 |

Bucktown | 216 Hammond Hwy. (Lake Ave.) | Metairie | 504-831-1248
Stuff yourself on "down-home cooking with an Italian flair" from the "affordable" menu that's a "mélange of New Orleans dishes" – particularly the "scrumptious" fried seafood and roast beef po' boys – along with "old-fashioned" pizzas and "killer" salads at this "suburban-style dive" in Bucktown; it's a bit "chaotic" and full of "people who've been going here for generations", so there's "always a wait, but it's worth it."

Red Fish Grill *Seafood*
| | 22 | 21 | 21 | $39 |

French Quarter | 115 Bourbon St. (Canal St.) | 504-598-1200 | www.redfishgrill.com
"Before opening the menu" at this "mildly upscale" French Quarter seafooder, order the "to-die-for double chocolate bread pudding" (it takes time to cook), then try to "save room" for it as you dig into "daydream"-worthy BBQ oysters followed by its eponymous fish served in a variety of "decadent" ways; the "sprawling", "funky" space is "noisy" and "packed with tourists" who feel "spoiled" by the "bevy" of servers.

Refuel Ⓜ *Eclectic*
| | ▽ 22 | 19 | 20 | $14 |

Riverbend | 8124 Hampson St. (S. Carrollton Ave.) | 504-872-0187 | www.refuelcafe.com
"Fabulous breakfasts", brunches and lunches – the latter starring "interesting sandwiches" and "gigantic salads" made with "always fresh ingredients" – fuel Riverbenders at this Eclectic "family-run" "sleeper"; the "delightful staff" and "lovely modern decor" also make it a "comfortable" spot to "hang out" while using the "free WiFi."

Reginelli's Pizzeria *Pizza*
| | 21 | 15 | 18 | $17 |

Garden District | 3244 Magazine St. (Pleasant St.) | 504-895-7272
Harahan | Citrus Palm Shopping Ctr. | 5608 Citrus Blvd. (Elmwood Park Blvd.) | 504-818-0111
Kenner | 817 W. Esplanade Ave. (Chateau Blvd.) | 504-712-6868
Lakeview | 874 Harrison Ave. (bet. General Diaz & Marshall Foch Sts.). | 504-488-0133
Uptown | 741 State St. (bet. Constance & Magazine Sts.) | 504-899-1414
www.reginellis.com
The "sauce has just the right zip" at this local pizza chain known for its "original" pies, "unique sandwiches" and "big salads"; it's "informal" and "cheerfully" staffed, making it an "easygoing" choice for families.

Remoulade ⓓ *Creole*
| | 18 | 15 | 18 | $25 |

French Quarter | 309 Bourbon St. (Bienville St.) | 504-523-0377 | www.remoulade.com
When "you're not feeling the white-tablecloth vibe but want better than a Lucky Dog", this Bourbon Street "down-to-earth cousin" of Arnaud's "without the dress code" is the place for "comforting" Creole "lunches or late-night snacks" on the "cheap"; it's fairly "touristy" and "not outstanding", but usually delivers an "enjoyable experience."

Restaurant des Familles Ⓜ *Cajun/Seafood*
| | 22 | 24 | 24 | $34 |

Crown Point | 7163 Barataria Blvd. (Lafitte Pkwy.) | 504-689-7834 | www.restaurantdesfamilles.com
"You may see an alligator swimming by" this "lovely" Crown Point Cajun providing "peaceful" "moonlit" views of the bayou and "fresh",

FOOD | DECOR | SERVICE | COST

"different" seafood ("I'm getting hungry just thinking about it"); the service is "prompt" and "accommodating" to groups, and while "it's a little out of the way", many feel "this is how" to savor the region's cuisine.

Rib Room *Steak* | 25 | 25 | 25 | $56 |

French Quarter | Omni Royal Orleans | 621 St. Louis St. (Chartres St.) | 504-529-7046 | www.omnihotels.com

"Seersucker suits and big hats" pack this "happening", high-ceilinged French Quarter "dining institution" in the Royal O to devour "fabulous prime rib" and other "quality" steaks, along with "must-try martinis"; for the full experience, go for a "power lunch" or "special-occasion" dinner, let the "top-notch", "traditional" staff take care of you and "get a table by the window to make everyone outside envious."

Riccobono's Panola Street Cafe *American* | - | - | - | I |

Carrollton | 7801 Panola St. (Burdette St.) | 504-314-1810

A Carrollton secret and offshoot of Metairie's Riccobono, it's less red-gravy Italian and more homestyle bacon and eggs at this former corner store complete with whirring ceiling fans, funky consignment art and schoolroom chairs on a linoleum floor; trad pancakes, chili cheese omelets and crab cakes Benedict, along with reasonably priced daily lunch specials, are served till 2 PM by a smiling young staff.

Riccobono's Peppermill *Creole/Italian* | 21 | 18 | 21 | $26 |
(aka Peppermill)

Metairie | 3524 Severn Ave. (12th St.) | 504-455-2266

It's "like eating at grandma's house" say fond fans of this "old-fashioned", inexpensive Metairie place where the "fantastic breakfasts" tend to outshine the "basic" Creole-Italian lunches and dinners; despite its "devoted" "older" following, detractors deem the fare "bland", "dated" and out of the "dark ages of TV trays and unimaginative food."

☑ RioMar ⧄ *Seafood* | 26 | 20 | 23 | $40 |

Warehouse District | 800 S. Peters St. (Julia St.) | 504-525-3474 | www.riomarseafood.com

Chef/co-owner Adolfo Garcia prepares "light, uncomplicated" ceviche among other "fantastic", seafood-centric Spanish and Latin-inspired plates at this Warehouse District "delight" that's "moderately priced for the quality"; warmed up by exposed-brick walls, it hosts a "hip", "dynamic" scene boosted by a "wonderful", group-friendly staff.

Ristorante Da Piero ⧄Ⓜ *Italian* | ▽ 27 | 24 | 24 | $52 |

Kenner | 401 Williams Blvd. (4th St.) | 504-469-8585 | www.ristorantedapiero.net

An "anomaly" in a "city full of Creole-Italians", this family-run "home of delectable delights" in Kenner provides "impeccable" Emilian cuisine served with "care" amid "refined yet extremely comfortable" environs; it's "fairly expensive" and can be a bit "slow", but many savor the "leisurely pace", along with occasional entertainment by an opera singer.

☑ Ristorante del Porto ⧄Ⓜ *Italian* | 26 | 24 | 24 | $49 |

Covington | 501 E. Boston St. (New Hampshire St.) | 985-875-1006 | www.delportoristorante.com

Married chef-owners Torre Bagalman and David Solazzo take guests on a "romantic", "Tuscan"-accented trip at this "rare" rustic Italian "nestled in the heart of Downtown Covington", where the "authentic", "innovative" dishes feature homemade pastas and local produce; given the "great wine and drink list", "top-notch" service and surroundings decorated with art from nearby galleries, even South Shore dwellers say it's "well worth the drive" and somewhat "expensive" check.

Ristorante Filippo ⑤ *Italian* ▽ 24 | 19 | 22 | $35

Metairie | 1917 Ridgelake Dr. (38th St.) | 504-835-4008

Enthusiasts find "everything you want in an evening" at this "hidden gem in Metairie" turning out "delicious" Italian food (with "extraordinary" red sauce) in a "cozy, romantic" atmosphere; since the service is "attentive" and "familiar" and tabs are moderate, it maintains a strong "local following."

Rock-n-Sake Bar & Sushi Ⓜ *Japanese* 23 | 21 | 19 | $32

Warehouse District | 823 Fulton St. (bet. Julia & St. Joseph Sts.) | 504-581-7253 | www.rocknsake.com

"SoHo comes to NOLA" at this Warehouse District "hot spot" (with an offshoot in NYC) whose "unexpectedly" winning menu boasts "out-of-this-world" Japanese dishes and "some of the most interesting rolls in the city"; it's "sophisticated" at lunch and a "hip" "babe market at night", complete with a "clublike vibe", "high-energy music" and "to-the-rim" drinks.

Rocky & Carlo's ⑤Ⓜ *Creole/Italian* 22 | 11 | 16 | $16

Chalmette | 613 W. St. Bernard Hwy. (Victor St.) | 504-279-8323

"Katrina couldn't keep this Chalmette favorite down" say diners from "da Parish" who declare it has "no decor, so you can concentrate on the gigantic portions" of "down-home" Creole-Italian food, including the "legendary" mac 'n' cheese with "red gravy"; since the "bills are small" and it's staffed by the "friendliest people around", it's earned its place as a "blue-plate" "institution."

Roly Poly *Sandwiches* 18 | 12 | 16 | $10

Central Business Dist. | One Shell Sq. | 701 Poydras St. (St. Charles Ave.) | 504-561-9800 ⑤

NEW **Metairie** | 3020 Veterans Memorial Blvd. (Ridgelake Dr.) | 504-872-0957

Uptown | 5409 Tchoupitoulas St. (Jefferson Ave.) | 504-891-8373

Mandeville | 3960 Florida St. (Devon Dr.) | 985-626-4892

www.rolypoly.com

A "bazillion combos" of "quick, healthy" wraps await at this soup-and-sandwich chain that's a "cut above" other fast-food options, making it a "favorite lunch spot" for many; despite the "guilt-free" prices, peeved patrons say it still has a "plastic quality" and is too "boring" for New Orleans.

Royal Blend Coffee & Tea *Coffeehouse* ▽ 16 | 16 | 15 | $10

French Quarter | 621 Royal St. (Toulouse St.) | 504-523-2716

Metairie | 204 Metairie Rd. (Friedrichs Ave.) | 504-835-7779

www.royalblendcoffee.com

Offering a "charming" "alternative" to the "more famous" java joints, these local coffeehouses in the French Quarter and Metairie pour "French roast that's a real treat" and have a "fantastic tea selection" to go with sandwiches and sweets; contented customers like to "sit and read for a while" in the "comfortable courtyard" on Royal Street, even if service is sometimes a buzzkill.

Royal China *Chinese*
24 | 11 | 18 | $23

Metairie | 600 Veterans Memorial Blvd. (Aris Ave.) | 504-831-9633 | www.royalchinarest.com

It's "best to bring a crowd, order too much and share everything" at this "authentic", "midrange" Chinese in Metairie dishing up "real dim sum" among other "delicious" food; though the setting "needs some work", "owner Shirley Lee makes you feel like a regular on your first visit", keeping "neighbors, politicos" and other "loyal" fans coming back.

NEW Ruby Slipper ⓜ *American*
▽ 23 | 21 | 22 | $19

Mid-City | 139 S. Cortez St. (Canal St.) | 504-309-5531 | www.therubyslippercafe.net

The "Southern breakfasts have just a little fancy thrown in" – and the "brandy milk punch at brunch makes drinking milk fun again" – at this "welcome" new daytime American in Mid-City, a neighborhood that "sorely needed a breakfast spot"; it's a "good value" too, and the "cute", "comfortable" "corner location" invites diners to "socialize as they wait" for a table.

rue de la course ◐⇄ *Coffeehouse*
19 | 18 | 18 | $9

Carrollton | 1140 S. Carrollton Ave. (bet. Oak & Zimpel Sts.) | 504-861-4343
Garden District | 3121 Magazine St. (9th St.) | 504-899-0242

Suffused with "European atmosphere" and an "intellectual, bohemian feel", these coffeehouses in Carrollton and the Garden District fill mugs with "fabulous" java, "fantastic iced coffee" and "great mochas" to match the "not-bad" pastries and lunch items; "quirky", "hip baristas" have "lots of attitude" and keep them open till midnight, when they're "overrun with med and law students cramming and caffeinating."

Russell's Marina Grill *Diner*
19 | 14 | 20 | $17

Lakefront | 8555 Pontchartrain Blvd. (Lake Marina Ave.) | 504-282-9999

"There's no place I'd rather be when hungover" confess customers of this Lakefront diner delivering "breakfast feasts" and "plain food cooked well" to a daytime "family" crowd; while the '50s-style space is merely "functional", it's full of "friendly faces."

Russell's Short Stop Po-Boys ⓑ *Po' Boys*
20 | 7 | 15 | $11

Metairie | 119 Transcontinental Dr. (Thrush St.) | 504-885-4572 | www.shortstoppoboys.com

A "long list of po' boys to fit any appetite", including "classic" "messy roast beef", means this "quintessential Metairie joint" "gets mobbed" (fortunately the "line moves quickly"); it's "out-of-the-way", but "decent" prices help make up for the hike; N.B. closes at 7:30 PM most weeknights.

Ⓩ Ruth's Chris Steak House *Steak*
26 | 22 | 25 | $62

NEW Central Business Dist. | Harrah's Hotel | 525 Fulton St. (Poydras St.) | 504-587-7099
Metairie | 3633 Veterans Memorial Blvd. (Hessmer Ave.) | 504-888-3600
www.ruthschris.com

"Rob a bank before you dine" at this "first-class" New Orleans–born chain in Metairie and now in the CBD's Harrah's Hotel, specializing in "mouthwatering" steaks "sizzling in butter" that "set the bar nation-wide"; the surroundings are "wonderfully decorated" and the staff "knows how to pamper" the "bigwigs", but some unrelenting reviewers say "Ruth must be turning in her grave" since corporate HQ "deserted New Orleans after the storm."

NEW Sailor's Seafood & Oyster Bar Seafood — | — | — | M

Mid-City | 133 N. Carrollton Ave. (Canal St.) | 504-483-3232
Early samplers say this Mid-City "neighborhood place" serves "sensational seafood" (the charred oysters in particular are "well prepared"), plus "interesting" Turkish specialties reflecting the owner's heritage; prices are appropriately modest for the casual, nautical-themed atmosphere.

Sake Cafe Japanese 23 | 23 | 21 | $29

Kenner | 817 W. Esplanade Ave. (Chateau Blvd.) | 504-468-8829
Metairie | Independence Mall | 4201 Veterans Memorial Blvd.
(bet. Independence St. & Lake Villa Dr.) | 504-779-7253
Uptown | 2830 Magazine St. (bet. 6th St. & Washington Ave.) |
504-894-0033 | www.sakecafeuptown.us
"Not your average sushi" specialist, this "stylish" Japanese trio turns out "imaginative" rolls and "modern" cooked dishes complemented by "fabulous" wines and cocktails; though the tabs strike some as "pricey", most find the "upscale" ambiance "worth it", especially at the separately owned Uptown locale boasting a "chic", "cavernous" dining area decked out with Dale Chihuly glass lamps.

Sal & Judy's M Creole/Italian 26 | 19 | 22 | $37

Lacombe | 27491 Hwy. 190 (14th St.) | 985-882-9443 |
www.salandjudys.com
"Locals love" this "authentic" Creole–Southern Italian "roadhouse" in Lacombe, vouching for its "traditional" pastas, steaks and other "food like you hoped your grandmother made", served in portions so ample "the plates must weigh a ton"; service is "attentive" and it's "unbeatable for the price", so to beat the "packed" crowd, "plan to make reservations a couple of weeks in advance."

Saltwater Grill S Seafood ∇ 16 | - | 17 | $22

Riverbend | 710 S. Carrollton St. (Maple St.) | 504-324-6640 |
www.saltwatergrillnola.com
"Plenty of seafood", "fun specials" and an "awesome bar staff" call crustacean-lovers to this affordable eatery that has relocated from Carrollton to the Riverbend; it's good for kids, as tables are covered in white butcher paper and set with crayons, but critics warn the food is "unpredictable" and the service uneven.

Sara's S M Asian/Creole ∇ 24 | 19 | 20 | $29

Riverbend | 724 Dublin St. (bet. Hampson & Maple Sts.) | 504-861-0565 |
www.sarasrestaurant.com
Riverbend foodies profess this "elegant" "date" spot's "stellar mixture of Indian" and Thai flavors elevates its Asian-Creole fusion fare to "sublime" status; to boot, the "relatively inexpensive" tabs, "accommodating" servers and "cool" "lounge"-like atmosphere (replete with "big, comfortable chairs") have them questioning how it remains "virtually undiscovered."

	FOOD	DECOR	SERVICE	COST

Semolina *Eclectic/Italian* | 17 | 17 | 18 | $22

Metairie | Clearview Mall | 4436 Veterans Memorial Blvd. (Clearview Pkwy.) | 504-454-7930
Mandeville | 2999 Hwy. 190 (St. Ann Dr.) | 985-626-8923
www.semolina.com

"Imaginative" "pasta variations" of world cuisines (BBQ chicken, jambalaya, pad Thai) is the concept of this "laid-back" Eclectic-Italian duo that "kids love" for the selection and adults appreciate for the "huge portions at moderate prices" and "ease of seating for large groups"; critics lament "hit-or-miss" quality – still, they "somehow end up coming back."

Semolina's Bistro Italia *Italian* | 17 | 19 | 18 | $27

Garden District | 3226 Magazine St. (Pleasant St.) | 504-895-4260 | www.semolina.com

At its latest venture, chain pasta purveyor Semolina "goes upscale" with "modern, sexy" decor, but stays true to its "bargain" roots with the "same" "huge portions" of noodles made with "interesting" sauces as its other eateries (additional Italian "comfort" fare is also served); if foodies find it "nothing special", grape nuts toast that many of the wines are "$25 a bottle", while spectators enjoy the sidewalk seating for "excellent" Garden District "people-watching."

Serranos Salsa Co. *Nuevo Latino* | 18 | 18 | 18 | $23

Metairie | Clearview Mall | 4436 Veterans Memorial Blvd. (Clearview Pkwy.) | 504-780-2354 | www.serranossalsacompany.com

Before catching a flick at the multiplex, Metairie amigos wash down "bottomless chips" dipped in "delicious salsa" with cocktails made from a "big selection of tequila and rum" at this vast Nuevo Latino "cantina" in the Clearview Mall; enthusiasts stay for what they call "colorful, flavorful", "relative-bargain" entrees, while "franchise"-phobics, who deem them "nothing remarkable", move along.

7 on Fulton *Contemp. Louisiana* | 22 | 22 | 22 | $48

Warehouse District | Wyndham Riverfront New Orleans | 701 Convention Center Blvd. (Girod St.) | 504-525-7555 | www.7onfulton.com

"Clever" and "cosmopolitan", the "pricey" Contemporary Louisiana fare at this Warehouse District hotel eatery is complemented by "modern, minimalist" surroundings with "effective" touches of candlelight; though critics cite "uneven" food, "inconsistent" service and a "lacking" atmosphere, it's a "pleasant" choice "if you're looking for privacy", since even fans note the "quiet" room has "never taken off with locals."

NEW Shane's Rib Shack *BBQ* | ∇ 18 | 17 | 22 | $24

Marrero | Belle Barataria Ctr. | 1855 Barataria Blvd. (bet. Oak & Richland Drs.) | 504-324-9701 | www.shanesribshack.com

"Solid BBQ" like pulled-pork sandwiches, racks of ribs and meat-topped salads sate starving shoppers at this chain shack-simile in Marrero's Belle Barataria Centre; but even "great prices" don't appease carpers who contend the 'cue is "characterless."

Shogun Japanese *Japanese* | 24 | 18 | 20 | $32

Metairie | 2325 Veterans Memorial Blvd. (Metairie Ct.) | 504-833-7477
Despite its "kitschy name", this "relaxed" longtime Japanese is, for many aficionados, still the "benchmark" in Metairie for "excellent"

"fresh" sushi, sashimi and "family-friendly" hibachi fare, presented with a "pretty good show at the grill"; the main concern is the service, which, while "courteous", "could be more accommodating."

Shula's *Steak*   20 | 19 | 20 | $57

Central Business Dist. | JW Marriott | 614 Canal St. (Camp St.) | 504-586-7211 | www.donshula.com

Expect "man-sized everything" at former NFL coach Don Shula's white-tablecloth chain beefery in the CBD's JW Marriott, where "quality steaks" are served with ample helpings of "sports memorabilia"; but it's "best left to the business traveler" caution locals who can find "no excuse for going" since it's "overpriced in all areas."

Siamese Restaurant *Thai*   ∇ 22 | 14 | 19 | $20

Metairie | 6601 Veterans Memorial Blvd. (Downs Blvd.) | 504-454-8752 | www.siamesecuisine.com

"Don't be thrown off by the strip-mall location" or short-on-charm atmosphere of this Metairie Thai serving "great" curries, noodles and seafood dishes; the voluminous menu provides strong variety and value, especially for group dining.

Singha ⊠ *Thai*   ∇ 22 | 12 | 17 | $20
(aka Singha Thai Cafe)

Central Business Dist. | 413 Carondelet St. (bet. Perdido & Poydras Sts.) | 504-581-2205

CBD lunchers storm this "popular" Thai for "consistent" fare with just "the right amount of spice"; though the space "isn't much", it's made up for by "bargain" prices and a "hard-working" staff that "customizes any dish to taste or dietary restriction."

Slice *Pizza*   23 | 15 | 18 | $16
(aka Slice Pizzeria)

Lower Garden Dist. | 1513 St. Charles Ave. (Melpomene Ave.) | 504-525-7437 | www.slicepizzeria.com

Not only does this Lower Garden District parlor "fill the need" for "fab" pizza by the slice ("hard to find" in the Crescent City), but it lets guests "customize individual" pieces with "fresh", "creative" toppings; its "twentysomething in-crowd" habitués also dig the whole pies, "awesome salads" and "fantastic calzones", which come via servers both "friendly" and "blasé."

Slim Goodies Diner ⊅ *American*   21 | 17 | 20 | $14

Garden District | 3322 Magazine St. (Toledano St.) | 504-891-3447

Like a "'50s-style diner" that's been "tattooed and pierced", this "oh-so-funky" Garden District breakfast-and-lunch nook serves an "interesting, locally influenced menu" of "reasonably priced", "stick-to-your-ribs" American comfort food "with many vegetarian options"; expect a "wait" "on weekend mornings", as "crowds line up" to be "set right after a night of too much fun" by the "delightful, hilarious" staff.

Smilie's Restaurant *Creole/Italian*   17 | 14 | 17 | $25

Harahan | 5725 Jefferson Hwy. (Edwards Ave.) | 504-733-3000 | www.smiliesrestaurant.com

"Senior citizens" love the "large", "reasonably priced" portions of seafood-heavy Creole-Italian eats (not to mention the "early-bird prix-fixe dinner") dished out at this "neighborhood place" in Harahan; on the other hand, "disappointed" whippersnappers say "nobody's smiling" here, what with the "nothing-special" fare and "boring decor."

St. Charles Tavern ● American | 14 | 11 | 15 | $17

Uptown | 1433 St. Charles Ave. (bet. Martin Luther King Jr. Blvd. & Thalia St.) | 504-523-9823

Sort of "like eating in a Tom Waits song", this "affordable" 24/7 American "dive" is a "godsend" to Uptown "policemen", "firemen" and other folks on the "night shift" who need some "greasy" "grub" "when everything else is closed"; but even drinking buddies admit it only "becomes appealing at about 2 AM" when "late-night cravings" trump "terrible surroundings."

Stein's Market & Deli Ⓜ Deli | 23 | 12 | 16 | $15

Lower Garden Dist. | 2207 Magazine St. (Jackson Ave.) | 504-527-0771 | www.steinsdeli.net

"Oversized-sandwich" lovers who feel the Lower Garden District "badly needed" "New York–quality pastrami", "divine corned beef" and other "delicious" "non-po'-boy-category" two-handers are thrilled with this "real deli", which also vends "hard-to-find-gourmet items"; though it may be "slightly pricey" for the type, it's "worth it for the quality."

🅩 Stella! American | 28 | 26 | 27 | $67

French Quarter | Hotel Provincial | 1032 Chartres St. (bet. St. Philip & Ursuline Sts.) | 504-587-0091 | www.restaurantstella.com

"The artistry and science that go into preparing the dishes is tops" at this "must-visit" New American in the French Quarter where "über"-chef-owner Scott Boswell creates "spectacular" dishes with an "avant-garde" "Asian backbeat"; "intelligent" wine choices, "engaged yet formal" servers who "knock themselves out to please" and a "soothing" setting pull together the "exceptional" meal, but "bring a fat wallet" since the check is equally "awe-inspiring."

Steve's Diner Ⓩ Diner | ▽ 16 | - | 12 | $14

Central Business Dist. | Place St. Charles | 201 St. Charles Ave., 2nd fl. (Common St.) | 504-522-8198 | www.steves-diner.com

Now moved to slightly larger quarters inside the food court of Place St. Charles in the CBD, this "reliable" diner still offers most of the same "decent" homestyle plate lunches, salads and a smattering of revolving daily specials to famished suits who say it's "always a good meal"; when it comes to the biscuits and other choice items, though, they often "run out of food too quickly."

🅩 St. James Cheese Company Ⓩ Continental | 26 | 18 | 21 | $18

Uptown | 5004 Prytania St. (Robert St.) | 504-899-4737 | www.stjamescheese.com

"Cheese-a-holics" rejoice over this Uptown "oasis" – an "adorable" "European"-style shop with a "fabulous" array of "international" *fromage*, cured meats and pâtés, a "helpful" staff "overflowing with knowledge" and a smattering of indoor and outdoor tables where foodies relax over "excellent" sandwiches, salads, cheese plates and charcuterie boards; it's a "perfect" salute to good weather, especially if you snag a worthy bottle from The Wine Seller next door; P.S. it closes early most nights, but Thursday "guest-chef dinners" are "lovely events."

🆕 Stop 9 Refueling Station & Culinary Specialties Ⓜ Eclectic
▽ 15 | 19 | 17 | $17

Lower Garden Dist. | 1432 St. Charles Ave. (Melpomene Ave.) | 504-267-3028 | www.stop9nola.com

This "cute" newcomer in the Lower Garden District offers an Eclectic hodgepodge of Spanish tapas and wines at night and "tasty sandwiches" during lunch on the weekends, as well as all-natural snowballs alongside "standard pastries and espresso drinks"; a retail area offers prepared foods for carryout and gourmet pantry items.

Store, The Ⓢ American
▽ 23 | 17 | 19 | $13

Central Business Dist. | 814 Gravier St. (Carondelet St.) | 504-701-4041 | www.thestoreneworleans.com

Inspired by an erstwhile eatery frequented by farmers in St. Landry Parish, this CBD daytimer puts "upscale" "tweaks" on New American fare like morning egg dishes, po' boys and salads; the digs are appropriately homey, "cool and funky", with beadboard paneling and church pews evoking simpler times, just like the "nice folks behind the counter."

☒ Sucré Dessert
25 | 26 | 21 | $13

Garden District | 3025 Magazine St. (bet. 7th & 8th Sts.) | 504-520-8311 | www.shopsucre.com

"Heavenly" gelato, "intricate chocolate creations" "to kill for", "exquisite pastries" – there are enough "delicious" treats to "satisfy any sweet tooth" at this "sleek", "absolutely gorgeous" teak-and-mint-green Garden District dessert bistro; "darn good sandwiches" provide savory sustenance 11 AM–4 PM, while wine and champagne help numb the "ouch!" of "pricey" tabs.

Sugar Park Tavern Pizza
▽ 25 | 10 | 15 | $13

Bywater | 800 France St. (Dauphine St.) | 504-940-6226

Pie partisans "brave" Bywater for the "delicious" "thin-crust" pizza – some of "the best" "for miles" – baked at this "dumpy" 21-and-over "dive bar with food"; there's also plenty of "cheap beer" and video poker, but practically "no service."

Sukho Thai Ⓜ Thai
- | - | - | M

Faubourg Marigny | 1913 Royal St. (Touro St.) | 504-948-9309 | www.sukhothai-nola.com

Both Quarterites and Marigny neighbors frequent this accommodating Asian serving satays and spicy curries in a sweet space decorated with colorful Thai decor; modest prices and a welcome BYO policy with no corkage fee make it all the more affordable.

Sun Ray Grill American
21 | 18 | 18 | $25

Gretna | Meadowcrest Ctr. | 2600 Belle Chasse Hwy. (Meadowcrest St.) | 504-391-0053
Metairie | 619 Pink St. (Focis St.) | 504-837-0055
Warehouse District | 1051 Annunciation St. (Andrew Higgins Dr.) | 504-566-0021
www.sunraygrill.com

There's "lots to choose from" at these "consistent" New American siblings, and though each proffers a slightly different menu, all offer a

	FOOD	DECOR	SERVICE	COST

"delectable" "fusion" of Asian, Caribbean, Mediterranean and Tex-Mex flavors along with "great value for the dollar"; the Warehouse District iteration has a vintage-industrial air, while the Gretna and Metairie locations are swathed in beige-and-orange island decor.

Superior Grill *Mexican*

20	19	19	$23

Uptown | 3636 St. Charles Ave. (Antonine St.) | 504-899-4200 | www.superiorgrill.com

"Knock-you-on-your-behind" margaritas and "tasty", "reasonably priced" Mex served in "large portions" draw "college students", "singles" and "large groups" to this "loud, fun" "party" place Uptown; indeed, it's "usually very busy", so it's quite a feat that "service usually doesn't suffer"; P.S. the "newly renovated" glass-enclosed porch is an ideal perch to "enjoy the view of the passing streetcars."

Surrey's Juice Bar Ⓜ⇗ *American*

25	16	18	$16

Lower Garden Dist. | 1418 Magazine St. (Euterpe St.) | 504-524-3828

"Delicious" "fresh-squeezed juices" and "creative", "organic-leaning" American dishes are "worth waiting for" ("which you will do", especially on weekends) at this "funky-crunchy" Lower Garden District breakfast and lunch "gem"; the "nice" staff adds to the charm, as does the "great art" for sale; N.B. cash only.

Sushi Brothers *Japanese*

25	17	23	$22

Lower Garden Dist. | 1612 St. Charles Ave. (bet. Euterpe & Terpsichore Sts.) | 504-581-4449 | www.sushibrothers.net

Some of "the best sushi deals in town" can be found at this Lower Garden District Japanese where "generous portions" of "fresh" sashimi and "creative rolls" are offered at "affordable prices"; it's "not the most exciting" setting, but the "aim-to-please" Vietnamese siblings who own it "more than make up" for that (plus "you can watch the streetcars pass" on St. Charles Avenue if you get bored).

Taco San Miguel *Mexican*

▽ 17	10	13	$13

NEW **Metairie** | 3517 20th St. (Arnoult Rd.) | 504-267-4027
Mid-City | 2120 N. Claiborne Ave. (Elysian Fields Ave.) | 504-473-3529

"It's a steal!" shout supporters of the "delicious, authentic" Mexican fare (tacos, gorditas, fajitas and the like) "made to order with fresh ingredients" at this "inexpensive" duo; the "tiny" Mid-City location proffers a more abbreviated menu than Metairie, but both are convenient places for "separate checks", since you get the goods "cafeteria-style."

Taj Mahal Indian Cuisine *Indian/Vegetarian*

▽ 22	13	19	$23

Old Metairie | 923 Metairie Rd. (Rosa Ave.) | Metairie | 504-836-6859

"Delicious sauces", "juicy tandoori meats", "great" naan and "fresh" vegetarian dishes are just some of the Indian fare "cooked to perfection" at this "quaint family restaurant" in Old Metairie; the "dumpy" setting's a hurdle that's easily "overcome" by "couldn't-be-friendlier" servers and cheap tabs (the lunch buffet is only $9.95); N.B. closed Tuesdays.

Tan Dinh *Vietnamese*

▽ 25	12	14	$18

Gretna | 1705 Lafayette St. (17th St.) | 504-361-8008

"One of the best Vietnamese restaurants in the greater metropolitan area", this "popular lunch spot" in Gretna dishes up "authentic" pho, curried goat and other "standouts" for "adventurous" eaters; it's all "well priced", so don't worry about the lowbrow digs – just "bring lots of people", explore the "large" menu and "try dishes you normally wouldn't think to order" for a "satisfying" meal; N.B. closed Tuesdays, and closes at 8 PM weeknights (9 PM weekends).

Taqueria Corona *Mexican*   21 | 13 | 18 | $17

Harahan | 1827 Hickory Ave. (Citrus Rd.) | 504-738-6722
Metairie | The Esplanade | 3535 Severn Ave. (W. Esplanade Ave.) | 504-885-5088
Uptown | 5932 Magazine St. (bet. Eleonore & State Sts.) | 504-897-3974

With a "bracing variety" of "flavorful tacos", flautas and burritos, preceded by "perfectly seasoned guac" and "delicious" *cebollitas* (cooked whole green onions), it's no wonder locals eat themselves into Mexican "food comas" at these "simple neighborhood joints"; "awesome margaritas by the pitcher" (not to mention "low prices") "go a long way toward making you forget" their "divey appearances."

Taqueria Guerrero Mexico *Mexican*   - | - | - | I

Mid-City | 208 N. Carrollton Ave. (bet. Bienville Ave. & Canal St.) | 504-484-6959

Those who've sampled this Mid-City Mexican report "authentic", even "amazing" tacos, tortas, chiles rellenos and more; light blue walls, a bar with arches and lots of windows help to offset fluorescent lighting and a loud television.

Taqueria Sanchez *Mexican*   - | - | - | I

Gretna | 46 Westbank Expwy. (Stephens St.) | 504-361-3050
Kenner | 2633 Williams Blvd. (bet. 26th & 27th Sts.) | 504-712-5234 ⌨
Metairie | 4432 S. I-10 Service Rd. W. (Concordia St.) | 504-883-2649

From one post-Katrina taco truck to its present multiple branches, the Sanchez family attracts budget-conscious Latinos and other fans for tacos, gorditos, enchiladas and even homemade Salvadorean pupusas for lunch or dinner; on the early side, hungry folks can also warm up with hearty huevos rancheros while catching the latest news *en español* on TV.

Theo's *Pizza*   24 | 15 | 19 | $17

Uptown | 4218 Magazine St. (Milan St.) | 504-894-8554 | www.theospizza.com

"Now that's some great pizza!" bellow boosters of this "funky", "urban" Uptown parlor's "crisp thin-crust" pies loaded with "zesty sauces" and "awesome", "out-of-the-ordinary toppings"; "great Italian salads" and "nicely priced" (albeit "limited") wines are two more reasons fans keep the "small", counter-service space "always booming."

13 Monaghan ☕ *Eclectic/Vegetarian*   19 | 15 | 16 | $18

Faubourg Marigny | 517 Frenchmen St. (bet. Chartres & Decatur Sts.) | 504-942-1345 | www.13monaghan.com

"Sober up after a night of partying on Frenchmen Street" or wake up to a "hangover lunch" of "darn good bar food" (including "lots of veg options") at this "neat place" with an Eclectic menu served till 4 AM; the decor is "simplistic" and the workers sometimes "slower than slow", but that just gives you time to explore the jukebox loaded with "the most obscure songs ever"; N.B. must be 21 or over.

DINING

	FOOD	DECOR	SERVICE	COST

Tomatillo's 🄼 *Mexican* | 16 | 20 | 20 | $24 |
Faubourg Marigny | 437 Esplanade Ave. (Frenchmen St.) | 504-945-9997
Eaters "enjoy the weather", live "Latin bands with dancing" (Friday–Sunday nights) and "really good" frozen margaritas in the "beautiful", spacious courtyard of this Faubourg Marigny Mexican with a "convenient" location across from the French Quarter; indeed, the music and the booze are "the real reasons anyone goes" here, being that the food is merely "average" and "not terribly authentic."

Tommy's Cuisine *Creole/Italian* | 25 | 24 | 25 | $48 |
Warehouse District | 746 Tchoupitoulas St. (bet. Girod & Julia Sts.) | 504-581-1103 | www.tommyscuisine.com
"You feel like the Sopranos could walk in any moment" at Tommy Andrade's "upscale" Warehouse District Creole-Italian, where the "old-school" surroundings set the stage for "phenomenal" fare and "plentiful" vino; "awesome" service ups its appeal for both "families" and "dates", while the adjoining wine bar provides an after-dinner option.

Tony Angello's Ristorante 🄯🄼 *Italian* | 24 | 20 | 21 | $42 |
Lakeview | 6262 Fleur de Lis Dr. (W. Harrison Ave.) | 504-488-0888
The cognoscenti at this "comfortable", "old-style" Lakeview Italian "pretend there is no menu" and say "feed me" to "Mr. Tony", who prepares 10–13 "sublime" small courses, each "more delicious than the last"; "warm" service and the house's "incredible character" have long made it a "favorite for small group celebrations."

Tony Mandina's 🄯🄼 *Italian/Seafood* | 22 | 18 | 22 | $27 |
Gretna | 1915 Pratt St. (Porter St.) | 504-362-2010 | www.tonymandinas.com
"Red-gravy" lovers say "ooh", "what a find" to this "romantic" Southern Italian in Gretna plating up "more-than-adequate portions" of "fabulous" fare that's strong on pasta and seafood; "personable" service and live piano on Friday–Saturday (the only nights dinner is served) lend it real "atmosphere" for a "leisurely" meal.

Tower of Pizza *Pizza* | - | - | - | I |
Metairie | 2410 Veterans Memorial Blvd. (Metairie Heights Ave.) | 504-833-9373
Opened in 1978, this "long-standing tradition" in Metairie "rocks" with "hand-flipped pizzas" and "great salads"; it's just one step up from a "dive", but that doesn't deter its die-hard fans, so "come early or wait."

Trey Yuen *Chinese/Seafood* | 23 | 23 | 21 | $28 |
Hammond | 2100 N. Morrison Blvd. (W. University Ave.) | 985-345-6789
Mandeville | 600 N. Causeway Blvd. (Monroe St.) | 985-626-4476
www.treyyuen.com
If you're gunning for "amazing Chinese", "shoot over" to one of these Hammond and Mandeville Mandarins for "top-notch" yet "affordable" fare featuring "local seafood"; "wonderful" service and "beautiful surroundings" (koi ponds, waterfalls, bamboo) further make it "worth the drive" over Lake Pontchartrain.

Trolley Stop Cafe *Diner*   ▽ | 20 | 10 | 18 | $15 |
Lower Garden Dist. | 1923 St. Charles Ave. (St. Andrew St.) | 504-523-0090
"Considering the price, you really can't beat" this "grungy" Lower Garden District diner doling out "solid breakfast at all hours" ("mon-

strous omelets", "strong coffee") and "darn good sandwiches" for lunch Sunday–Wednesday until 2 PM; since it's also open all night Thursday–Saturday, it's "just the place to detox" in the wee hours.

Tujague's *Creole*　　　21 | 20 | 21 | $41

French Quarter | 823 Decatur St. (Madison St.) | 504-525-8676 | www.tujagues.com

At this "memorable" French Quarter Creole, "one of the oldest restaurants in New Orleans", "entertaining servers" ferry a "reasonably priced", "wonderful five-course" table d'hôte menu that includes "fabulous shrimp rémoulade" and "the world's most tender beef brisket" ("you only have to make one choice: the entree"); even locals who dub it a "food museum" "for tourists" allow "everyone has to try" this "quintessential experience" at least once.

Two Tony's 🗷Ⓜ *Italian*　　　23 | 15 | 21 | $26
(aka Il Tony's)

Bucktown | 105 Hammond Hwy. (Lake Pontchartrain & 17th St. Canal) | Metairie | 504-831-0999 | www.two-tonys.com

Lusty marinara sauce "so rich and wicked" "they should bottle it" and other Italian fare "served with pride", including "fabulous" seafood, are delivered in "large portions for a reasonable cost" at this "comfortable" Bucktown father-and-son "hole-in-the-wall"; the staff adds a "friendly" touch to the "nostalgic" "local atmosphere" that's "relaxing" for both "couples and families."

Ugly Dog Saloon & BBQ *BBQ*　　　20 | 11 | 15 | $17

Warehouse District | 401 Andrew Higgins Dr. (Tchoupitoulas St.) | 504-569-8459 | www.uglydogsaloon.net

A cross "between a family restaurant and a biker bar", this "shoddy"-looking, "self-service" Warehouse District joint smokes "fantastic BBQ" paired with "abundant sides"; "awesome prices" draw everyone from "federal judges to construction workers" for lunch, while "several large-screen TVs" make it a "catch-the-game" "hangout."

🆉 Upperline Ⓜ *Contemp. Louisiana*　　　26 | 24 | 25 | $50

Uptown | 1413 Upperline St. (bet. Prytania St. & St. Charles Ave.) | 504-891-9822 | www.upperline.com

"Inspired" Contemporary Louisiana fare like the "incredible" "fried green tomatoes with shrimp rémoulade" makes fans want to grab chef Ken Smith and "kiss him square on the lips" at this "high-end", slightly "off-the-wall" bistro where owner and "doting" "eminence rouge" JoAnn Clevenger "visits every table" and "makes sure the place runs like a Swiss clock"; set in an "elegant" 19th-century house chock-a-block with "unique" local art, it's a "classic date spot" that's "hugely popular" among the Uptown set.

Vega Tapas Cafe *Mediterranean*　　　24 | 21 | 22 | $36

Old Metairie | 2051 Metairie Rd. (bet. Beverly Garden Dr. & Bonnabel Blvd.) | Metairie | 504-836-2007 | www.vegatapascafe.com

"Try six dishes in one night" at this Old Metairie Mediterranean where the "imaginative" seasonal small plates are made with "the freshest, most tantalizing ingredients", the wine list is "enthralling" and the "hip, stylish" digs are augmented with "ever-revolving art on the walls"; of course, it's "a bit overpriced for the portions, but that's tapas, isn't it?"

	FOOD	DECOR	SERVICE	COST

Venezia *Italian* | 22 | 16 | 20 | $25

Jefferson | 587 Central Ave. (1 block north of Jefferson Hwy.) | 504-734-3991 🗷
Mid-City | 134 N. Carrollton Ave. (Canal St.) | 504-488-7991 Ⓜ
www.venezianeworleans.com

"Huge portions" of "tasty", "traditional red-gravy" Italian and "great pizza" draw "families" to these "popular" Mid-City and Jefferson "standbys"; sure, the settings are "not fancy", but with such "consistency" and "friendly" service, wallet-watchers wonder "why pay more?"

Vincent's *Italian* | 24 | 18 | 22 | $35

Metairie | 4411 Chastant St. (W. Esplanade Ave.) | 504-885-2984 🗷
Uptown | 7839 St. Charles Ave. (Fern St.) | 504-866-9313 Ⓜ
www.vincentsitaliancuisine.com

"Perfectly prepared" Southern Italian dishes and "seafood to remember", including "gotta-have" corn and crabmeat bisque, lure locals to this "fairly priced" Metairie mainstay and its more "intimate" Uptown cousin with a "sensational" "old-world" atmosphere; the staff "looks the part" and always "takes care of you", lending both locales lots of "neighborhood charm."

🅉 Vizard's 🗷Ⓜ *Contemp. Louisiana* | 26 | 22 | 24 | $51

Uptown | 5015 Magazine St. (Robert St.) | 504-895-2246
Inside "secluded" new Uptown digs, chef-owner and "viable force" on the culinary scene Kevin Vizard continues to wow a "faithful following" with his "wonderful", "distinctive" Contemporary Louisiana cuisine delivered by a "knowledgeable" staff; add in a "festive" and "dressy" (if "crowded") setting decorated with the "fascinating" artwork of Beth Lambert (Vizard's sister), and most don't mind the "pricey" tab.

Voodoo BBQ *BBQ* | 20 | 14 | 16 | $18

Lower Garden Dist. | 1501 St. Charles Ave. (Martin Luther King Jr. Blvd.) | 504-522-4647
St. Rose | 100 James Dr. E. (Airline Hwy.) | 504-464-1880
www.voodoobbqandgrill.com

Partisans pinpoint the "tender brisket", "delicious" pulled pork and "tasty variety of sauces and sides" like the "legendary corn pudding" as reasons this duo (Lower Garden District is counter-serve only, St. Rose has a broader menu) is "fall-off-the-bone" "fine" for BBQ; however, certain connoisseurs are "not impressed", "cheap" prices notwithstanding.

Vucinovich 🗷 *Seafood* | – | – | – | I

New Orleans East | 4510 Michoud Blvd. (Chef Menteur Hwy.) | 504-254-5246
Fans of fried fish flock to this out-of-the-way New Orleans East old-timer for crispy seafood platters and overstuffed po' boys with creamy potato salad that rivals yo' mama's; set inside a plain Cajun-style cottage, it offers lunch only in casual order-at-the-counter style.

Walker BBQ 🗷Ⓜ🗷 *BBQ* | ▽ 25 | 11 | 19 | $18

New Orleans East | 10828 Hayne Blvd. (bet. Lady Gray & Lafourche Sts.) | 504-241-8227
From the "folks who make the famous cochon de lait po' boy at Jazz Fest", this New Orleans East BBQ plies fans with the "finger-lickin' good" shredded pork sandwich "the other 50 weeks of the year" – but

only for lunch Wednesday–Friday ("go early", because when they "run out", they close); ribs, beef brisket, half chickens and sides are also "tops", but the digs are "hovel"-like, so grab the goods and keep walking.

Wasabi 🗷 Japanese

| 24 | 16 | 19 | $27 |

Faubourg Marigny | 900 Frenchmen St. (Burgundy St.) | 504-943-9433 | www.wasabinola.com

It's "well worth the stop" on Frenchmen Street for the "well-prepared" "fresh sushi" and "interesting" entrees at this casual Japanese; decor-scorers "can't think of anything unique to point out" (unless you're into video poker), but stay-at-homes give credit for "fast delivery."

NEW West Indies Cafe 🗷 Pan-Latin

| – | – | – | M |

Lower Garden Dist. | 1600 St. Charles Ave. (bet. Euterpe & Terpsichore Sts.) | 504-571-2015

Hidden on the first floor of a health club, this Lower Garden District sleeper is the latest stylish venture from chef-owner Hernan Caro (ex the shuttered Baru Café), whose spicy Caribbean and Pan-Latin menu ranges from chilled jerk shrimp salad to crisp yuca pies; tropical colors, courtyard tables and live jazz on the weekends lend extra enticement.

Whole Foods Market Eclectic

| 23 | 17 | 19 | $17 |

Metairie | 3420 Veterans Memorial Blvd. (Severn Ave.) | 504-888-8225
Uptown | 5600 Magazine St. (Arabella St.) | 504-899-9119
www.wholefoods.com

These Metairie and Uptown outposts of the "foodie"-grocery-store chain also vend "delicious", "healthy" and "organic" prepared fare – "oven-fresh pizzas", "delicious baked goods", "primo salads", "the list goes on" – all to be carried out or eaten in the "small dining areas"; though relatively "pricey" tabs earn it the moniker "Whole Paycheck", "you get what you pay for", no?

Whole Hog Café 🗷 BBQ

| ▽ 23 | 13 | 15 | $18 |

Central Business Dist. | Entergy Corporate Headquarters | 639 Loyola Ave. (Poydras St.) | 504-525-4044 | www.wholehogcafe.com

Lunchtimers "go whole hog" at this "BBQ lover's dream" in the lobby of a CBD office building by topping a "delicious" pulled pork, chicken or beef brisket sandwich (piled about "three-inches thick") with one of seven sauces and pairing it with a "great stuffed potato"; while a meal here is a true "guilty pleasure", it's also a "value."

Willie Mae's Scotch House 🗷🗷 Soul Food

| 25 | 14 | 16 | $19 |

Treme | 2401 St. Ann St. (N. Tonti St.) | 504-822-9503

"Take a cab" to Treme for lunch at this "legendary" bit of "New Orleans history", the "bare-bones" (though "immaculate") soul fooder founded by nonagenarian Willie Mae Seaton and celebrated for its "phenomenal fried chicken", "terrific" red beans and rice and other "wonderful" eats; but go "only when you have" about "two hours" to spare, because the mostly "friendly" service is always "extremely slow"; N.B. no credit cards and, despite the name, no hooch.

NEW Wolfe's 🗷🗷 Contemp. Louisiana

| – | – | – | E |

French Quarter | 1041 Dumaine St. (N. Rampart St.) | 504-593-9535

Chef-owner Tom Wolfe has retained the calm, distinctive interior of the former Peristyle, complete with historic wall murals and ceiling fans, while transforming the menu at this French Quarter restaurant into a more personal expression of Contemporary Louisiana–New American cuisine; both regional and international accents mingle in dishes like Kobe beef short ribs and slow-roasted duck, while a happy hour with small plates served at the bar invites sophisticated sipping and nibbling.

Wolfe's in the Warehouse *Creole*   21 | 20 | 19 | $44

Warehouse District | New Orleans Marriott at the Convention Ctr. | 859 Convention Center Blvd. (St. Joseph St.) | 504-613-2882

Chef-owner Tom Wolfe studs his "pleasing" menu with signature duck dishes and "wonderfully prepared fish" at this Creole in the Marriott at the Convention Center; "reasonably priced wines" and "accommodating" service also entice – so why is it "never crowded"?

Ye Olde College Inn ⑤Ⓜ *Creole/Southern*   21 | 19 | 21 | $25

Carrollton | 3000 S. Carrollton Ave. (bet. Earhart Blvd. & Fig St.) | 504-866-3683 | www.collegeinn1933.com

This "classed-up" "reincarnation" of the "iconic" Carrollton establishment (the original opened in 1933) gets kudos for the "creative" additions to its menu of Creole-Southern "comfort food", and while the "prices are somewhat higher", it's still "not too expensive"; though it "bears no resemblance to it's olde self" (the digs are "more upscale" now), the "personal service" hasn't changed a bit.

Young's ⑤Ⓜ *Steak*   24 | 14 | 20 | $46

Slidell | 850 Robert Blvd. (Marche Blvd.) | 985-643-9331

Bloodhounds who sniff out the "secret" Slidell location of this "high-priced" chophouse with "no sign out front" are rewarded with "super steaks"; the "cozy" setting may "need a face-lift", but not the servers (they're "mostly young", and "adequate" to boot); P.S. no reservations mean often "long waits for tables", so you may want to "dine early."

🆕 Yuki Izakaya ❶Ⓜ⌀ *Japanese*   – | – | – | I

Faubourg Marigny | 525 Frenchmen St. (Decatur St.) | no phone

A minuscule, slightly chaotic izakaya (or tavern) decorated with old Japanese movie posters, this Frenchmen Street newcomer pulls in a hip, diverse crowd for small plates of fried, grilled and pickled dishes as well as a limited variety of sashimi; more than a dozen sakes are available as well as barley- and sweet potato-based shochus and Japanese beers.

Zea Café *Eclectic*   23 | 20 | 20 | $25

Harahan | 1655 Hickory Ave. (Citrus Rd.) | 504-738-0799

Zea Rotisserie *Eclectic*

Lower Garden Dist. | 1525 St. Charles Ave. (Terpsichore St.) | 504-520-8100

Zea Rotisserie & Brewery *Eclectic*

Metairie | Clearview Mall | 4450 Veterans Memorial Blvd. (Clearview Pkwy.) | 504-780-9090

Zea Rotisserie & Grill *Eclectic*

Kenner | Esplanade Mall | 1401 W. Esplanade Ave. (Arizona Ave.) | 504-468-7733

🆕 **Harvey** | 1121 Manhattan Blvd. (bet. Apache & Ute Drs.) | 504-361-8293

www.zearestaurants.com

"You name it, they make it sing" at these Eclectic mini-chain eateries where the "mouthwatering rotisserie meats", "spicy" Thai ribs, "hummus that really hums" and "incredible corn grits" are the "habit-forming" standouts on the "ample menu"; "spot-on service", "comfortable atmospheres" and "reasonable prices" make for equally enjoyable "business lunches" and "nights out with the family"; P.S. the Metairie branch pours "first-rate" house-brewed suds.

Zeke's ⌧ *Seafood* | 17 | 14 | 18 | $22 |

Old Metairie | 1517 Metairie Rd. (Bonnabel Blvd.) | Metairie | 504-832-1133
Perhaps it's nostalgia for "old-time seafood" (mostly "boiled or fried") or the fact that they "always feel welcome" in the "busy", "cozy" digs, but many Old Metairie locals "like this place a lot"; however, loyalists still in mourning for its namesake founder, who died in 2005, lament it has "never been more than passable" since.

Zoë *Contemp. Louisiana*   ∇ | 22 | 22 | 21 | $41 |

Central Business Dist. | W New Orleans | 333 Poydras St. (S. Peters St.) | 504-207-5018 | www.whotels.com
The "beautiful, contemporary" setting and "creative", "delicious" fare at this Contemporary Louisianan in the CBD's W hotel make it a chic destination for the business lunch set; some sniff at its high-end "chain" trappings, however, calling it "mediocre" and "somewhat pretentious."

NIGHTLIFE

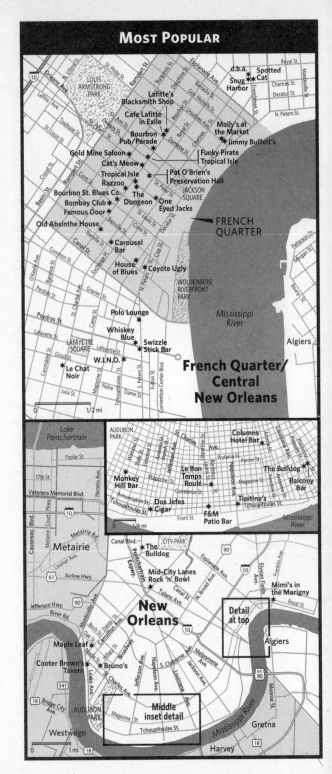

MOST POPULAR

Detail at top

d.b.a. · Spotted Cat
Snug Harbor

Lafitte's Blacksmith Shop
Cafe Lafitte in Exile
Bourbon Pub/Parade
Gold Mine Saloon
Cat's Meow
Tropical Isle
Razzoo
Bourbon St. Blues Co.
Bombay Club
Famous Door
The Dungeon
One Eyed Jacks
Old Absinthe House

Molly's at the Market
Jimmy Buffett's
Funky Pirate
Tropical Isle
Pat O'Brien's
Preservation Hall

JACKSON SQUARE

FRENCH QUARTER

Carousel Bar
House of Blues
Coyote Ugly

WOLDENBERG RIVERFRONT PARK

Mississippi River

Algiers

Polo Lounge
Whiskey Blue
Swizzle Stick Bar
W.I.N.O.
Le Chat Noir

LAFAYETTE SQUARE

French Quarter/ Central New Orleans

0   1/2 mi

Lake Pontchartrain

AUDUBON PARK

Columns Hotel Bar

Monkey Hill Bar
Le Bon Temps Roulé
The Bulldog
Balcony Bar
Tipitina's
Dos Jefes Cigar
F&M Patio Bar

Mississippi River

0   1/4 mi

Metairie

The Bulldog
CITY PARK
Mid-City Lanes Rock 'n' Bowl

Mimi's in the Marigny

New Orleans

Detail at top

Algiers

Maple Leaf
Cooter Brown's Tavern
Bruno's

AUDUBON PARK

Middle inset detail

Westwego

Gretna

Harvey

0   1 mi

40,000 places to eat, drink, stay & play – free at ZAGAT.com

Most Popular

❶	Pat O'Brien's	㉒	Spotted Cat
❷	Lafitte's Blacksmith	㉓	Bourbon St. Blues
❸	Columns Hotel	㉔	Dungeon
❹	Tipitina's	㉕	Polo Lounge*
❺	Mid-City Lanes	㉖	Dos Jefes Cigar
❻	House of Blues	㉗	Tropical Isle*
❼	Carousel Bar	㉘	W.I.N.O.*
❽	Bulldog	㉙	Coyote Ugly
❾	Snug Harbor	㉚	F&M Patio Bar*
❿	d.b.a.	㉛	Mimi's*
⓫	Maple Leaf	㉜	Famous Door
⓬	Jimmy Buffett's	㉝	Molly's at Market
⓭	Preservation Hall	㉞	One Eyed Jacks
⓮	Old Absinthe House	㉟	Bruno's
⓯	Cooter Brown's	㊱	Gold Mine Saloon*
⓰	Bourbon Pub/Parade	㊲	Swizzle Stick
⓱	Cat's Meow*	㊳	Le Chat Noir
⓲	Bombay Club	㊴	Monkey Hill
⓳	Whiskey Blue	㊵	Cafe Lafitte in Exile
⓴	Balcony Bar	㊶	Razzoo*
㉑	Funky Pirate	㊷	Le Bon Temps Roulé

It should go without saying that New Orleans is famous for its night-life. Though a few popular bars and clubs can be pricey, budget-conscious nightcrawlers will have no trouble finding what they seek here. To help them, we have included a list of the Best Buys at the bottom of page 94.

KEY NEWCOMERS

Our editors' take on the year's top arrivals.

Bar Tonique	Live Bait
Bar UnCommon	Pravda
Garden District Pub	W.I.N.O.

* Indicates a tie with place above

Top Ratings

Excludes places with low votes, unless indicated by a ▽.

APPEAL

28	Preservation Hall
27	Vaughan's Lounge
	Polo Lounge
	Tipitina's
	Columns Hotel
26	Mid-City Lanes
	Le Chat Noir
	Lafitte's Blacksmith
	Snug Harbor
	Swizzle Stick

DECOR

27	Polo Lounge
	Loa
26	Columns Hotel
	Swizzle Stick
	Carousel Bar

Whiskey Blue

25	Tommy's Wine
	Bombay Club
24	Pat O'Brien's
23	Le Chat Noir

SERVICE

26	Polo Lounge
25	Swizzle Stick
24	45 Tchoup
	W.I.N.O.
	Finn McCool's
	Tommy's Wine
	Carousel Bar
	Le Chat Noir
	Bombay Club
23	Old Point Bar

BY CATEGORY

Listed in order of Appeal ranking.

COCKTAIL EXPERTS

27	Polo Lounge
	Columns Hotel
26	Swizzle Stick
	Carousel Bar
24	Loa

26	Swizzle Stick
	(Loews)
	Carousel Bar
	(Hotel Monteleone)
24	Loa
	(International House)

DANCE CLUBS

24	Bourbon Pub/Parade
23	One Eyed Jacks
22	Dungeon
21	Oz
19	Ampersand

JAZZ CLUBS

28	Preservation Hall
26	Snug Harbor
	Maison Bourbon▽
25	Spotted Cat
	Donna's B&G

DIVES

27	Vaughan's Lounge
25	Maple Leaf
23	Snake & Jake's
22	Le Bon Temps Roulé
	Mayfair

LOCAL FAVORITES

27	Tipitina's
	Columns Hotel
26	Mid-City Lanes
25	Maple Leaf
21	Molly's at Market

HOTEL BARS

27	Polo Lounge
	(Windsor Court)
	Columns Hotel

BEST BUYS

1. Ms. Mae's	6. Snake & Jake's
2. Finn McCool's	7. Kingpin
3. Dragon's Den	8. Old Point Bar
4. Saturn Bar	9. 45 Tchoup
5. Avenue Pub	10. Vaughan's Lounge

Nightlife

Ratings & Symbols

Appeal, Decor and **Service** are rated on the Zagat 0 to 30 scale.

Cost reflects surveyors' estimated price of a typical single drink. For places listed without ratings, the price range is as follows:

⌐ below $5	Ⓔ $11 to $14
Ⓜ $5 to $10	ⓋⒺ $15 or more

Abbey, The ⊅   15 | 12 | 15 | M
French Quarter | 1123 Decatur St. (bet. Governor Nicholls St. & Ursuline Ave.) | 504-523-7177
A "cheap", "grimy delight", this 24/7 "dive" in the French Quarter "can attract a dodgy crowd in the pre-dawn hours"; it draws a few "Hollywood celebrities" too ("shhh, don't tell anyone"), but jaded types say "just because Angelina went there doesn't make it any less disgusting."

Ampersand   19 | 19 | 16 | M
Central Business Dist. | 1100 Tulane Ave. (S. Rampart St.) | 504-587-3737 | www.clubampersand.com
"Beautiful people", "fake-bakers" and other "weekend partyers" slip through the "roped-off lines" into this "sexy" nightclub inside a former CBD bank, complete with private "little nooks and crannies" and a "living-large Miami Beach" feel; it boasts an impressive "caliber of DJ talent", with a "mind-blowing sound system" that blasts hip-hop beats on Fridays and grooves of "top global electronic artists" on Saturdays.

Apple Barrel ⊅   21 | 10 | 16 | M
Faubourg Marigny | 609 Frenchmen St. (bet. Chartres & Royal Sts.) | 504-949-9399
"Awesome" musicians playing "gypsy jazz" and "down 'n' dirty blues" draw an overflow crowd of neighbors and "scruffy older white" folks to this "tiny", "smoky" Frenchmen Street "dump" stocking a "decent", "inexpensive" beer selection; "you'll be lucky if you can find room to stand", but if not you can always "hang out and people-watch on the bench right outside."

Avenue Pub   20 | 16 | 22 | M
Lower Garden Dist. | 1732 St. Charles Ave. (Polymnia St.) | 504-586-9243
The balcony above St. Charles Avenue makes this Lower Garden District "dive" a favorite for "parade viewing", but outside of Carnival season it's a round-the-clock "locals hangout" with "bartenders of the friendly neighborhood variety", a "classic" jukebox and 30 draft beers for not a lot of scratch; "mini-tacos" and other "late-night food" make it a "great place to go after the after-party."

Balcony Bar, The   20 | 15 | 19 | M
Uptown | 3201 Magazine St. (Harmony St.) | 504-895-1600
At this "nothing-fancy" Uptown bar, "only a set of rickety stairs" separates the first-floor crowd of "pool sharks, arm-wrestling women and

other assorted New Orleans characters" from the "Tulane and Loyola" undergrads and "professional students" above on the balcony, taking in the "Magazine Street scene"; both floors feature "nice" bartenders, "good tunes" and drinks for "frugal" budgets.

Balcony Music Club
▽ 18 | 15 | 15 | M

French Quarter | 504 Esplanade Ave. (Decatur St.) | 504-599-7770
This "local" venue on the far edge of the Quarter (once El Matador and most recently Harry Anderson's magic club) books "eclectic acts" playing everything from blues to bluegrass with occasional comedy too; denizens also dig the late-night eats and "good happy-hour specials."

Banks Street Bar & Grill
▽ 22 | 12 | 22 | M

Mid-City | 4401 Banks St. (S. Alexander St.) | 504-486-0258 | www.banksstreetbar.com
"A first-class dive in a still semi-abandoned area" of Mid-City, this "little neighborhood music bar" featuring nightly, no-cover shows lets fans "get up close and personal" with the acts; since it also serves a limited bar menu, plus gratis red beans and rice on Mondays and oysters on Thursdays, it's a "fun place for friends and food."

NEW Bar Tonique
- | - | - | M

French Quarter | 820 N. Rampart St. (St. Ann St.) | 504-324-6045
Located on the French Quarter's somewhat forlorn back border, this intimate new lounge, an offshoot of Uptown's Delachaise, is an oasis of style with its horseshoe-shaped bar in the center, white vinyl booths along the walls and Tiffany blue ceiling above; in addition to offering a deep list of wines and whiskeys, the skilled bartenders mix a selection of classic cocktails, some of which are made with homemade tonic water.

NEW Bar UnCommon
- | - | - | E

(fka Jazz Lounge)

Central Business Dist. | Renaissance Pere Marquette Hotel | 817 Common St. (Baronne St.) | 504-525-1111 | www.marriott.com
The legendary mixologist and cocktail historian Chris McMillian (ex the now-private Library Lounge) is again shaking up classic sours, fizzes and juleps at this recently renovated CBD boîte; its ultramodern decor of glittering blue alcoves, a glowing, glass-topped bar and an ocean of blown-glass bulbs suspended from the ceiling attracts both trendy travelers and in-the-know imbibers.

Big Top Gallery
▽ 20 | 23 | 18 | M

Central City | 1638 Clio St. (bet. Carondelet St. & St. Charles Ave.) | 504-569-2700 | www.3rcp.com
"Three cool women" run this "always-interesting" Central City venue where a gallery of "modern art" is the backdrop for film, performances and bands; though "parking can be difficult" and the schedule a bit unpredictable, it draws a varied crowd that appreciates the nonsmoking space and "early-evening family entertainment on Fridays."

Blue Nile
23 | 19 | 20 | M

Faubourg Marigny | 532 Frenchmen St. (Decatur St.) | 504-948-2583 | www.bluenilelive.com
You can "get your groove on" at this "cool big daddy" on Frenchmen Street, because "there's room to dance" to some of the "best live mu-

sic New Orleans has to offer", yet it's still "quiet enough in back to have a conversation"; "no-frills", "funky and down-home", it "feels like a genuine old blues club."

Bombay Club
25 | 25 | 24 | E

French Quarter | 830 Conti St. (bet. Bourbon & Dauphine Sts.) | 504-586-0972 | www.thebombayclub.com

At this "haven from the craziness of Bourbon Street", "bartenders who really care about their craft" mix a long list of "pricey" martinis and the kitchen cooks Contemporary Louisiana cuisine for an "older" crowd; imbibers sink into leather chairs and lovers retreat to the "private enclosed booths" as "sophisticated live piano" and jazz set the "civilized" tone.

Boot, The
14 | 9 | 13 | M

Uptown | 1039 Broadway (Zimpel St.) | 504-866-9008

"Dance all night with young college kids" at this "smoky", "smelly and grungy" Uptown "dive", which sits "closer to the Tulane dorms than most classrooms"; true, it's a "beloved sanctuary" from scholarly pursuits for "beefed-up frat boys in tight T-shirts and drunk sorority girls", but "not so great if you're over the age of 25."

Bourbon Pub/Parade ⌗
24 | 19 | 22 | M

French Quarter | 801 Bourbon St. (St. Ann St.) | 504-529-2107 | www.bourbonpub.com

It's a "party all night" at this "lively" French Quarter gay bar in the center of Bourbon Street's "lavender lane", filled with plenty of "cute, cut" "eye candy" as well as "clever videos" on display; "two floors with different music" plus "good pours" by "welcoming" bartenders seal the deal for "dancing in/out-of-towners who are either in/out of the closet."

Bourbon Street Blues Company
21 | 16 | 17 | M

French Quarter | 441 Bourbon St. (St. Louis St.) | 504-566-1507 | www.bourbonstbluesco.com

"Rousing" live blues (which beats most of the music "permeating the strip") lures a crowd to this Bourbon Street "tourist stop", which also invites "squeezing your way onto the nice balcony" to make believe it's Mardi Gras by "throwing beads"; with "three-for-one beers upstairs", many consider it a "must-go."

Bridge Lounge
21 | 20 | 19 | M

Lower Garden Dist. | 1201 Magazine St. (Erato St.) | 504-299-1888

"Hang out and howl with the dogs" at this "cozy and chic" but still "very casual" canine-friendly "paradise" in the Lower Garden District; even poochless "young professionals" swear by the "best mojitos" and other "specialty cocktails", though a few wags warn of "slow" service and "sketchy" surroundings.

Bruno's
20 | 18 | 19 | M

Uptown | 7538 Maple St. (Hillary St.) | 504-861-7615 | www.brunostavern.com

"Generations of New Orleanians" from "college kids" to folks their "parents' age" mingle at this relocated (from across the street) and "revamped" Uptown sports bar whose 10 plasma TVs make it a natural for "watching the game"; "darts, shuffleboard" and elevated pub

grub like "Boudreaux fries" are additional perks, though some surveyors say "Newno's" lacks the "soul and vibe" of the original.

Bulldog, The

24 | 20 | 20 | M

Mid-City | 5135 Canal Blvd. (City Park Ave.) | 504-488-4191
Uptown | 3236 Magazine St. (Pleasant St.) | 504-891-1516
www.draftfreak.com

"Hardworking bartenders" pull pints of "awesome" "microbrews"
among "scores of unique beers" (50 on tap and 100 in bottles) for
"grad students and other professionals" at this Mid-City and Uptown
duo with a "convivial atmosphere"; since "four-legged friends" are al-
lowed on the patio at both branches, lucky dogs might sneak a bite of the
"decent" pub food off their owners' plates; P.S. "go on Wednesdays
and you get to keep your glass."

Cafe Lafitte in Exile

21 | 18 | 22 | M

French Quarter | 901 Bourbon St. (Dumaine St.) | 504-522-8397 |
www.lafittes.com

"The drinks are strong and the men are weak and begging for more" at
this "granddaddy" of a French Quarter gay bar catering to an over-30
crowd for "trash disco" tunes on Sunday and plenty of "cruising" every
night; since the "scene can be sleazy" in the wee hours, just "watch out
for what happens in the dark corners."

Cajun Cabin

▽ 20 | 18 | 21 | M

French Quarter | 503 Bourbon St. (St. Louis St.) | 504-529-4256 |
www.cajuncabin.com

Game guests say "you'll have a blast" on Bourbon Street dancing to
the Cajun and zydeco acts that might just coax you on stage and hand
you "two spoons to play the washboard"; the "attentive" bartenders
keep the pricey beer flowing, and there's bayou-inspired food to soak
it up too.

Carousel Bar

26 | 26 | 24 | M

French Quarter | Hotel Monteleone | 214 Royal St. (bet. Bienville Ave. &
Iberville St.) | 504-523-3341 | www.hotelmonteleone.com

"Stop in for a round or two" at this rotating "respite" delivering
"instant aesthetic satisfaction" with its "retro" merry-go-round look
inside the French Quarter's Hotel Monteleone; it gets "crowded", but
with "well-versed" bartenders mixing vintage cocktails for the local
"elite" and other "beautiful people", most agree it's "worth a whirl."

Carrollton Station

22 | 18 | 21 | M

Carrollton | 8140 Willow St. (Dublin St.) | 504-865-9190 |
www.carrolltonstation.com

"Artists young and old" play "real music that isn't preprocessed for
tourists" at this "funky", "hidden" venue with a "neighborhood feel";
its "large carved wooden bar" offers a "nice beer selection" and "decent" mixed drinks, plus "late-night food" is served too, making for a
"cozy" Carrollton stop.

Cat's Meow

20 | 16 | 16 | M

French Quarter | 701 Bourbon St. (St. Peter St.) | 504-523-2788 |
www.701bourbon.com

"Forget about class and join the party" "caterwauling" "cheesy country tunes and classic rock" at this "raucous" Bourbon Street karaoke

bar where nearly every night "wasted tourists", "a dozen brides-to-be" and even locals indulging in a "guilty pleasure" get whipped up into a singing and dancing "frenzy"; since it's usually "jammed", some critics caw the "service is Darwinian: only the strong imbibe."

Checkpoint Charlie's
17 | 12 | 18 | M

French Quarter | 501 Esplanade Ave. (Decatur St.) | 504-281-4847
"Where else can you drink, play pool and do your laundry?" ask amused multitaskers who mix among "Quarter dwellers, service folks and alternatives" at this 24-hour bar, eatery and Laundromat that also hosts nightly "live hardcore and rock music"; it's "loud" and a "real dive", but comes through for night owls as the "best place to be from 3 AM to dawn, at least on a Tuesday."

Chocolate Bar
- | - | - | VE

Mid-City | 540 S. Broad St. (Gravier St.) | 504-373-5636
At this Mid-City club, an upscale African-American crowd finds "contemporary decor but a laid-back atmosphere" and a bar that mixes "extremely creative drinks"; live jazz and DJ sets give it plenty to "love"; N.B. closed Tuesday–Wednesday.

Circle Bar
22 | 20 | 22 | M

Warehouse District | 1032 St. Charles Ave. (Lee Circle) | 504-588-2616
"The crumbling edifice doesn't give much of a hint of what's inside" this "tiny" Warehouse District watering hole where "tattooed hipsters" sip "cheap" drinks "under the K&B sign" and get "up close to up-and-coming bands" playing "alt-country and indie" tunes; between sets, the "killer jukebox" adds to the "groovy vibe."

⚡ Columns Hotel Bar
27 | 26 | 21 | M

Uptown | Columns Hotel | 3811 St. Charles Ave. (bet. General Taylor & Peniston Sts.) | 504-899-9308 | www.thecolumns.com
"Debs" and "dates" "drink up the Southern heritage" along with plenty of "Pimm's Cups" at this "must-see" lounge inside a "grand old hotel" with a "large, tree-shaded porch facing St. Charles Avenue"; boasting "awesome ambiance", bartenders with "character" and "delicious" live music, it's a true "treasure in the heart of Uptown."

Cooter Brown's Tavern
21 | 15 | 19 | M

Carrollton | 509 S. Carrollton Ave. (St. Charles Ave.) | 504-866-9104 | www.cooterbrowns.com
Flat-screen "TVs as far as the eye can see" along with a selection of "hundreds of brews" make this "dingy, worn and terrific" Carrollton "hole-in-the-wall" a "staple for college students, working-class cognoscenti" and "beer lovers" to cheer for the home team; the kitchen also keeps bellies full with pub grub and half-shell delicacies from the "understated (and underrated) oyster bar."

Corner Pocket ⊄
- | - | - | M

French Quarter | 940 St. Louis St. (Burgundy St.) | 504-568-9829 | www.cornerpocket.net
Curious customers "sate their interest for scantily clad boys" at this French Quarter gay bar with nightly strip shows and "always interesting drag queens employed to keep things moving"; those who prefer "classier" entertainment caution it's "not for the faint of heart."

	APPEAL	DECOR	SERVICE	COST

Coyote Ugly

| 16 | 14 | 15 | E |

French Quarter | 225 N. Peters St. (bet. Bienville Ave. & Iberville St.) | 504-561-0003 | www.coyoteuglysaloon.com

Bartenders "dance on the bar" while "horndogs" do "ever-popular body shots" at this "cheesy" French Quarter chain link compared to the nightlife "version of Hooters"; some are game for the "pretty stupid fun", but others say it feels too much like a "bad movie", with a "rude" staff that "likely flunked out of stripper school."

d.b.a.

| 24 | 20 | 20 | M |

Faubourg Marigny | 618 Frenchmen St. (bet. Chartres & Royal Sts.) | 504-942-3731 | www.drinkgoodstuff.com

"Everything is top-shelf" at this "dark, warm" and "delightful" NYC import that's a "neat" place to sip single malts and sample suds from a "phenomenal" beer list in the "bohemian" surroundings of the Marigny; it regularly books "first-rate New Orleans" acts and since "all manner of people flow through" – "locals, out-of-towners who know their music" and the "occasional celebrity" – it's "where everyone meets, but no one knows your name."

Donna's Bar & Grill ⊯

| 25 | 13 | 20 | M |

French Quarter | 800 N. Rampart St. (St. Ann St.) | 504-596-6914 | www.donnasbarandgrill.com

Enthusiasts say "everyone should have a Donna's experience" because this "joint" on the Rampart edge of the French Quarter "jumps with energy" from "heart-pounding" "brass-band jazz"; it's "tiny, hot, sweaty and way too crowded" with "regulars who love the music" and the "soul food", and transform it into a "party with friends"; N.B. currently open Thursday–Sunday only.

Dos Jefes Uptown Cigar Bar

| 23 | 19 | 21 | M |

Uptown | 5535 Tchoupitoulas St. (bet. Joseph & Octavia Sts.) | 504-891-8500

Free sets by the city's "better-known musicians" fill the air at this Uptown cigar bar with "surprisingly little haze to annoy nonsmokers" (thanks to a "great air-filtering system"); an "older, laid-back crowd" "hangs out and listens to jazz" inside or retires to the "fantastic patio" with "porch swings" and "plenty of space to sit and talk."

Dragon's Den

| 22 | 19 | 18 | M |

Faubourg Marigny | 435 Esplanade Ave. (Frenchmen St.) | 504-949-1750

Vintage-loving visitors advise "dress like you fell off a 1929 circus wagon to fit in" at this "esoteric" lounge whose "Oriental atmosphere" makes it the "sultriest club in America's sultriest city", while the balcony entices too with its view "overlooking Marigny"; it "traffics in avant-garde sounds, everything from reggae to free jazz", and late at night "musicians from all over town" arrive to "jam."

Dungeon, The

| 22 | 22 | 18 | M |

French Quarter | 738 Toulouse St. (bet. Bourbon & Royal Sts.) | 504-523-5530 | www.originaldungeon.com

Devotees of "headbanger music, thrash metal" and other "loud" beats "get their Goth on" and get down on the "close" dance floor at this "dark", "scary" French Quarter "maze" "where NOLA's vampires dwell"; the scene starts "late", so it's not uncommon after a few "Dragon's Blood shots" to "stumble out to greet a new day well under way."

	APPEAL	DECOR	SERVICE	COST

Famous Door
19 | 13 | 16 | M

French Quarter | 339 Bourbon St. (bet. Bienville Ave. & Conti St.) | 504-598-4334 | www.thebestofbourbonstreet.com

"Get the Bourbon Street experience" at this French Quarter club where "strangers ask you to dance" to the cover band's version of "'Sweet Home Alabama' a couple of times each night"; some find the staff "aggressive" and the drinks "overpriced", but it's still a "favorite" for party people who say it's "tough to have a bad time here."

F&M Patio Bar
21 | 12 | 16 | M

Uptown | 4841 Tchoupitoulas St. (Lyons St.) | 504-895-6784 | www.fandmpatiobar.com

"Tulane kids" and other "late, late bar hounds" "get trashed and dance on pool tables" at this "crazy" Uptown "meat market", a "last stop" that barely gets going till after "2 AM"; the jukebox blasting "cheesy" music is topped only by the "alcohol-absorbing" but "artery-clogging cheese fries", which really "hit the spot after a night of imbibing."

Fat Harry's Bar
17 | 13 | 19 | M

Uptown | 4330 St. Charles Ave. (Napoleon Ave.) | 504-895-9582

"Always slammed on the weekends" (and a popular place to "catch Mardi Gras on the parade route"), this "iconic joint" Uptown has "quick bartenders" serving up "reasonable" drinks; "if you're over 25", it's "not bad for happy hour" and "watching the game" on "old-ass TVs", but "don't bother after 9 PM" when it's "time to move along, fogies."

Finn McCool's
22 | 19 | 24 | M

Mid-City | 3701 Banks St. (S. Telemachus St.) | 504-486-9080 | www.finnmccools.com

An "awesome trivia night every Monday", "good Guinness on draft" and lots of "bar games" add to the flavor of this "welcoming" Irish pub in Mid-City; it's "neighborhood-friendly" and often chock-full of frenzied "European sports" fans, especially during the "World Cup."

☑ 45 Tchoup
21 | 17 | 24 | M

Uptown | 4529 Tchoupitoulas St. (Jena St.) | 504-891-9066

"Everyone is welcome" at this Uptown watering hole where the owners "remember your name, what you drink and who you cheer for"; the prices are "low, low, low", the vibe is "mellow" and a Monday trivia night "completes the scene."

French 75
▽ 25 | 25 | 24 | E

French Quarter | Arnaud's Restaurant | 813 Bienville St. (bet. Bourbon & Dauphine Sts.) | 866-230-8895 | www.arnauds.com

The "barkeeps are artists" at this vintage place to "get a glass of something great" (with cigars for sale too) attached to Arnaud's restaurant in the French Quarter; customers call the "cozy" surroundings with "eclectic decoration" "very French" and a little "pricey", but "perfect for the cocktail moment" before dinner.

Fritzel's European Jazz Pub
23 | 16 | 19 | M

French Quarter | 733 Bourbon St. (bet. Orleans & St. Ann Sts.) | 504-586-4800

Guests "groove" to "consistently outstanding" "trad jazz" at this Dixieland destination that, despite its Bourbon Street address, doesn't

	APPEAL	DECOR	SERVICE	COST

attract "too many drunkards"; the "tight", "outrageously under-decorated" space has "dilapidated charm" and a "pure New Orleans vibe" paired with a German theme, so "order a Jäger with a beer back" and enjoy the "fine" tunes.

Funky Pirate

21 | 14 | 17 | M

French Quarter | 727 Bourbon St. (bet. Orleans & St. Ann Sts.) | 504-523-1960 | www.tropicalisle.com

"Locals still go" to hear "legend" Big Al Carson, nearly a quarter ton of talent, "belt out the blues" (with lots of "dirty ditties") at this Bourbon Street "staple"; though snarky stowaways say it's "kind of a dive" that "should be called the Junky Pirate", the "friendly waitresses" sling potent Hand Grenades that "get you where you want to go in a hurry."

NEW Garden District Pub

▽ 19 | 19 | 21 | E

Lower Garden Dist. | 1916 Magazine St. (St. Mary St.) | 504-267-3392 | www.gardendistrictpub.com

"Catch up with old friends or make a new one" at this "low-key", dog-friendly hangout in the Lower Garden District, occupying a refurbished site that the owners' parents once ran as a pub in the 1960s; with its exposed-brick walls and copper-topped bar, the vibe is "cool and quaint", which perfectly "reflects the community."

Gold Mine Saloon

20 | 14 | 16 | M

French Quarter | 701 Dauphine St. (St. Peter St.) | 504-586-0745 | www.goldminesaloon.net

After a few too many "awesome flaming Dr. Pepper shots", customers "cut a rug" and "dance off the pain" to tunes "reminiscent of a late '90s prom" at this "sweaty" "final stop" in the French Quarter; even if the service is lacking, it's "carried some through school and into adulthood (I still go, but maybe I shouldn't)"; N.B. open Thursday–Saturday only.

Good Friends Bar

21 | 18 | 22 | M

French Quarter | 740 Dauphine St. (St. Ann St.) | 504-566-7191 | www.goodfriendsbar.com

At this "mellow" gay bar in the French Quarter, an "older crowd" (and boys "looking for a sugar daddy") ensures that it's "civilized" while the "cute, frisky bartenders keep the place jumping" and whip up "out-of-this-world" frozen drinks; with a second floor for "delightful" piano sing-alongs on Sundays (4–8 PM) and "comfortable balcony seating", it encourages a feeling of "camaraderie."

Handsome Willy's

▽ 16 | 15 | 20 | M

Central Business Dist. | 218 S. Robertson St. (Cleveland Ave.) | 504-525-0377 | www.handsomewillys.com

"Lots of free food" on Fridays until 10 PM and low-cost weeknight specials make for a "cheap" outing at this "hipster hangout" in the "no-man's-land of the CBD"; the scene is rounded out with DJs, a "nice" patio and bartenders with "MFAs in poetry slinging your drinks", and though it's usually closed Sundays, it stays open during Saints games.

Hi Ho Lounge

▽ 17 | 17 | 21 | M

Faubourg Marigny | 2239 St. Claude Ave. (Marigny St.) | 504-945-4446

"Memorable music-making" by "up-and-coming jazz and indie" acts (and post-show happy hours) fuel the "arty" scene at this Marigny club that's "comfortable and cleaner" after a post-K renovation; be aware, though, that it's "way off the beathen path" in a "rough part of town", so cautious customers advise "don't come alone."

Hookah Café
21 | 23 | 19 | M

Faubourg Marigny | 500 Frenchmen St. (Decatur St.) | 504-943-1101 | www.hookah-cafe.com

"Swanky", "dark and mellow", this Frenchmen Street hookah bar "delivers when it comes to quality shisha and a relaxed-friendly atmosphere" enhanced by DJs, live music and belly dancers; the martinis and beers are "top-notch" too, though a few puffers paint it as a "pricey place to smoke from pipes that don't get you high"; N.B. some tables require bottle service.

House of Blues
23 | 22 | 19 | E

French Quarter | 225 Decatur St. (bet. Bienville Ave. & Iberville St.) | 504-529-2583 | www.hob.com

The "formula works anywhere" admit fans of this French Quarter chain link whose "mind-blowing entertainment" makes it "the spot to see nationally known bands in New Orleans", even if you need to "stand for the entire concert"; while critics say it's "overpriced", "theme-parky" and the "layers of security are ridiculous", most agree that the "acoustics are fantastic" and there's "not a bad view in the place", plus the revived "great gospel brunch" is a Sunday highlight.

Howlin' Wolf
20 | 15 | 19 | M

Warehouse District | 907 S. Peters St. (Diamond St.) | 504-529-5844 | www.thehowlinwolf.com

"Cavernous", "clean" and "well-run", this music club in the Warehouse District is a "pleasure" for "partying" "when your favorite band is playing" since "you're never too far from the stage"; though some say it has "little decor or any real local flavor", it delivers "big shows with big crowds (and big-ticket prices)" during Jazz Fest.

Igor's Bar & Grill
19 | 12 | 18 | M

Lower Garden Dist. | 2133 St. Charles Ave. (Jackson Ave.) | 504-568-9811

"Characters abound" at this 24-hour "dive bar" in the Lower Garden District "no-man's-land", where "cheap drinks" (the "best Bloody Mary"), "ginormous" burgers and "energy around the clock" are the draws; the room's not much to look at, but there's a patio and "good people-watching on the Avenue."

Jimmy Buffett's Margaritaville Cafe
20 | 21 | 18 | M

French Quarter | 1104 Decatur St. (Ursuline Ave.) | 504-592-2565 | www.margaritaville.com

Wannabe beach bums "get wasted away on 'ritas and fried food" at this "tacky" but "upbeat" French Quarter outpost of the tropical chain, featuring "lively" bands downstairs and "tire swings" upstairs so you can sway "while you sip"; critics call it "notoriously overpriced" (could it be that "Jimmy is related to Warren"?), adding that "Parrotheads" and "middle-aged conventioneers" are the standard crowd, but the "drunk tourists can be fun to watch."

	APPEAL	DECOR	SERVICE	COST

Johnny White's Sports Bar
21 | 13 | 20 | M

French Quarter | 720 Bourbon St. (Orleans St.) | 504-524-4909

"All hail" this "always-open" French Quarter sports bar, a "lovable dump" that "will be remembered" "as the place that never closed during Katrina"; customers cheer the "clued-in" bartenders pouring "cheap drinks", and say that while "you may worry about the DNA on the ripped seat covers, you'll never worry about getting a cold beer."

Kerry Irish Pub
20 | 16 | 21 | M

French Quarter | 331 Decatur St. (bet. Bienville Ave. & Conti Sts.) | 504-527-5954 | www.kerryirishpub.com

It's St. Paddy's Day year-round at this "loud, friendly", "locally priced" French Quarter pub where neighbors "meet up" for an "authentic Guinness" and "stay for the music" with a Celtic lilt; most agree that with its "crazy bartenders and nasty decor – you can't beat it."

Kingpin
22 | 19 | 21 | M

Uptown | 1307 Lyons St. (Perrier St.) | 504-891-2373 | www.kingpinbar.com

"Tucked away in a freakishly cool corner" of Uptown, this drinkery with "off-the-wall" decorations, frequent "live music" and "shuffleboard!" is a "favorite watering hole for locals in-the-know" and the home base for a group of "Elvis impersonators on scooters" (a sub-Krewe of the Muses parade); a "warm staff and cold beer" are always waiting, but it's also in the running for "smokiest bar in town."

☑ Lafitte's Blacksmith Shop
26 | 23 | 21 | M

French Quarter | 941 Bourbon St. (bet. Dumaine & St. Philip Sts.) | 504-593-9761

This "epic" registered historic landmark in the French Quarter "would be a museum with a shop selling postcards and snowglobes" anywhere else, but in New Orleans it remains a "dark", "sly" and "magical" candlelit bar with "lots of character" at the "quietest location on Bourbon Street"; visitors and natives alike sip "dangerous Voodoo Daiquiris" poured by "friendly, efficient" bartenders, and say it's "a stitch" to "sit around the piano" in back and "sing along."

La Nuit/Box Office
- | - | - | M

Uptown | 5039 Freret St. (Soniat St.) | 504-899-0336 | www.nolacomedy.com

Though it's hard to take this Uptowner seriously, that's exactly the hope of the intrepid comedy troupe behind this intimate theater with regular performances from local and visiting laugh masters; buy tickets at the adjacent, and aptly named, new Box Office bar, which doubles as a comfortable lounge to sip a pint and swap jokes even on nights when there's no show next door.

Le Bon Temps Roulé
22 | 14 | 17 | M

Uptown | 4801 Magazine St. (Bordeaux St.) | 504-895-8117

It's "run-down and dirty looking, and that often includes the clientele" after they "sweat two gallons" dancing to the "fantastic music" at this "wild", "hot as hell" Uptown "dive"; vets advise it gets "super crowded on Thursdays" when brass band favorite the Soul Rebels play until late, but the menu of "pub grub" "can help you get through the night."

☑ Le Chat Noir

26 | 23 | 24 | M

Warehouse District | 715 St. Charles Ave. (bet. Girod & Julia Sts.) | 504-581-5812 | www.cabaretlechatnoir.com

"Start spreading the news" about this "chic little" cabaret in the Warehouse District where "dressed-up people" catch "unique" music and comedy shows with "satirical" "New Orleans appeal"; "there's not a bad seat in the house" and the "yummy" cocktails are delivered with "unobtrusive and professional table service"; N.B. open Friday-Sunday, with additional shows during the week.

Le Phare Bar

▽ 22 | 24 | 20 | M

Central Business Dist. | Loft 523 | 523 Gravier St. (bet. Camp & Magazine Sts.) | 504-636-1889 | www.lepharenola.com

The "20-to-30 crowd" "dresses to impress" at this "dark", "clubby" and "high-end" hotel lounge in the CBD where there's "plenty of room to dance" to DJ sets or escape to the "seating areas and chill with friends" in smoke-free surroundings; happy-hour drink specials and "dance lessons" on salsa and tango nights are more reasons it "hits the mark."

NEW Live Bait Bar & Grill

- | - | - | I

Bucktown | 200 Hammond Hwy. (Lake Ave.) | Metairie | 504-840-0902

You could almost cast a lure into Lake Pontchartrain from the patio of this Bucktown newcomer that caters to sailors with its tiki touches, fish mounted on the walls and list of more than 100 rums; Cajun and zydeco bands play often, the kitchen specializes in deep-fried, drinking-friendly fare and the thick crowds get rowdy when the hometown Saints take the field.

☑ Loa

24 | 27 | 21 | M

Central Business Dist. | International House Hotel | 221 Camp St. (Gravier St.) | 504-553-9550 | www.ihhotel.com

"Are we in LA?" ask transported tipplers about this "sexy", "modern" CBD hotel lounge that's "hip, but not annoyingly so" with "plush" furnishings, an altarlike bar and "lots of candles to look beautiful by"; indeed, it's "the place to see and be seen in NOLA" sipping "fantastic" but "expensive" drinks, like the signature Loatini, paired with food from the newly opened Rambla.

Madigans

19 | 16 | 16 | M

Carrollton | 800 S. Carrollton Ave. (Maple St.) | 504-866-9455

It's easy to "have a drink with one or eight people" on the patio at this "college" haunt in Carrollton "near the Tulane campus"; a pool table and bar eats lend it extra "hangout" appeal, though blasé bar-hoppers call it "nothing special."

Maison Bourbon Jazz Club

▽ 26 | 23 | 23 | E

French Quarter | 641 Bourbon St. (bet. St. Peter & Toulouse Sts.) | 504-522-8818

"Trad jazz" "right in the heart of the action" wins over visitors who "stop in and enjoy the music" at this French Quarter club featuring an "amazing stream" of talent; the cover is one "overpriced" drink per set – not a bad deal for the "nice atmosphere" and the escape from the "mobs of drunk teenagers" on Bourbon Street.

APPEAL | DECOR | SERVICE | COST

Maple Leaf Bar
25 | 16 | 18 | M

Carrollton | 8316 Oak St. (Dante St.) | 504-866-9359

"Dance and sweat to some funky, funky music", like the "world-renowned" Rebirth Brass Band on Tuesdays, at this "monstrously fun" "must-visit venue" that rolls "late" into the night with a crowd of Carrollton "college kids" and an "interesting group of regulars" who know not to "expect a 10 PM show to start on time"; with a "pressed-tin ceiling" and a "fantastic little garden of overgrown palms", it's not "swanky" by any stretch, but it's a "real" "classic."

Markey's Bar
∇ 23 | 18 | 24 | I

Bywater | 640 Louisa St. (Royal St.) | 504-943-0785

"Blue collar and hipster meet" at this "always packed" "local hangout in the Bywater" that supporters call "one of more underrated neighborhood bars" in the city; there are seven flat-screen TVs, the drinks are "some of the cheapest" around and the staff "turnover is slow so the bartender will know you", plus it "just gets better" with a hearty menu too.

Mayfair, The ⌀
22 | 20 | 21 | M

Uptown | 1505 Amelia St. (Prytania St.) | 504-895-9163

"You'll run into an old friend and make 10 more" when you "ring the doorbell" and enter this "quirky" "little Uptown pool hall" with a "fantastic jukebox"; admirers approve of the bartenders who "know how to pour a drink", and say you may "get a kiss from Ms. Gertie", the "famous" "geriatric owner in leather pants who hits on the college boys."

⚡ Mid-City Lanes Rock 'n' Bowl
26 | 21 | 21 | M

Mid-City | 4133 S. Carrollton Ave. (Tulane Ave.) | 504-482-3133 | www.rocknbowl.com

"Red-and-green shoes with numbers on them" are "coming back into style" at this "one-of-a-kind" Mid-City "music and dance venue inside a vintage bowling alley" that's "a total hoot"; the "cool music" ranges from rock to zydeco, the "drinks don't drain your wallet" and owner John Blancher is the "quintessential host" who sometimes "takes the stage for Tom Jones and Elvis imitations."

Milan Lounge
∇ 17 | 15 | 19 | M

Uptown | 1312 Milan St. (bet. Perrier & Prytania Sts.) | 504-895-1836

Those who "stumble into" this Uptown tavern "near the parade route" discover the "official home of the Chicago Cubs in New Orleans" along with "friendly" barkeeps and "inexpensive" drinks; still, the "cliquish" crowd can be "territorial", so "if you feel like you don't belong here you probably don't."

Mimi's in the Marigny
24 | 20 | 20 | M

Faubourg Marigny | 2601 Royal St. (Franklin Ave.) | 504-872-9868

This "hot spot" in the Marigny is "like a house party" filled with a "young", "interesting crew on both sides of the bar"; "downstairs is a funky dive with a sophisticated edge", and upstairs is a "wonderfully intimate space to see a small band tear it up" while feasting on "tasty but pricey tapas."

	APPEAL	DECOR	SERVICE	COST

Molly's at the Market
`21` `19` `21` `M`

French Quarter | 1107 Decatur St. (Ursuline Ave.) | 504-525-5169 |
www.mollysatthemarket.net

"Kick back with the friendly, heavily tattooed bartenders" at this French
Quarter "watering hole" and let them pour you a pint of the many "ales
and beers on tap", a shot from the "delectable choice of Irish whiskey"
or a cup of the frozen Irish coffee; it's a "warm place" where "everyone
is treated like an old friend" and the regulars shout "come in, get a
drink, be social – or don't be social, we don't give a damn."

Monkey Hill Bar
`21` `22` `21` `M`

Uptown | 6100 Magazine St. (Webster St.) | 504-899-4800 |
www.crescentcitytattooco.org

An "often overlooked, swanky-ass little bar" Uptown, this is a "vener-
able meat market" for the "beautiful" "20–30 crowd" ("I thought I died
and went to yuppie hell"); "you usually have to elbow your way to the
bar", but when you get there the "excellent" bartenders can fix you
something from the "incredible" list of martinis, wines and scotches.

Ms. Mae's The Club ⊄
`17` `11` `20` `I`

Uptown | 4336 Magazine St. (Napoleon Ave.) | 504-218-8035

It "endured a fire last year" but this Uptown 24-hour "dive", voted Best
Bang for the Buck in nightlife, still delivers the "cheapest and hardest
drinks in town" to an "eclectic" crowd of "bikers, hippies, freaks, college kids and even a guy in a suit from time to time"; just be sure to
"wash your hands when you get out" and "don't do anything illegal, because the police station is only a sand wedge away."

Neutral Ground Coffeehouse ⊄
`19` `17` `18` `M`

Uptown | 5110 Danneel St. (bet. Dufossat & Soniat Sts.) | 504-891-3381 |
www.neutralground.org

Even if it looks like "some hippie moved his Pacific Northwest tree-
house" to Uptown, this "quirky", sofa-strewn nighttime coffeehouse
has a "soul that's pure New Orleans", featuring "enjoyable" entertainment by a "wide array of aspiring musicians"; since no alcohol is
served, it's ideal for "under-21s" as well as an "older crowd" catching
up over espresso and pastries.

Ohm Lounge
`-` `-` `-` `M`

Central Business Dist. | Royal St. Charles Hotel | 135 St. Charles Ave.
(bet. Canal & Common Sts.) | 504-587-1330 | www.ohm-lounge.com

A "cool Asian aesthetic" informs this "upscale" yet "comfortable" CBD
lounge offering sake, "specialty drinks" and a "fishbowl" view onto
St. Charles Avenue; DJ nights add to the stylish vibe, and it "even
smells great" too.

Old Absinthe House
`23` `19` `19` `M`

French Quarter | 240 Bourbon St. (bet. Bienville Ave. & Iberville St.) |
504-523-3181 | www.oldabsinthehouse.com

"More history than one place can hold" comes with the Herbsaint at this
French Quarter "institution" "abounding in characters" and succeeding
in making the "sleaze that makes up much of Bourbon Street completely disappear"; it "doesn't look like a place to have a well-made
cocktail, but the bartenders know what they're doing", so "order an
absinthe frappé and pretend it's 1894 again."

	APPEAL	DECOR	SERVICE	COST

Old Point Bar · 23 17 23 M

Algiers | 545 Patterson Dr. (Olivier St.) | 504-364-0950 |
www.oldpointbar.com

"Beware of drinking sailors" at this Algiers Point "neighborhood place
for a cold beer on a hot night" that's "well worth" the "lovely ferry ride"
from Downtown; the "music can't be beat for the pass-the-hat-around
price", and during a set break you can "walk up the levee" and watch
ships pass on the Mississippi.

One Eyed Jacks · 23 20 19 M

French Quarter | 615 Toulouse St. (Chartres St.) | 504-569-8361 |
www.oneeyedjacks.net

"Dark, quirky" and "reminiscent of a 19th-century brothel", this "happening" club hosts a "crowd of Gen-Xers, French Quarter regulars"
and occasional "famous people" dancing to "modern music" by a
"wide array" of local and touring acts; it's an "intimate setting" that
also features "other surprising events", including burlesque shows
and a "crazy" '80s night on Thursdays.

Oz ⊅ · 21 18 18 M

French Quarter | 800 Bourbon St. (St. Ann St.) | 504-593-9491 |
www.oznewworleans.com

"A chicken coop in a town full of roosters and tourist foxes", this
French Quarter gay bar is a hit for "late-night dancing" "when the music is right and the hot men's shirts are off"; it's also popular for "drag
bingo", "people-watching from the balcony" and generally "losing
track of time" before "walking into the sunlight"; N.B. open 24 hours
on the weekends.

Pal's Lounge · - - - I

Faubourg St. John | 949 N. Rendon St. (St. Philip St.) | 504-488-7257
At this designer update on the corner dive, populated by Faubourg
St. John hipsters and the occasional movie star, vintage pinups hang
on the blue and nicotine-brown walls and each bathroom is plastered
with gender-appropriate retro porn; try your luck at video poker, chal-
lenge a friend to a game of air hockey or just chat with a neighbor from
down the street.

⊠ Pat O'Brien's · 25 24 21 M

French Quarter | 718 St. Peter St. (Royal St.) | 504-525-4823 |
www.patobriens.com

This "well-oiled fun machine" in the French Quarter "never changes",
and "yeah, it's a tourist trap, but it's also a locals trap" voted the city's
Most Popular nightspot; you can sing along to the "dueling" piano
players who "honor all requests", relax on the "beee-yootiful" courtyard with a "fire-breathing fountain" and get a souvenir from "roving
photographers", but "watch out for the surprisingly potent trademark
Hurricanes – they really pack a punch!"

Phoenix, The ⊅ · - - - M

Faubourg Marigny | 941 Elysian Fields Ave. (bet. Burgundy &
N. Rampart Sts.) | 504-945-9264 | www.phoenixneworleans.com

"So sleazy it could only exist in a gay fantasy" say regulars of this
Marigny "gay leather" "cruise club"; open 24/7, it's "dark and sexy"
("just the way I like my men!") and "best late at night."

	APPEAL	DECOR	SERVICE	COST

☑ Polo Lounge
`27` `27` `26` `E`

Central Business Dist. | Windsor Court Hotel | 300 Gravier St. (S. Peters St.) | 504-523-6000 | www.windsorcourthotel.com

"Keep that pinky up" at this "grand" CBD hotel lounge (voted No. 1 for both Service and Decor) frequented by "movers and shakers from New Orleans and afar" who "relax" over "to-die-for" martinis mixed by "knowledgeable" bartenders; with "dark walls and comfortable chairs" out of a vintage "drawing room", it's a "classic" for savoring live piano and jazz combos too (Thursday–Saturday).

NEW Pravda
`▽ 22` `24` `21` `M`

French Quarter | 1113 Decatur St. (Ursuline Ave.) | 504-525-1818

"Set to the tune of Soviet Russia", this "sleek", new French Quarter nightspot with an Eastern Bloc aesthetic is perfect when you're in a "Eurotrashy mood"; 50 vodkas and a half-dozen "expensive" absinthes dominate the bar, while the "romantic courtyard" suits a "quiet" night out.

☑ Preservation Hall ⊄
`28` `20` `17` `M`

French Quarter | 726 St. Peter St. (bet. Bourbon & Royal Sts.) | 504-522-2841 | www.preservationhall.com

"If you can't get in, press your nose against the glass" to "get your fill of blissful" "traditional jazz" by "talented" musicians at this "must-see" French Quarter "bastion of New Orleans heritage", voted No. 1 for Appeal in nightlife; it has an "unmistakable effervescence and energy", but expect "long lines, no drinks" (it's all-ages) and a room "so intimate that you'll want to make sure you applied your deodorant"; N.B. all shows are $10.

Rawhide 2010 ⊄
`▽ 25` `17` `25` `M`

French Quarter | 740 Burgundy St. (St. Ann St.) | 504-525-8106 | www.rawhide2010.com

Randy regulars have a "funky raw time" at this "rough-hewn", "muscle/leather rainbow bar" in the French Quarter that wins bear-hugs for its "incredibly warm and hospitable bartenders"; though some say it's "not nearly as cruisy at the name would imply", for those who like "watching gay male porn, shooting pool and drinking beer", "you've found your place."

Ray's Boom Boom Room
`20` `14` `16` `E`

Faubourg Marigny | 508 Frenchmen St. (bet. Decatur & Royal Sts.) | 504-309-7137

At this "spacious" room for "good music" in the Marigny with a "'30s-'40s atmosphere", the "local jazz" bands blow while fans "chill" and re-fill with dishes of Creole comfort food; some find the staff too "slow" and the surroundings hot and uninviting, but loyalists "love it" just the same.

Razzoo Bar & Patio
`18` `16` `17` `M`

French Quarter | 511 Bourbon St. (bet. St. Louis & Toulouse Sts.) | 504-522-5100 | www.razzoo.com

Have a "flashback to your college days" at this French Quarter bar where "packs" of "raucous" youngsters "dance" and mix inside, then "cool off" on the patio (or "warm up" next to the fire fountain); complete with an "energizing house cover band" and "DJs on stage who taunt the crowd into reality TV stunts", some sniff it's "perfect for the tourists looking to see what New Orleans isn't, but rather what they believe it to be."

R Bar

19 | 18 | 20 | M

Faubourg Marigny | Royal Street Inn | 1431 Royal St. (Kerlerec St.) | 504-948-7499 | www.royalstreetinn.com

There's mad "mojo" at this "out-of-the-way" Marigny "artist joint" whose "cool crowd, cool vibe and cool location" make it a "terrific spot to hang out" "late, late" or on "Mardi Gras morning"; set in the 1890s building housing the Royal Street Inn, it's been recently refurbished ("they got rid of my favorite airplane seats!"), but still features an antique barber chair for a $10 haircut and shot on Mondays.

Red Eye Bar & Grill

15 | 11 | 18 | M

Metairie | 1057 Veterans Memorial Blvd. (Sena Dr.) | 504-833-6900
Warehouse District | 852 S. Peters St. (bet. Julia & St. Joseph Sts.) | 504-593-9393
www.redeyegrill.net

A "young crowd" gets "wild on the weekend" at this Warehouse District and Metairie duo where even older drop-ins "shake their money maker" to a "mix of oldies and rap" (though some complain that "it's the same five songs on rotation all night"); with "cheap, cold beer" on tap, it works for mellower "day drinking" too.

Republic New Orleans

16 | 17 | 13 | M

Warehouse District | 828 S. Peters St. (bet. Julia & St. Joseph Sts.) | 504-528-8282 | www.republicnola.com

It "feels like a movie set" at this Warehouse District club complete with a "velvet rope" and "chandeliers upstairs in the V.I.P. area", attracting the "cash-flow endowed" to "dress to impress" and "dance their cares away" to DJs and indie rock bands; some feel it's "cheesy" and "tries too hard", while others admire it for the "awesome atmosphere."

Rivershack Tavern

22 | 21 | 21 | M

Jefferson | 3449 River Rd. (Shrewsbury Rd.) | 504-834-4938 | www.therivershacktavern.com

"You'd have to be on the ferry to get any closer to the river" than this "rollicking roadhouse" in Jefferson where real "characters" get down to live rock and R&B; a "tacky ashtray" collection and "hilarious" barstools are trademarks, while the "large variety of beer" and pub grub provide sustenance.

Rusty Nail

▽ 22 | 21 | 23 | M

Warehouse District | 1100 Constance St. (John Churchill Chase St.) | 504-525-5515 | www.therustynail.org

This "hidden" "saloon-style venue" amid the "urban blight" of the Warehouse District draws "eclectic crowds" from nearby condos for live music, bingo nights, a small bar menu and scotch offerings, like the classic namesake cocktail; while the $5 cover most weekends may deter some, fans feel it's "getting close to finding its groove."

Saturn Bar

22 | 18 | 18 | M

Bywater | 3067 St. Claude Ave. (Clouet St.) | 504-949-7532

"Talk about strange decor" at this "funky but famous" Bywater "dive" whose "classic attic-explosion decorating scheme" features plenty of "bizarre paintings" and bric-a-brac to bolster "surreal experiences";

"it's very off the beaten path", making it a "great place to kick back, hide from the rest of the world" and catch the occasional punk rock show.

Snake & Jake's Christmas Club Lounge   23 | 13 | 21 | M

Uptown | 7612 Oak St. (Hillary St.) | 504-861-2802 | www.snakeandjakes.com

Bar-hoppers on a bender "break on through to the dark side" at this Uptown "after-hours place" ("I've never been before 4 AM") lit with "Christmas lights" and filled with "furniture that might have been fished out of your great-grandmother's" house; often full of "bartenders and staff from other establishments", it's a "true original" that boasts well-mixed drinks and the promise of a "story to tell" the next day.

Snug Harbor Jazz Bistro   26 | 19 | 21 | M

Faubourg Marigny | 626 Frenchmen St. (Chartres St.) | 504-949-0696 | www.snugjazz.com

Revelers "rejoice in hearing" both the "up-and-coming and internationally known stars" of the "modern jazz" world, like Charmaine Neville and members of the Marsalis family, at this "dark, romantic" Marigny club with a "focus on the music"; it's "snug" indeed with tables right "on top of each other", but that also means you get to "sit about 10 feet from the performers"; P.S. you can "grab a burger before the band" in the adjoining dining room.

Spotted Cat ⊘   25 | 15 | 19 | M

Faubourg Marigny | 623 Frenchmen St. (Chartres St.) | 504-943-3887

"Duck in" to this "chill" Marigny "hole-in-the-wall" ("really, there may be holes in the walls") to hear bands playing "quirky, old-fashioned jazz" and imagine that it's "New Orleans 50 years ago"; the bartenders sometimes seem "a bit hassled", but they whip up martinis with "infused vodkas" for "great sippin' and listening."

St. Joe's Bar   20 | 20 | 19 | M

Uptown | 5535 Magazine St. (bet. Joseph & Octavia Sts.) | 504-899-3744

The room's "tight fit" means this Uptown "natives' hangout" with "eclectic" "religious decor" can make you feel like you're "getting drunk in a closet", but the "gorgeous tropical back patio" offers space to spread out; "cool" for kicking back and "talking with your friends", it gets a boost from "knowledgeable bartenders" whose "blueberry mojitos are the bomb."

☒ Swizzle Stick Bar   26 | 26 | 25 | E

Central Business Dist. | Loews | 300 Poydras St. (S. Peters St.) | 504-595-3305 | www.cafeadelaide.com

They "know what they're doing with a shaker" at this "beautiful" "new classic" in the CBD's Loews hotel with a "whole menu worth trying" of "fancy, inventive drinks" ("get one of each, and cab it home"); the "regulars do their best to be entertaining in spite of being outnumbered by visitors", though a few object to the "tourist prices."

☒ Tipitina's   27 | 19 | 19 | M

Uptown | 501 Napoleon Ave. (Tchoupitoulas St.) | 504-895-8477 | www.tipitinas.com

The "holy grail" of New Orleans funk, this Uptown "granddaddy of the city's music clubs" with a "rich history" also "hosts everything from hip-hop to the blues", along with a Sunday evening "fais do-do" when "all the Cajuns come with their dancing shoes"; the space "feels somewhat barn-ish" and it "might take awhile to get a drink", but it remains a "marvelous venue" whose devotees declare "don't miss this unique place."

Tommy's Wine Bar

24 | 25 | 24 | E

Warehouse District | 752 Tchoupitoulas St. (Notre Dame St.) | 504-525-4790 | www.tommyscuisine.com

Sippers stumble on a "sophisticated experience" at this high-end Warehouse District boîte (adjoining Tommy's Cuisine) that's ideal for "unwinding after a long day, or a long week", while also "quiet and dark enough for a romantic date"; along with a strong wine list, it also pleases palates with cognac and scotch, and the regular "piano music provides a relaxing background."

Tropical Isle

20 | 16 | 20 | M

French Quarter | 600 Bourbon St. (Toulouse St.) | 504-529-1728
French Quarter | 721 Bourbon St. (Orleans St.) | 504-529-4109
www.tropicalisle.com

"Home of the infamous" "radioactive" Hand Grenade that's "sure to get you bombed", this "cheesy" French Quarter duo looks and sounds "unaware that the '80s ended"; it's "frat meathead central", but the bartenders are "entertaining" and even the haters admit the 721 branch has "one of the best balconies in town."

☑ Vaughan's Lounge

27 | 18 | 20 | M

Bywater | 800 Lesseps St. (Dauphine St.) | 504-947-5562

Fans trumpet "if you haven't experienced Kermit Ruffins'" Thursday night "house party" at this "neighborhood joint", then "you haven't experienced New Orleans"; the "real deal in the Bywater", it's a "great dive bar" in a "building that looks like it could blow away in a frail breeze."

Whiskey Blue

23 | 26 | 19 | E

Central Business Dist. | W New Orleans | 333 Poydras St. (bet. S. Peters & Tchoupitoulas Sts.) | 504-525-9444 | www.gerberbars.com

"Young", "pretty peacocks get all fluffed up" to make an appearance at this "expensive", "fun and flirty" CBD lounge inside the W hotel, where the "distant" bartenders are nonetheless "well-versed in all the right drinks"; it's decked out with "contemporary fine lines" and "sleek surfaces", but critics sniff "there's one of these in every city and they're all the same."

NEW W.I.N.O.

24 | 21 | 24 | E

Warehouse District | 610 Tchoupitoulas St. (Lafayette St.) | 504-324-8000 | www.winoschool.com

Cork dorks feel like "kids in a candy store" at this "inventive" Warehouse District wine bar equipped with "self-serve" "vending machines" that that let you create a "DIY flight" from 80 different bottles; the "crowd is upscale", and the "knowledgeable" staffers "don't swirl their glasses and look down" their noses at newbies; N.B. beers, cheeses and chocolates are also served, and the bar offers tasting classes too.

SITES & ATTRACTIONS
DIRECTORY

Sites & Attractions

Ratings & Symbols

Appeal, Facilities and **Service** are rated on the Zagat 0 to 30 scale.

Cost reflects the attraction's high-season price range for one adult admission, indicated as follows:

$0 Free		**E** $26 to $40	
I $10 and below		**VE** $41 or more	
M $11 to $25			

MOST POPULAR

1. Audubon Aquarium
2. French Market
3. Audubon Zoo
4. National WWII Museum
5. Audubon Park

TOP APPEAL

29 National WWII Museum
28 Audubon Zoo
27 Audubon Aquarium
Jackson Square
Audubon Park

Ashé Cultural Arts Center   - | - | - | I

Central City | 1712 Oretha Castle Haley Blvd. (Euterpe St.) | 504-569-9070 | www.ashecac.org

Established and emerging African-American painters, performers and writers gather in this community-oriented, multiuse Central City facility that brings together art exhibits and plays with drumming circles and dance classes in a sleek, lofty 6,600-sq.-ft. space.

☒ Audubon Aquarium of the Americas   27 | 26 | 24 | M

French Quarter | 1 Canal St. (Convention Center Blvd.) | 504-581-4629 | 800-774-7394 | www.auduboninstitute.org

Surveyors rate this "wonderful", "exotic" aquarium on the Mississippi River edge of the French Quarter the city's Most Popular attraction for its "world-class exhibits" that some say are "second only to Monterey, CA"; "fantastic fins", "entertaining eels", an "amazing" white alligator and a "caring staff" make a visit here "a blast for kids and grown-ups alike."

NEW Audubon Insectarium   - | - | - | M

French Quarter | U.S. Custom House | 423 Canal St. (N. Peters St.) | 504-410-2847 | 800-774-7394 | www.auduboninstitute.org

There are big bugs and little bugs, termites and spiders, winged creatures and a plethora of pesky pests at this new museum – North America's largest of its kind – that's guaranteed to make kids squeal and parents squeamish; all can learn about insects from ancient history to the modern day through exhibits including a Japanese butterfly garden and simulated underground environment, before wishing each other 'bug appétit' as they catch a snack in the Tiny Termite Café.

Audubon Park   27 | 21 | 16 | $0

Uptown | 6500 St. Charles Ave. (bet. Calhoun & Walnut Sts.) | 504-581-4629 | 800-774-7394 | www.auduboninstitute.org

"Dripping with Spanish moss and Southern charm", "ancient" oaks "still standing after Katrina" create a "green oasis" in this "jewel of

Uptown New Orleans" with its "well-kept" "bike and walking paths" and "fabulous golf course"; "adjacent to the zoo", it's a "serene", "wonderful" place to "feed the ducks", "ride bikes", play tennis or just "waste away a day" "with a good book."

⁊ Audubon Zoo
`28` `26` `23` `M`

Uptown | 6500 Magazine St. (Exposition Blvd.) | 504-861-2537 | 800-774-7394 | www.auduboninstitute.org

"Da monkeys, dey all aks fo' you" at this "outstanding" zoo, a "modern marvel" Uptown that's deemed a "great family attraction" with a "dedicated staff" and "user-friendly layout"; for a real New Orleans experience, catch some "local flavor" at the "not-to-be-missed" swamp exhibit that's "so authentic they post nutria recipes."

Beauregard-Keyes House
`21` `22` `20` `I`

French Quarter | 1113 Chartres St. (Ursuline St.) | 504-523-7257

A visit to this little known, "nicely restored" Vieux Carré mansion is "a must for fans of [author] Francis Parkinson-Keyes" and appealing to "history buffs"; aside from an "extensive doll collection" it's "not riveting for kids", but "informative" docents provide an "interesting glimpse" into ante- and postbellum French Quarter life.

Cabildo
`23` `23` `20` `I`

French Quarter | Louisiana State Museum | 701 Chartres St. (St. Peter St.) | 504-568-6968 | 800-568-6968 | lsm.crt.state.la.us

"Fascinating" any time of year but a particularly "cool respite" on Jackson Square when it's hot, this "exquisite" 1790s Spanish-style building – where the Louisiana Purchase was signed – is the flagship of the Louisiana State Museum complex; Napoleon's death mask is one "highlight", but "you can spend a day" learning what NOLA was like "before the Hurricane – the drink, not the natural disaster – hit Bourbon Street."

Chalmette Battlefield & National Cemetery
`-` `-` `-` `$0`

Chalmette | Jean Lafitte National Historical Park | 8606 W. St. Bernard Hwy. (Jean Lafitte Pkwy.) | 504-281-0510 | www.nps.gov/jela

This site of the Battle of New Orleans, which marked the American victory over the British at the end of the War of 1812, is still undergoing major repair and restoration due to damage from hurricanes Katrina and Rita, but the Chalmette Monument, historic cannon and nearby adjacent National Cemetery are still worth seeing; parts of the battlefield may be closed at certain times for reconstruction, so it's best to call ahead before heading out.

Contemporary Arts Center
`22` `24` `21` `I`

Warehouse District | 900 Camp St. (bet. Andrew Higgins Dr. & St. Joseph St.) | 504-528-3805 | www.cacno.org

"Hip" and "vibrant", this "ultracool" Warehouse District space showcases "great" "local artwork" and "interesting" traveling shows that "push the envelope in the best way"; though critics contend that "it doesn't compare with New York City or Chicago" galleries, CAC fans "highly recommend" it for its "eclectic" program of "plays, music, exhibits", "performance art", film and dance offered year-round.

1850 House

`-` | `-` | `-` | `I`

French Quarter | Louisiana State Museum, Lower Pontalba Building | 523 St. Ann St. (bet. Chartres & Decatur Sts.) | 504-568-6968 | lsm.crt.state.la.us

Entry to this historic New Orleans property is a bargain (at $3) for visitors looking to view an antebellum row house furnished in mid-19th-century rococo revival style; built by Baroness Micaela Almonester de Pontalba in 1850, its parlor, dining room, bedrooms and nursery have all been re-created by the Louisiana State Museum.

⚡ French Market

`23` | `17` | `18` | `$0`

French Quarter | N. Peters St. (bet. Esplanade Ave. & Jackson Sq.) | 504-522-2621 | www.frenchmarket.org

"Kitschy yet cool", this French Quarter "shopper's paradise" makes a "great stroll full of history" with an "eclectic gumbo" of "wonderful spices", T-shirts, "irresistible mementos" and "beads, beads, beads"; though the "charmingly displayed junk" can be "hit-or-miss", fans come to "wander, people-watch" and "haggle with vendors" for a "unique experience" that's "touristy, but in a good way"; its post-Katrina renovation has brought some crisp new shopping areas, plus a farmer's market is set to open soon.

French Quarter Visitor Center

`-` | `-` | `-` | `$0`

French Quarter | Jean Lafitte National Historical Park | 419 Decatur St. (bet. Conti & St. Louis Sts.) | 504-589-2636, ext. 1 | www.nps.gov/jela

Several small exhibitions focus on local music and dialects at this French Quarter–based visitor center of Jean Lafitte National Historical Park that also carries brochures and information about its other family-friendly sites scattered across southern Louisiana; early birds can learn more about the history of New Orleans with a ranger-led, one-hour walking tour along the Mississippi River departing daily at 9:30 AM (free tickets are given out beginning at 9 AM).

Gallier House

∇ `26` | `24` | `23` | `I`

French Quarter | 1132 Royal St. (bet. Governor Nicholls & Ursuline Sts.) | 504-525-5661 | www.hgghh.org

The former home of James Gallier, Jr., one of the city's "premier architects", this "exquisitely detailed and maintained" French Quarter house museum boasts "several innovative" features (for the 1800s) such as running hot and cold water, skylights and copper bathtubs; "informative guides", seasonal decorative "dressings" reminiscent of "the old times" and a "great gift shop" make it "fun for the entire family."

Hermann-Grima House

`26` | `26` | `24` | `I`

French Quarter | 820 St. Louis St. (bet. Bourbon & Dauphine Sts.) | 504-525-5661 | www.hgghh.org

This "very well-preserved" and faithfully restored mid-19th-century French Quarter mansion, complete with a courtyard and stable, offers a close "look into the lifestyles" of the era's rich and famous Creole families, as well as edification for those "interested in the history of architecture"; the "great docents" lead lively tours, and the particularly memorable cooking demonstrations at the outdoor "pre-Civil War working kitchen" (every Thursday, October–May) "make you realize how different things used to be."

	APPEAL	FACIL.	SERVICE	COST

Historic New Orleans Collection

25 | 25 | 24 | $0

French Quarter | 533 Royal St. (bet. St. Louis & Toulouse Sts.) | 504-523-4662 | www.hnoc.org

"A diamond in the midst of the Quarter", this "enlightening" museum holds an "amazing collection of artifacts and books" that are "painstakingly kept by professionals who care"; its multiple buildings encompass the Williams Gallery, Research Center and Residence (a former "not-so-humble abode"), which all provide a fascinating "archive of New Orleans" along with "interesting special events"; N.B. tours are $5.

Houmas House Plantation

- | - | - | M

Darrow | 40136 Hwy. 942 | 225-473-9380 | www.houmashouse.com

Once the largest sugar plantation in America, this rarefied River Road estate sold its goods at a clip until the great flood of 1927 and the ensuing Depression, and was restored in 2003 when new owners decorated the Greek Revival mansion with period antiques and enlivened its surrounding 12-acre site with elaborate gardens; leisurely afternoon tours often lead to dinner on the grounds at Latil's Landing Restaurant (reservations recommended), or Southern drinks at Turtle Bar.

Jackson Square

27 | 18 | 15 | $0

French Quarter | Chartres to St. Ann Sts., Decatur to St. Peter Sts. | www.jackson-square.com

"Hundreds of years of history" unfold throughout this "picturesque" park and "heart of the city", named for hometown hero Andrew Jackson (depicted in the central equestrian sculpture) and bordered by the Mississippi River and St. Louis Cathedral; in addition to its "amazing architecture" and some of the "best street theater" in town ("the starving artists, fortune tellers, performers are sprinkling back"), it makes a "lovely place for people-watching" to the rhythm of "horses pulling carriages" and "sweet jazz played on the corner."

Jean Lafitte National Historical Park & Preserve

26 | 20 | 19 | $0

Marrero | 6588 Barataria Blvd. | 504-589-2330, ext. 10 | www.nps.gov/jela

Named for one of the most colorful Barataria pirates of old, this "swamp setting" with its "lush marshland" in Marrero is a "gem" of greater New Orleans; both locals and tourists tout it as a "terrific place to see some gators and enjoy the bayou" while taking "wonderful walking paths" and guided canoe tours with "informed rangers" – and it's "especially gorgeous" in the spring when the wildflowers are "in bloom"; N.B. the park has six locations across southern Louisiana – see its website for more information.

Lafayette Cemetery No. 1

▽ 25 | 14 | 12 | $0

Garden District | 1400 Washington Ave. (Prytania St.) | 888-721-7493 | www.saveourcemeteries.org

Amid the mansions of the Garden District lies a "whole different world" "unlike anything you've ever seen" – this 19th-century site of "beautiful" above-ground tombs, which reflect the "weight of history and lives past"; guided tours for $6 are offered Mondays, Wednesdays, Fridays and Saturdays at 10:30 AM, and it makes a smart stop before lunch at Commander's Palace (right across the street); closes at 2:30 PM weekdays and noon on Saturday (closed Sunday).

APPEAL | FACIL. | SERVICE | COST

Longue Vue House & Gardens
26 | 25 | 24 | I

Old Metairie | 7 Bamboo Rd. (bet. Metairie Rd. & Palmetto St.) | Metairie | 504-488-5488 | www.longuevue.com

The "absolutely beautiful, extremely well-kept" and flower-filled gardens designed by Ellen Biddle Shipman are the highlights of this Old Metairie national landmark – an "incredible city estate" constructed in 1939 for Edgar Bloom Stern, a cotton broker, and his wife, Edith Rosenwald Stern, a Sears-Roebuck heiress; "renewed" post-Katrina, it remains a "wonderful hidden treasure" enhanced by the "great children's discovery area", gift shop "without equal" and events that enchant "in the spring", fall and "around the holidays."

Louisiana Children's Museum
- | - | - | I

Warehouse District | 420 Julia St. (bet. Magazine & Tchoupitoulas Sts.) | 504-523-1357 | www.lcm.org

Families flock to this most playful of places for a variety of hands-on hijinks – like piloting a tugboat down the Mississippi and stepping into Mr. Rogers' Neighborhood – and even the littlest of visitors have a special nook for climbing and hiding; art programs, exhibitions and a well-stocked museum shop round out the experience at this Warehouse District establishment, which often plays host to birthday parties.

Louisiana's Civil War Museum at Confederate Memorial Hall
20 | 16 | 16 | I

Warehouse District | 929 Camp St. (bet. Andrew Higgins Dr. & St. Joseph St.) | 504-523-4522 | www.confederatemuseum.com

Founded by Confederate veterans, this "strange" Warehouse District museum is "controversial" for sure, but history buffs say it "deserves to be better known" for its "huge, varied collection of Civil War memorabilia"; many find it an "interesting" "balance to the World War II Museum" nearby, even if it's "not worth a stop by itself"; N.B. the museum is currently completing renovations, so call before visiting.

🆕 Museum of the American Cocktail
- | - | - | I

Central Business Dist. | Southern Food & Beverage Museum, Riverwalk Mktpl. | 1 Poydras St., Ste. 169 (Julia St. entrance) | 504-569-0405 | www.museumoftheamericancocktail.org

Since history records the cocktail was invented in N'Awlins, it's more than appropriate that there be a museum in its honor offering informative mixology presentations and a treasure trove of artifacts ranging from vintage cocktail shakers to absinthe accoutrements to rare bartender's manuals and all manner of memorabilia; be warned, though, that this little newcomer, entered through the Southern Food & Beverage Museum in the Riverwalk Marketplace, does not sell booze.

☒ National World War II Museum
(fka National D-Day Museum)
29 | 29 | 26 | M

Warehouse District | 945 Magazine St. (Andrew Higgins Dr.) | 504-527-6012 | www.nationalww2museum.org

"Moving, inspiring and humbling", this "world-class" Warehouse District "must-see" (founded by historian Stephen Ambrose as the National D-Day Museum, and currently in the middle of an expansion) presents an "outstanding" collection that spans "everything from rationing to V-E Day", "diary entries to uniforms", and "doesn't pull any punches" in conveying the "terror and trauma of war"; rated No. 1 for Appeal among Attractions, it features exhibits covering the "European and Pacific theaters" as well as the domestic front, and engaging docents ("a highlight") who "fascinate even the non-history buff", leaving visitors with a "great appreciation for the men and women who served."

New Orleans Botanical Garden
26 | 24 | 21 | I

Mid-City | City Park | Victory Ave. (off Roosevelt Mall Dr.) | 504-483-9386 | www.neworleanscitypark.com

"Still rebounding" from the hurricane, this WPA-era City Park garden has been replanted to become a "post-Katrina oasis of beauty" that's "soothing to the soul"; its "great array" of "native plants", notably its forest of "ancient" live oaks (the largest in the world), is complemented by Enrique Alferez's sculptures, a miniature train garden that operates on the weekends and seasonal traditions like "music in the summer and pretty lights during the holidays."

New Orleans City Park
23 | 16 | 15 | $0

Mid-City | 1 Palm Dr. (Marconi Dr.) | 504-482-4888 | www.neworleanscitypark.com

It was "hit tremendously hard by Katrina" and "a lot of work" still needs to be done, but this 1,300-acre Mid-City "treasure", one of the largest urban parks in the country, is "slowly being restored" by "scores of volunteers"; home to the New Orleans Museum of Art, the Sydney and Walda Besthoff Sculpture Garden, Botanical Garden and Storyland amusement park (crafted by Mardi Gras float designers), it's "still a great place to walk, jog or bike" and to visit during December's light-festooned Celebration in the Oaks.

New Orleans Jazz
National Historical Park
- | - | - | $0

French Quarter | 916 N. Peters St. (St. Philip St.) | 504-589-4806 | www.nps.gov/jazz

Still a work in progress, the only national park dedicated solely to the enjoyment of jazz is scheduled to move its visitor's center in mid-2009 from the French Quarter to the historic, renovated Perseverance Hall in Louis Armstrong Park; in the meantime, it hosts a variety of live music performances, demonstrations and Saturday morning kids' programs in which children are invited to join the Treme Brass Band with their own instruments.

New Orleans Museum of Art
26 | 26 | 23 | I
(aka NOMA)

Mid-City | City Park | 1 Collins Diboll Circle (Esplanade Ave.) | 504-488-2631 | www.noma.org

"One of the city's greatest assets", this "beautiful beaux arts building" and its "very fine collection" fortunately remain "intact" despite Katrina's impact on surrounding City Park; its "awesome glass display", "extensive" European and American paintings and pre-Columbian pieces "will keep you riveted for hours", but be sure to leave time for the "spectacular" sculpture garden, perhaps "the number one way to introduce young people to art while giving them room to run around"; N.B. free to Louisiana residents.

APPEAL | FACIL. | SERVICE | COST

Oak Alley Plantation

`-` | `-` | `-` | M

Vacherie | 3645 Hwy. 18 (3 mi. west of Hwy. 20) | 225-265-2151 |
www.OakAlleyPlantation.com

Countryside trekkers have a soft spot for this "incredible
antebellum plantation", which offers a "great tour" of its "magnificent" oak allée and grand Southern mansion ("where *Interview with the
Vampire* was filmed"); you can rent a car and plan for a "full-day of activity" on 'Plantation Road' (River Road) – "just be sure you have
a good map."

Ogden Museum of Southern Art

24 | 27 | 24 | I

Warehouse District | 925 Camp St. (Howard Ave.) | 504-539-9600 |
www.ogdenmuseum.org

"Southern arts and crafts" that go beyond "the usual suspects" win
raves for this new museum – a "marvelous" edifice that's "one of the
few great modern buildings" in the Warehouse District and part of the
University of New Orleans; its "impressive" permanent collection and
special exhibits, from glass to pottery to photography, "form a clear
picture [without] overwhelming", and it's a real treat to swing by
"after hours on Thursday night" and have a glass of wine while
"local musicians" play.

Old Ursuline Convent

`-` | `-` | `-` | I

French Quarter | 1100 Chartres St. (Ursuline St.) | 504-529-3040

This "lovely" landmark, "one of the oldest buildings in the Mississippi
Valley" and the embodiment of "history with a capital H", offers a
"cool lesson" about the early-18th-century arrival of the French
Ursuline nuns and the cross-cultural schools they founded in New
Orleans; it also features seasonal, changing exhibits, and the herb garden and courtyard serve as a "tranquil escape from the boisterous"
surrounding French Quarter.

Old U.S. Mint

`-` | `-` | `-` | I

French Quarter | Louisiana State Museum | 400 Esplanade Ave.
(N. Peters St.) | 504-568-6968 | 800-568-6968 | lsm.crt.state.la.us

In a magnificent Greek Revival building adjacent to the French
Market, this national historic landmark features examples of the
gold and silver coins produced here from its beginnings in
1835 until it ceased operations as a mint in 1909; a collection of
artifacts including an 1868 coining press and an extraordinary
bullion scale are all on the first floor, while the second floor
features changing exhibitions.

Presbytere

25 | 23 | 19 | I

French Quarter | Louisiana State Museum | 751 Chartres St. (St. Ann St.) |
504-568-6968 | lsm.crt.state.la.us

Designed as a monastery to flank St. Louis Cathedral and match the
Cabildo on the opposite side, this 1813 cornerstone of Jackson Square
now houses a "wonderful" museum providing an "excellent (and
G-rated) look at Mardi Gras" in a permanent, costume-rich collection
that "shows off Louisiana's unique culture" in a way that "kids love"
and Carnival connoisseurs say is "not to be missed", particularly if
you've never seen the real thing; an exhibit honoring the 100-year-old
Krewe of Zulu will be featured in 2009.

	APPEAL	FACIL.	SERVICE	COST

NEW Southern Food & Beverage Museum

| | − | − | − | I |

Central Business Dist. | Riverwalk Mktpl. | 1 Poydras St., Ste. 169 (Julia St. entrance) | 504-569-0405 | www.southernfood.org

Food lovers can peruse vintage tools, cookbooks and menus among other collected treasures at this new celebration of Southern culinary culture in the Riverwalk Marketplace; special exhibitions, demonstrations and tastings are often featured, plus admission includes entry to the adjacent Museum of the American Cocktail.

St. Louis Cathedral

| | 26 | 25 | 19 | $0 |

French Quarter | Jackson Sq. | 615 Pere Antoine Alley (Chartres St.) | 504-525-9585 | www.stlouiscathedral.org

"One of the great cathedrals in a country that doesn't have many", this 18th-century Jackson Square centerpiece is a "historical must" for most; along with admiring the extraordinary stained-glass windows depicting the life of Louis IX and the glorious Renaissance-style painted ceiling, you can acquire amulets like a "medal with your patron saint" from the gift shop, though sinful types might do better to "view the beautiful church, then pray for what you did on Bourbon Street the night before."

St. Louis Cemetery No. 1

| | 25 | 15 | 13 | $0 |

French Quarter | 420 Basin St. (bet. Conti & St. Louis Sts.) | 504-596-3050 | www.saveourcemeteries.org

Visiting one of the South's oldest cemeteries, whose dead are buried above ground inside "beautiful old statuary", is a "one-of-a-kind experience found nowhere else in the USA"; its "decadent decay" is "disturbing", "ghostly" and "poetic" (see the grave of "voodoo queen" Marie Laveau), but experienced explorers offer just one caution: this "city of the dead" is in a "sketchy neighborhood" bordering the French Quarter, so visitors should take the $12 guided tour (Sundays at 10 AM) instead of going alone.

Woldenberg Riverfront Park

| | 24 | 19 | 15 | $0 |

French Quarter | Bienville St. (The Mississippi River) | 504-565-3033

"One of the coolest spots in town (literally)", this "lovely" "linear" "green space on the banks of the Mississippi River" is a fine place to "get a real look at Ol' Man River" and "watch the ships go by"; it's nothing fancy, but suited to simple French Quarter pleasures like "munching on a po' boy" and savoring "the only place with a breeze in the city."

40,000 places to eat, drink, stay & play – free at ZAGAT.com

HOTEL
DIRECTORY

Hotels

Ratings & Symbols

Rooms, **Service**, **Dining** and **Facilities** are rated on the Zagat 0 to 30 scale.

Cost reflects the hotel's high-season rate for a standard double room. It does not reflect seasonal changes.

🧒 children's programs
✕ exceptional restaurant
ⓗ historic interest
🍳 kitchens
🐾 allows pets

👀 views
Ⓢ notable spa facilities
🏊 swimming pool
🎾 tennis

TOP OVERALL*

25 Windsor Court	W French Quarter
24 Ritz-Carlton	21 Monteleone, Hotel
22 Omni Royal Orleans	W New Orleans

Bienville House ✕🐾👀🏊   –   –   –   – $189

French Quarter | 320 Decatur St. | 504-529-2345 | fax 504-525-6079 | 800-535-9603 | www.bienvillehouse.com | 80 rooms, 3 suites

Frequent French Quarter lodgers note the "nice" staff as one reason they "return every time" to this "pet-friendly" boutique hotel with a nearly 200-year-old history; some guests find the rooms "Gothic" (balcony-blessed dwellers deem them "richly appointed", while those in "quiet", windowless interior quarters call them "creepy"), and while "there's not much to speak of in the amenities department" (save for a pool), it now offers New American dining at the well-rated Iris restaurant.

Bourbon Orleans ⓗ👀🏊   ▽ 18 | 20 | 16 | 20 | $139

French Quarter | 717 Orleans St. | 504-523-2222 | fax 504-571-4666 | www.bourbonorleans.com | 177 rooms, 41 suites

A "super", "accessible" location "close to Jackson Square and the action on Bourbon Street", as well as two-story suites with balconies, earn points for this former Wyndham housed in an 1817 French Quarter building by the river; still, some say the "loud street noise" (get a room "overlooking the courtyard" if you want to sleep) and "variable" quarters that "need improvement" "despite the renovations" make it hard to "recommend."

Chateau Sonesta 👀🏊   ▽ 22 | 23 | 20 | 22 | $279

French Quarter | 800 Iberville St. | 504-586-0800 | fax 504-586-1987 | www.chateausonesta.com | 226 rooms, 25 suites

Operating behind an 1849 neo-Classical facade, this French Quarter hotel sports "lovely" common areas, a courtyard and a prime location right near Bourbon and Dauphine streets; even if the "rooms vary in size" and "loud" acoustics are an issue (depending on which area of the hotel you're staying in), most agree it's a "wonderful" choice.

---

* Based on overall average scores

HOTELS

	ROOMS	SERVICE	DINING	FACIL.	COST

Doubletree Hotel New Orleans ≈ | 19 | 20 | 18 | 19 | $161

Central Business Dist. | 300 Canal St. | 504-581-1300 | fax 504-212-3141 |
800-222-8733 | www.doubletree.com | 359 rooms, 8 suites
Overlooking the Mississippi, across from the casino and next to the
French Quarter, this "right-by-all-the-action" mid-rise is "solid in all
ways"; the "basic" rooms are small, but the beds boast "crisp linens"
and "down comforters and pillows"; more "discouraging" are the "hidden"
charges for valet-only parking (which "feels like a rip-off"),
fridges and Internet; luckily, the "helpful service" is included.

Harrah's New Orleans ✕♨ | ∇ 23 | 24 | 22 | 24 | $139

Central Business Dist. | 228 Poydras St. | 504-533-6000 | fax 504-593-8010 |
800-427-7247 | www.harrahs.com | 366 rooms, 84 studios
"Centrally located" "close to the Convention Center" "without being in
the chaos of Bourbon Street", this "Vegas South" hotel "surprises"
with "lovely rooms", "good service", a "gorgeous lobby" and "great entertainment"
(there's a "casino right there"); despite having "no pool"
and "no spa", this "value" is "well worth the stay."

Hilton New Orleans Riverside ⚲♨≈⚲ | 19 | 18 | 16 | 19 | $219

Central Business Dist. | 2 Poydras St. | 504-561-0500 | fax 504-584-3989 |
800-445-8667 | www.hilton.com | 1540 rooms, 76 suites
"Lounge at the riverfront pool and watch the barges float by" suggest
supporters of this "sprawling" "convention hotel" in a "convenient,
safe location" "attached to a unique mall"; some rooms boast "tremendous
views" of the Mississippi, the staff is "well trained" and
there's an "amazing health club", but many deem the dining just "ok",
aside from Drago's "highly recommended" oysters.

Hilton St. Charles Ave. ✕≈ | - | - | - | - | $369

Central Business Dist. | 333 St. Charles Ave. | 504-524-8890 |
fax 504-524-8889 | 800-445-8667 | www.hilton.com | 225 rooms, 25 suites
Dining at Lüke is "reason enough to stay" at this "tidy" convention
property, formerly Kimpton's Hotel Monaco, where you can "eat and
drink extremely well" and be served by a "professional staff"; overall,
fans find a "good value" for a "convenient" city location.

Iberville Suites ⚲Ⓢ | ∇ 20 | 21 | - | 19 | $249

French Quarter | 910 Iberville St. | 504-523-2400 | fax 504-524-1321 |
866-229-4351 | www.ibervillesuites.com | 232 suites
Thrifty travelers "on a Courtyard budget" enjoy high-end perks "at a
fraction of the cost" at this "quaint" hotel on the "upper end of the
French Quarter" that's "adjoined to the Ritz-Carlton" and has "access" to
its amenities; "spacious rooms" with "nice furnishings" and "friendly
service" "make it easy to forget" there's "no bar or dining room", just
a "genteel lobby" "graced" with "oriental carpets and antiques."

InterContinental ⚲♨≈ | ∇ 23 | 21 | 17 | 21 | $499

Central Business Dist. | 444 St. Charles Ave. | 504-525-5566 |
fax 504-523-7310 | 888-424-6835 | www.interconti.com | 458 rooms,
21 suites
"It never disappoints" say road warriors of this "tried-and-true" convention
hotel "centrally located" in the CBD and on the Mardi Gras
"parade route"; while some dis the "nondescript" dining, they toast

the "stellar service", "nice gym on the top floor" and "immaculate" but "smallish" rooms with "good amenities", deeming this "a steal" despite "insane" "parking prices."

International House ✕ 🏄   ▽ 20 | 23 | - | 19 | $249

Central Business Dist. | 221 Camp St. | 504-553 9550 | fax 504-553-9560 | 800-633-5770 | www.ihhotel.com | 113 rooms, 4 suites

"Like a mini-W but more quaint", this "hip", "West Coast"-style boutique hotel situated in the CBD lures "beautiful people" to its "very cool bar, Loa"; surveyors say the accommodations are "nice" but "impossibly small", except for the penthouse suites that boast river views, and the staff is "warm and personal"; N.B. the chic Rambla restaurant opened in fall 2008, serving French and Spanish small plates.

JW Marriott 🏄🍸   19 | 20 | 17 | 18 | $189

Central Business Dist. | 614 Canal St. | 504-525-6500 | fax 504-525-8068 | 800-771-9067 | www.marriott.com | 487 rooms, 7 suites

The "lobby bar with soaring ceilings" is the "best place to rebuild New Orleans one drink at a time" jest guests of this "typical conference hotel" "right in the heart of things" in the CBD and "convenient to the French Quarter"; "small" but "well-furnished" rooms and "competent" service have most calling it "pleasant", though a few deem it "devoid of style."

Le Pavillon Hotel 🏄🍸   ▽ 19 | 25 | 18 | 19 | $279

Central Business Dist. | 833 Poydras St. | 504-581-3111 | fax 504-620-4130 | 800-535-9095 | www.lepavillon.com | 219 rooms, 7 suites

Guests of this CBD "grande dame" feel like they're "staying at Tara" thanks to the "columned entrance", the "old-world luxury" of the "magnificent lobby" and, most of all, the "top-notch" (and top-hatted) staff delivering "a heavy dose of New Orleans charm" and complimentary "nighttime snacks of peanut-butter-and-jelly sandwiches"; rooms are "smallish but comfortably appointed", and while "parking leaves a lot to be desired", the location is "one block from the streetcar."

Loews 👫 🍴 🏄 ⑤ 🍸   ▽ 26 | 26 | 25 | 25 | $249

Central Business Dist. | 300 Poydras St. | 504-595-3300 | fax 504-595-3310 | 800-235-6397 | www.loewshotels.com | 273 rooms, 12 suites

"You can't go wrong" praise patrons of this "well-located" business hotel in the CBD deemed "practically perfect in every way" from the "spacious rooms" with "huge baths" to the "accommodating" staff to the "fabulous food" (including "room service by the Brennan" restaurant group); "contemporary Southern design" defines the "absolutely beautiful" public spaces, including a "fabulous bar and lounge area" with "great people-watching" and a "lovely indoor Jacuzzi and pool" – indeed, it's all so "wonderful", you'll want to "check back in" next week.

Maison de Ville & the Audubon Cottages ✕ ⑪ 🏄 🍸   ▽ 22 | 22 | 24 | 17 | $179

French Quarter | 727 Toulouse St. | 504-561-5858 | fax 504-528-9939 | 800-634-1600 | www.hotelmaisondeville.com | 14 rooms, 7 cottages, 2 suites

The former quarters of Tennessee Williams and James Audubon are about as "authentic" as you can get for N'Awlins, so book a stay at this "old-time" Vieux Carré hotel and get a load of the local "'wow' factor"; if "staff shortages" have affected the level of service a bit, at least the cottages are still "nice" and the courtyard is as "beautiful" as ever.

	ROOMS	SERVICE	DINING	FACIL.	COST

Maison Dupuy ♨≋

▽ | 22 | 24 | 23 | 19 | $109

French Quarter | 1001 Toulouse St. | 504-586-8000 | fax 504-525-5334 | 800-535-9177 | www.maisondupuy.com | 187 rooms, 12 suites, 1 cottage
"Perfectly charming" aptly sums up this "budget" boutique whose "excellent" location in the French Quarter provides a retreat from all the ongoing activities on nearby Bourbon Street; clients adore the "inviting" atmosphere and courtyard pool, "quick" service, "excellent" fare at Dominique's and "cozy", if also "small", rooms; P.S. expect to see a lot of "wedding receptions."

Marriott Metairie at Lakeway ♨≋

– | – | – | – | $195

Metairie | 3838 N. Causeway Blvd. | 504-836-5253 | fax 504-836-5258 | 888-465-4329 | www.neworleanslakesidehotel.com | 186 rooms, 34 suites
Enjoy room service overlooking Lake Pontchartrain at this "newly redone" "beautiful property", where the visitors who like the dining, "on-site exercise facility" and "walks along the levee" say they'd prefer "never to leave"; the tastefully refurbished rooms feature 32-inch plasma HDTVs with Internet, signature Revive bedding with allergy-tested duck down and work areas with ergonomic chairs.

Marriott New Orleans ♨≋

▽ | 18 | 19 | 15 | 19 | $375

French Quarter | 555 Canal St. | 504-581-1000 | fax 504-523-6755 | 888-771-4429 | www.marriott.com | 1275 rooms, 55 suites
A $38-million renovation has spruced up this smoke-free French Quarter lodging "right in the middle of everything"; the chambers feature "improved bedding" (the chain's signature Revive brand) and large workstations, but "if you're spending time in your room this close to Bourbon Street, you're missing the point" say celebrating surveyors; expect "decent" food, a "lively" wine bar and a "very W" "new lobby" complete with its own Starbucks.

Marriott New Orleans Convention Center ≋

21 | 20 | 18 | 20 | $299

Warehouse District | 859 Convention Center Blvd. | 504-613-2888 | fax 504-613-2890 | 800-228-9290 | www.marriott.com | 320 rooms, 11 suites
Just across from the Convention Center and 15 minutes' walking distance to the French Quarter, this "smoke-free" Warehouse District hotel proves "excellent for business or pleasure" with "comfortable, luxurious rooms" and an "amazing" lobby; some reviewers find the staff "superb" while others complain of "rude" service, but most agree that the daily valet parking fee of about $28 is on the "high side" – and there's "no self-parking available."

Monteleone, Hotel ⑪♨Ⓢ≋

22 | 23 | 19 | 21 | $319

French Quarter | 214 Royal St. | 504-523-3341 | fax 504-681-4491 | 800-535-9595 | www.hotelmonteleone.com | 530 rooms, 40 suites
"As comforting as a beignet and café au lait on a cold morning", this French Quarter "landmark" is known for its "independent ethos, amiable staff" and one-of-a-kind "revolving" Carousel Bar, which keeps "your head spinning and your beverages swirling"; admirers appreciate the "fantastic spa", "exquisite rooftop pool", "grand" public spaces "full of antiques" and "elegant" suites that bear the names of authors who once stayed here.

HOTELS

	ROOMS	SERVICE	DINING	FACIL.	COST

Ⓩ Omni Royal Orleans ♥♥✕⅍♨≈ | 21 | 24 | 21 | 23 | $279

French Quarter | 621 St. Louis St. | 504-529-5333 | fax 504-529-7089 |
888-444-6664 | www.omniroyalorleans.com | 321 rooms, 25 suites
"Sipping drinks and watching paddleboats on the Mississippi" from
the "marvelous rooftop terrace and pool" is a must at this "gracious"
"old French Quarter hotel" say fans, who also praise the "perfect location" "in the center of everything" (yet "far enough from Bourbon"),
"wonderful staff" and "excellent" eats from the Rib Room ("a favorite
with the local lunch crowd"); rooms, though "comfortable and elegant", "could do with a bit of an upgrade."

Prince Conti Hotel | - | - | - | - | $189

French Quarter | 830 Conti St. | 504-529-4172 | fax 504-636-1046 |
800-366-2743 | www.princecontihotel.com | 73 rooms, 3 suites
Set in a historic building with an "outstanding" French Quarter location
"one block from Bourbon Street", this property boasts "great antiques"
and other "unique features you won't find anywhere else for the
price"; its nouveau Creole bistro, the Bombay Club, is cozy for eats and
drinks, and the "nice" staff is "helpful in recommending places to go."

Provincial, Hotel ⓗ≈ | - | - | - | - | $259

French Quarter | 1024 Chartres St. | 504-581-4995 | fax 504-581-1018 |
800-535-7922 | www.hotelprovincial.com | 82 rooms, 11 suites
It's "like having your own French Quarter place" boast those in-the-
know who return time and again to this "off-the-beaten-path" "historic"
property far enough away from Bourbon Street for a "quiet" night's
sleep, yet close enough to get in on the action easily; "hospitable service", landscaped courtyards, two pools and the "excellent" Stella!
restaurant keep guests pampered and entertained both day and night.

Renaissance Arts Hotel ♨≈ | - | - | - | - | $179

Warehouse District | 700 Tchoupitoulas St. | 504-613-2330 |
fax 504-613-2331 | 800-431-8634 | www.renaissanceartshotel.com |
210 rooms, 7 suites
Erudite excursionists say this "superb" place "lives up to its name"
since it's "like staying in an art gallery": installations (including
"Chihuly glass") adorn "the rooms, lobby and restaurant, and there's
a sculpture garden inside"; the "ideal location" in the Warehouse
District and the on-site Creole seafooder, La Côte Brasserie, are further reasons why this chainster comes "highly recommended."

Renaissance Pere Marquette ♨≈ | 19 | 20 | 16 | 17 | $329

Central Business Dist. | 817 Common St. | 504-525-1111 |
fax 504-525-0688 | 800-372-0482 | www.marriott.com | 268 rooms, 4 suites
"For convenience, you can't beat this hotel" within "walking distance
of the Superdome, French Quarter and Canal Street" that mirrors the
city's "cool, jazzy feel" in its "modern" rooms and chic dining at MiLa;
"individual attention" is key and customer service ranks as "excellent", but the $28-per-night parking fee is overly "expensive."

Ⓩ Ritz-Carlton, The ♥♥✕⅍♨Ⓢ | 25 | 24 | 22 | 25 | $519

French Quarter | 921 Canal St. | 504-524-1331 | fax 504-670-2884 |
800-241-3333 | www.ritzcarlton.com | 491 rooms, 36 suites
"The little touches really add up" at this "ultra-luxe" French Quarter
hotel deemed "better than ever" after a "gorgeous renovation" that's

resulted in "flawless rooms", "de-lish food" and "amazing facilities" like a "fantastic spa" and "lively courtyard" "complete with parrot"; though a few picky patrons cite "post-Katrina issues" (the staff is "still learning"), most say extras, like the "amazing piano bar entertainment", are "icing on the cake."

Royal Sonesta ⌂♨≋

| 20 | 21 | 21 | 21 | $250 |

French Quarter | 300 Bourbon St. | 504-586-0300 | fax 504-586-0335 | 800-766-3782 | www.sonesta.com | 478 rooms, 22 suites

You can be "in the middle of the action" and "stay up all night" if you book balcony quarters "above Bourbon Street" at this French Quarter veteran, but "if you want to sleep" get a "beautiful room overlooking the courtyard"; it "retains its old-world charm" say fans, and the staff "labors tirelessly" to keep service "excellent."

Sheraton ⌂♨≋

| - | - | - | - | $289 |

Central Business Dist. | 500 Canal St. | 504-525-2500 | fax 504-595-5552 | 800-325-3535 | www.sheraton.com | 1057 rooms, 53 suites

Views of the Mississippi River and adjacent French Quarter are one of the perks of staying in this sizable CBD hotel where guests can take a dip in the outdoor pool and have a tipple at the lobby's Pelican Bar; overlooking the atrium, Roux Bistro offers a moderately priced Creole menu.

Sheraton Metairie New Orleans ≋

| 19 | 19 | 16 | 20 | $149 |

Metairie | 4 Galleria Blvd. | 504-837-6707 | fax 504-837-6906 | 800-325-3535 | www.sheraton.com | 179 rooms, 2 suites

The briefcase brigade is "pleasantly surprised" by the "excellent" service and "friendliness of the staff" at this "elegant but not stuffy" hotel with "easy access to I-10 and Causeway Boulevard"; "new, spacious" rooms are "modern and tasteful" with "comfortable" beds, and work-out enthusiasts praise the "incredible fitness room"; the "free parking" also earns raves, while some call the "food the only problem."

Soniat House ⊕♨

| ▽ 26 | 26 | 16 | 22 | $265 |

French Quarter | 1133 Chartres St. | 504-522-0570 | fax 522-7208 | 800-544-8808 | www.soniathouse.com | 33 rooms, 12 suites, 1 cottage

Quintessentially "refined" and utterly "genteel", this luxury boutique comprising three 1830s townhouses in the lower, residential French Quarter is "top-notch in every respect"; expect "lovely flowers all around" and "charming" rooms (some with balconies overlooking Chartres Street) decorated in "fine" period furnishings and stocked with Frette linens; in short, this member of Small Luxury Hotels of the World is a true "New Orleans experience" that makes you feel like "a royal"; N.B. the proprietors also own the adjacent antique shop.

Westin New Orleans Canal Place ⌂♨≋

| ▽ 21 | 20 | 17 | 21 | $200 |

(fka Wyndham at Canal Place)

Central Business Dist. | 100 Iberville St. | 504-566-7006 | fax 504-553-5120 | 800-937-8461 | www.westin.com | 398 rooms, 40 suites

A location that's "wonderfully convenient to the Quarter or Warehouse District" and across the street from Harrah's Casino is the draw at this CBD convention hotel with "breathtaking views of the Mississippi"

| | ROOMS | SERVICE | DINING | FACIL. | COST |

from the lobby and from some of the "huge" rooms; though many moan that it's "understaffed", the "friendly" crew "tries to be helpful."

W French Quarter ⚐♨≋ | 23 | 21 | 20 | 22 | $489 |

French Quarter | 316 Chartres St. | 504-581-1200 | fax 504-523-2910 | 877-946-8357 | www.whotels.com | 94 rooms, 2 suites, 2 carriage houses

"Everything you expect in a W and more (or less?)" is how fans describe this typically "sparse-but-cool" spot "in the heart of the French Quarter" with "large", "modern" rooms and "outstanding" food at Bacco restaurant; some find the "beautiful courtyard" with a "wonderful pool" the "main attraction" of this "oasis from the chaos", but others pout over the "'whatever, whenever' attitude of the staff."

Whitney, A Wyndham Historic Hotel | 20 | 18 | 15 | 18 | $89 |

Central Business Dist. | 610 Poydras St. | 504-581-4222 | fax 504-207-0100 | 877-999-3223 | www.wyndham.com | 70 rooms, 23 suites

Set in a restored old bank, this hotel with plenty of "old-world elegance" "fits in with the experience of New Orleans" say its fans, who like the CBD location "close enough to walk to most of the interesting places"; rooms are "small but sumptuous" and the staff is "friendly and social", which more than makes up for what some consider "expensive" valet parking charges.

🛇 Windsor Court Hotel ✕🕮⚐♨≋ | 24 | 25 | 24 | 25 | $250 |

Central Business Dist. | 300 Gravier St. | 504-523-6000 | fax 504-596-4513 | 888-596-0955 | www.windsorcourthotel.com | 56 rooms, 266 suites

"The good times are rollin' again" assert aficionados who rank this "sophisticated" CBD spot a "first choice" thanks to its "beautiful, spacious rooms", "unrivaled" service and "out-of-this-world" dining that includes an "old-world" "high tea in the lobby"; if aesthetes find it all a "tad shabby", fans who "could live here" simply see "lots of patina" and suggest "spending more for a club level room."

W New Orleans ⚐♨≋ | 23 | 22 | 18 | 21 | $469 |

Central Business Dist. | 333 Poydras St. | 504-525-9444 | fax 504-581-7179 | 877-946-8357 | www.whotels.com | 400 rooms, 23 suites

This "chic" hotel "right outside of the French Quarter" gets "two thumbs up" from the "young professional crowd" and "tourists with a need for contemporary consistency" who appreciate its "modern ambiance" and "boutique-hotel" feel despite its "large" size; the "nicely decorated", "intimate" rooms (some say "claustrophobic") with "great amenities" ("love the bath products") and "good views of the Mississippi" are enhanced by a "trendy" staff and rooftop pool.

Wyndham Riverfront New Orleans ✕🕮 | ▽ 23 | 22 | 20 | 19 | $299 |

Warehouse District | 701 Convention Center Blvd. | 504-524-8200 | fax 504-524-0600 | 800-996-3426 | www.wyndham.com | 190 rooms, 12 suites

Fresh from a $9-million total renovation, this "big conference hotel" is "surprisingly nice" gush groupies who savor the "comfortable" rooms with pillow-top mattresses and ergonomic work chairs (the "corner" units are particularly "spacious"); other pluses include "reasonable" dining, some of "the best river views" and a Warehouse District location just a few blocks from the French Quarter that's "great for shopping."

INDEXES

Dining Cuisines

Includes restaurant names, locations and Food ratings.

AMERICAN (NEW)

Z Bayona | **French Qtr**	28
Bistro Daisy | **Uptown**	26
NEW Copeland's Social | **Metairie**	-
NEW Country Club | **Bywater**	22
Z Dakota | **Covington**	28
Etoile | **Covington**	22
Z Gautreau's | **Uptown**	28
Z Herbsaint | **Warehouse**	26
Iris | **French Qtr**	25
NEW Lago | **Lakeview**	24
Z Le Parvenu | **Kenner**	26
One Rest. | **Riverbend**	25
Patois | **Uptown**	25
Z Pelican Club | **French Qtr**	26
NEW Pellicano | **Kenner**	-
Z Stella! | **French Qtr**	28
Store | **CBD**	23
Sun Ray Grill | **multi.**	21
NEW Wolfe's | **French Qtr**	-

AMERICAN (TRADITIONAL)

Betsy's Pancake | **Mid-City**	22
Blue Plate Cafe | **Lower Garden**	22
Bubba Gump | **French Qtr**	13
Bywater BBQ | **Bywater**	16
Camellia Grill | **Riverbend**	23
Cannon's | **Uptown**	16
Chad's Bistro | **Metairie**	18
Coffee Pot | **French Qtr**	21
Come Back Inn | **multi.**	19
Copeland's Cheesecake | **multi.**	19
Ernst Cafe | **Warehouse**	16
Feelings Cafe | **Faub Marigny**	21
GB's Patio B&G | **Riverbend**	17
Gordon Biersch | **CBD**	16
Hard Rock Cafe | **French Qtr**	13

Houston's | **multi.**	22
Mother's | **CBD**	22
NEW New Orleans Cake | **Faub Marigny**	-
Oak St. Cafe | **Carrollton**	-
O'Henry's | **multi.**	13
Oscar's | **Old Metairie**	19
P&G | **CBD**	17
Parasol's | **Irish Channel**	24
Popeyes | **multi.**	22
Port of Call | **French Qtr**	24
Raising Cane's | **Metairie**	18
Riccobono's Panola St. | **Carrollton**	-
NEW Ruby Slipper | **Mid-City**	23
Slim Goodies | **Garden**	21
St. Charles Tav. | **Uptown**	14
Surrey's Juice | **Lower Garden**	25

ARGENTINEAN

Z La Boca | **Warehouse**	27

ASIAN

Sara's | **Riverbend**	24

ASIAN FUSION

Hipstix | **Warehouse**	21

BAKERIES

Croissant d'Or | **French Qtr**	24
Z La Boulangerie | **Uptown**	28
La Madeleine | **multi.**	20
NEW New Orleans Cake | **Faub Marigny**	-

BARBECUE

Bywater BBQ | **Bywater**	16
Corky's BBQ | **Metairie**	19
Hillbilly BBQ | **River Ridge**	23
NEW J'anita's | **Lower Garden**	23
Joint | **Bywater**	25

NEW Shane's Rib Shack	**Marrero**	18
Ugly Dog	**Warehouse**	20
Voodoo BBQ	**multi.**	20
Walker BBQ	**New Orleans E**	25
Whole Hog	**CBD**	23

BELGIAN

Clémentine	**Gretna**	24

BRAZILIAN

Fire of Brazil	**French Qtr**	21

BURGERS

Beachcorner	**Mid-City**	21
Bud's Broiler	**multi.**	20
Clover Grill	**French Qtr**	21
GB's Patio B&G	**Riverbend**	17
Hard Rock Cafe	**French Qtr**	13
Lakeview Harbor	**Lakeview**	20
Lee's Hamburgers	**multi.**	20
New Orleans Hamburger	**multi.**	17
Oscar's	**Old Metairie**	19
Port of Call	**French Qtr**	24

CAJUN

Alpine	**French Qtr**	18
Big Al's Seafood	**multi.**	19
Bon Ton Café	**CBD**	24
Cafe Beignet	**French Qtr**	20
Cafe Pontalba	**French Qtr**	18
Cochon	**Warehouse**	25
Coop's Place	**French Qtr**	22
Copeland's	**multi.**	19
Franky & Johnny's	**Uptown**	20
Kosher Cajun Deli	**Metairie**	21
Z K-Paul's	**French Qtr**	27
La Thai	**Uptown**	22
Mother's	**CBD**	22
Mulate's	**Warehouse**	19
New Orleans Food	**multi.**	22
Oak Alley	**Vacherie**	19
Petunia's	**French Qtr**	22
Rest. des Familles	**Crown Pt**	22
Vucinovich	**New Orleans E**	-

CALIFORNIAN

Lucy's Surfer's	**multi.**	14

CARIBBEAN

NEW West Indies	**Lower Garden**	-

CENTRAL AMERICAN

Pupuseria Divino	**Gretna**	21

CHEESE SPECIALISTS

Z St. James Cheese	**Uptown**	26

CHICKEN

Popeyes	**multi.**	22
Raising Cane's	**Metairie**	18

CHINESE

(* dim sum specialist)

August Moon	**Uptown**	17
Z Café East	**Metairie**	22
China Doll	**Harvey**	22
Doson's	**Mid-City**	19
Five Happiness	**Carrollton**	22
Great Wall	**Old Metairie**	22
NEW Hoshun	**Lower Garden**	23
Imperial Garden	**Kenner**	-
Kim Son	**Gretna**	24
Nine Roses	**Gretna**	24
P.F. Chang's	**Metairie**	20
Royal China*	**Metairie**	24
Trey Yuen	**multi.**	23

COFFEEHOUSES

Z Café Du Monde	**French Qtr**	24
Caffe! Caffe!	**multi.**	22
CC's Coffee	**multi.**	19
Chateau Coffee	**multi.**	19
Churros Café	**Metairie**	-
Coffea Cafe	**Bywater**	-
NEW Lakeview Brew	**Lakeview**	-
Morning Call	**Metairie**	25
PJ's Coffee	**multi.**	19
Royal Blend	**multi.**	16
rue de la course	**multi.**	19

DINING

CUISINES

COFFEE SHOPS/ DINERS

Bluebird Cafe	**Uptown**	22
Clover Grill	**French Qtr**	21
Coffee Rani	**multi.**	23
Elizabeth's	**Bywater**	24
Frosty's Caffe	**Metairie**	25
Russell's Marina	**Lakefront**	19
Slim Goodies	**Garden**	21
Steve's Diner	**CBD**	16
Trolley Stop	**Lower Garden**	20

COLOMBIAN

Barú Bistro	**Uptown**	23

CONTEMPORARY LOUISIANA

NEW Alligator Pear	**Harvey**	_
NEW Beebe's	**Lakefront**	25
Z Brigtsen's	**Riverbend**	28
Café Amelie	**French Qtr**	23
NEW Creole Skillet	**Warehouse**	_
Crescent City Brew	**French Qtr**	17
Z Dakota	**Covington**	28
Dante's Kitchen	**Riverbend**	25
Z Emeril's	**Warehouse**	25
NEW Gott Gourmet Café	**Garden**	_
Grocery	**Garden**	_
La Côte	**Warehouse**	22
Z La Petite Grocery	**Uptown**	26
Mat & Naddie's	**Riverbend**	23
Mélange	**French Qtr**	19
Z MiLa	**CBD**	26
Z Mr. B's Bistro	**French Qtr**	25
New City Grille	**Metairie**	22
New Orleans Grill	**CBD**	24
Z NOLA	**French Qtr**	26
Oak St. Cafe	**Carrollton**	_
Z Ralph's/Park	**Mid-City**	25
7 on Fulton	**Warehouse**	22
Z Upperline	**Uptown**	26
Z Vizard's	**Uptown**	26

NEW Wolfe's	**French Qtr**	_
Zoë	**CBD**	22

CONTINENTAL

Z August	**CBD**	28
Z Cuvée	**CBD**	26
Flaming Torch	**Uptown**	23
Z St. James Cheese	**Uptown**	26

CREOLE

Abita Brew	**Abita Springs**	19
Alpine	**French Qtr**	18
Z Antoine's	**French Qtr**	24
Z Arnaud's	**French Qtr**	25
Austin's	**Metairie**	_
Begue's	**French Qtr**	24
Bistro/Maison	**French Qtr**	26
Z Brennan's	**French Qtr**	24
Z Broussard's	**French Qtr**	25
Café Adelaide	**CBD**	24
Cafe Atchafalaya	**Irish Channel**	19
Cafe Pontalba	**French Qtr**	18
Café Sbisa	**French Qtr**	_
Z Clancy's	**Uptown**	27
Coffee Pot	**French Qtr**	21
Z Commander's	**Garden**	27
Copeland's	**multi.**	19
Court/Sisters	**French Qtr**	20
Crystal Room	**CBD**	_
Z Cuvée	**CBD**	26
Z Cypress	**Metairie**	27
NEW Daniel's on Bayou	**Faub St. John**	_
Dante's Kitchen	**Riverbend**	25
Z Dick & Jenny's	**Uptown**	26
Dooky Chase	**Treme**	24
Dunbar's Creole	**Uptown**	25
Eleven 79	**Lower Garden**	25
Z Emeril's Delmonico	**Lower Garden**	26
Feelings Cafe	**Faub Marigny**	21
Felix's Oyster Bar	**French Qtr**	_

Fiorella's Café | **French Qtr**	21
Fury's | **Metairie**	23
Z Galatoire's | **French Qtr**	27
Grand Isle | **Warehouse**	19
Gumbo Shop | **French Qtr**	21
Ignatius Eatery | **Uptown**	21
Impastato's | **Metairie**	23
Z Jacques-Imo's | **Carrollton**	26
Joey K's | **Garden**	19
Julie's Little Indian | **Bywater**	18
NEW La Famiglia | **Metairie**	-
Z La Provence | **Lacombe**	27
Le Citron | **Lower Garden**	23
Z Le Parvenu | **Kenner**	26
Li'l Dizzy's | **multi.**	22
Liuzza's by Track | **Faub St. John**	23
Liuzza's Rest. | **Mid-City**	21
Mandina's | **multi.**	23
Mr. Ed's | **Metairie**	20
Z Muriel's | **French Qtr**	23
Napoleon House | **French Qtr**	19
Oak Alley | **Vacherie**	19
Olivier's | **French Qtr**	21
Palace Café | **French Qtr**	24
Petunia's | **French Qtr**	22
Remoulade | **French Qtr**	18
Riccobono's | **Metairie**	21
Rocky & Carlo's | **Chalmette**	22
Sal & Judy's | **Lacombe**	26
Sara's | **Riverbend**	24
Smilie's | **Harahan**	17
Tommy's Cuisine | **Warehouse**	25
Tujague's | **French Qtr**	21
Vucinovich | **New Orleans E**	-
Wolfe's/Warehouse | **Warehouse**	21
Ye Olde College | **Carrollton**	21

CUBAN

Churros Café | **Metairie**	-
Country Flame | **French Qtr**	18
Liborio Cuban | **CBD**	21

DELIS

Johnny's Po-Boy | **French Qtr**	-
Kosher Cajun Deli | **Metairie**	21
Stein's | **Lower Garden**	23

DESSERT

Z Angelo Brocato | **Mid-City**	28
Z Café Du Monde | **French Qtr**	24
Caffe! Caffe! | **multi.**	22
Coffee Rani | **multi.**	23
Copeland's Cheesecake | **multi.**	19
Croissant d'Or | **French Qtr**	24
Dong Phuong | **New Orleans E**	23
Gelato Pazzo | **Carrollton**	25
Z Hansen's Sno-Bliz | **Uptown**	28
La Crêpe Nanou | **Uptown**	24
Z La Divina | **multi.**	26
La Madeleine | **multi.**	20
Morning Call | **Metairie**	25
rue de la course | **multi.**	19
Z Sucré | **Garden**	25

ECLECTIC

Abita Brew | **Abita Springs**	19
NEW Arabesque | **Mid-City**	23
Cafe Rani | **Garden**	20
Z Dick & Jenny's | **Uptown**	26
Marigny Brass. | **Faub Marigny**	22
Refuel | **Riverbend**	22
Semolina | **multi.**	17
NEW Stop 9 | **Lower Garden**	15
13 Monaghan | **Faub Marigny**	19
Whole Foods | **multi.**	23
Zea | **multi.**	23

FONDUE

Melting Pot | **Lower Garden**	19

FRENCH

Z Antoine's | **French Qtr**	24
Z August | **CBD**	28
Begue's | **French Qtr**	24
Bistro/Maison | **French Qtr**	26

Broussard's | **French Qtr**	25
Café Minh | **Mid-City**	25
Crêpes à la Cart | **Uptown**	25
Crystal Room | **CBD**	–
Dominique's | **French Qtr**	25
Flaming Torch | **Uptown**	23
Galatoire's | **French Qtr**	27
Gautreau's | **Uptown**	28
Herbsaint | **Warehouse**	26
NEW Hostel | **French Qtr**	–
La Provence | **Lacombe**	27
Patois | **Uptown**	25
NEW Rambla | **CBD**	–

FRENCH (BISTRO)

Café Degas | **Faub St. John**	24
Chateau du Lac | **Old Metairie**	25
Ciro's Côté Sud | **Uptown**	–
Delachaise | **Uptown**	22
Etoile | **Covington**	22
La Crêpe Nanou | **Uptown**	24
La Madeleine | **multi.**	20
La Petite Grocery | **Uptown**	26
Lilette | **Uptown**	26
Martinique | **Uptown**	26
Meauxbar | **French Qtr**	24
Orleans Grapevine | **French Qtr**	22

FRENCH (BRASSERIE)

Lüke | **CBD**	23

GERMAN

NEW Jager Haus | **French Qtr**	–

GREEK

Acropolis | **Metairie**	24
Mr. Gyros | **Metairie**	24

HEALTH FOOD

(See also Vegetarian)
Whole Foods | **multi.**	23

HONDURAN

Islas Roatan | **Mid-City**	–
Jazz Tacos | **French Qtr**	16

HOT DOGS

Easy Dogs | **Gretna**	19

ICE CREAM PARLORS

Angelo Brocato | **Mid-City**	28
Gelato Pazzo | **Carrollton**	25
Hansen's Sno-Bliz | **Uptown**	28
La Divina | **multi.**	26

INDIAN

Julie's Little Indian | **Bywater**	18
Nirvana Indian | **Uptown**	21
Taj Mahal | **Old Metairie**	22

IRISH

Parasol's | **Irish Channel**	24

ITALIAN

(N=Northern; S=Southern)
Adolfo's | S | **Faub Marigny**	24
Andrea's | N | **Metairie**	21
Anselmo's | S | **Metairie**	19
Bacco | **French Qtr**	24
Bravo! | **Metairie**	20
Brick Oven | **Kenner**	21
Cafe DiBlasi | **Terrytown**	21
Cafe Giovanni | **French Qtr**	24
Cafe Roma | **multi.**	20
Carmine's | **Metairie**	20
NEW Daniel's on Bayou | **Faub St. John**	–
Eleven 79 | **Lower Garden**	25
Fausto's Bistro | **Metairie**	22
Fazzio's | **Mandeville**	20
Fellini's | **Mid-City**	20
Fury's | **Metairie**	23
Gelato Pazzo | **Carrollton**	25
NEW Il Posto Café | **Uptown**	24
Impastato's | **Metairie**	23
Irene's Cuisine | S | **French Qtr**	26
NEW Italian Barrel | **French Qtr**	–
Italian Pie | **multi.**	17
La Divina | **multi.**	26
NEW La Famiglia | **Metairie**	–
La Vita | **Faub St. John**	13

Le Citron | **Lower Garden**	23
Leonardo Tratt. | S | **Warehouse**	–
Liuzza's Rest. | **Mid-City**	21
Louisiana Pizza | **multi.**	22
Mandina's | **Mandeville**	23
Maple St. Cafe | **Carrollton**	22
Mona Lisa | **French Qtr**	23
Z Mosca's | **Avondale**	26
Mr. Ed's | **Metairie**	20
Nuvolari's | **Mandeville**	24
Pascal's Manale | **Uptown**	23
R & O's | **Bucktown**	21
Riccobono's | **Metairie**	21
Rist. Da Piero | N | **Kenner**	27
Z Rist. del Porto | **Covington**	26
Rist. Filippo | **Metairie**	24
Rocky & Carlo's | **Chalmette**	22
Sal & Judy's | S | **Lacombe**	26
Semolina | **multi.**	17
Semolina's Bistro Italia | **Garden**	17
Smilie's | **Harahan**	17
Tommy's Cuisine | **Warehouse**	25
Tony Angello's | S | **Lakeview**	24
Tony Mandina's | S | **Gretna**	22
Two Tony's | **Bucktown**	23
Venezia | **multi.**	22
Vincent's | S | **multi.**	24

JAMAICAN

Boswell's Jamaican | **Mid-City**	–

JAPANESE

(* sushi specialist)

NEW Gimchi* | **Metairie**	19
Hana Japanese* | **Riverbend**	21
Horinoya* | **CBD**	24
NEW Hoshun* | **Lower Garden**	23
Kanno* | **Metairie**	28
Kyoto | **Uptown**	24
Kyoto II | **Harahan**	22
Little Tokyo* | **multi.**	24
Mikimoto* | **Carrollton**	–
Miyako* | **Lower Garden**	21
NINJA* | **Carrollton**	24
Rock-n-Sake* | **Warehouse**	23
Sake Cafe | **multi.**	23
Shogun | **Metairie**	24
Sushi Brothers* | **Lower Garden**	25
Wasabi* | **Faub Marigny**	24
NEW Yuki Izakaya | **Faub Marigny**	–

KOREAN

(* barbecue specialist)

NEW Gimchi* | **Metairie**	19
Korea House* | **Metairie**	24

KOSHER

Casablanca | **Metairie**	21
Kosher Cajun Deli | **Metairie**	21

LEBANESE

Lebanon's Café | **Carrollton**	23

MEDITERRANEAN

Acropolis | **Metairie**	24
Angeli/Decatur | **French Qtr**	20
Byblos | **multi.**	22
Fellini's | **Mid-City**	20
Fresco Cafe | **Uptown**	19
Jamila's Cafe | **Uptown**	24
La Vita | **Faub St. John**	13
Maple St. Cafe | **Carrollton**	22
Napoleon House | **French Qtr**	19
Vega Tapas | **Old Metairie**	24

MEXICAN

Carreta's Grill | **multi.**	19
Casa Garcia | **Metairie**	20
Country Flame | **French Qtr**	18
El Gato Negro | **French Qtr**	21
Felipe's Taqueria | **multi.**	–
Juan's Burrito | **multi.**	21
Lucy's Surfer's | **multi.**	14
Nacho Mama's | **multi.**	15
Pupuseria Divino | **Gretna**	21
Superior Grill | **Uptown**	20
Taco San Miguel | **multi.**	17
Taqueria Corona | **multi.**	21
Taqueria Guerrero | **Mid-City**	–

Taqueria Sanchez | **multi.** | __-__
Tomatillo's | **Faub Marigny** | __16__

MIDDLE EASTERN

Babylon Café | **Uptown** | __21__
Byblos | **multi.** | __22__
Mona's Cafe | **multi.** | __19__

MOROCCAN

Casablanca | **Metairie** | __21__

NUEVO LATINO

Barú Bistro | **Uptown** | __23__
Serranos Salsa Co. | **Metairie** | __18__

PAN-ASIAN

Hipstix | **Warehouse** | __21__

PAN-LATIN

NEW Daniel's on Bayou | __-__
    Faub St. John
Fiesta Latina | **Kenner** | __-__
Mayas | **Lower Garden** | __-__
Pupuseria Macarena | **Metairie** | __-__
NEW West Indies | **Lower Garden** | __-__

PIZZA

Angeli/Decatur | **French Qtr** | __20__
Cafe Roma | **multi.** | __20__
Ciro's Côté Sud | **Uptown** | __-__
Fresco Cafe | **Uptown** | __19__
Italian Pie | **multi.** | __17__
La Vita | **Faub St. John** | __13__
Louisiana Pizza | **multi.** | __22__
Mark Twain's | **Old Metairie** | __22__
New York Pizza | **Uptown** | __21__
R & O's | **Bucktown** | __21__
Reginelli's | **multi.** | __21__
Slice | **Lower Garden** | __23__
Sugar Park | **Bywater** | __25__
Theo's | **Uptown** | __24__
Tower of Pizza | **Metairie** | __-__
Venezia | **multi.** | __22__

PO' BOYS

Cafe Maspero | **French Qtr** | __19__
Z Central Grocery | **French Qtr** | __25__
Come Back Inn | **multi.** | __19__

Z Crabby Jack's | **Jefferson** | __26__
Deanie's | **multi.** | __22__
Z Domilise's | **Uptown** | __26__
Franky & Johnny's | **Uptown** | __20__
Galley | **Old Metairie** | __24__
Grocery | **Garden** | __-__
Ignatius Eatery | **Uptown** | __21__
Joey K's | **Garden** | __19__
Johnny's Po-Boy | **French Qtr** | __-__
NEW Mahony's | **Uptown** | __-__
Mike Serio's | **CBD** | __19__
Parasol's | **Irish Channel** | __24__
Parkway Bakery | **Mid-City** | __25__
Russell's Short Stop | **Metairie** | __20__

PUB FOOD

Beachcorner | **Mid-City** | __21__
Gordon Biersch | **CBD** | __16__
Lakeview Harbor | **Lakeview** | __20__
Sugar Park | **Bywater** | __25__

SANDWICHES

Audubon Park | **Uptown** | __15__
Cafe Maspero | **French Qtr** | __19__
Z Central Grocery | **French Qtr** | __25__
Z Crabby Jack's | **Jefferson** | __26__
DiMartino's | **multi.** | __22__
Z Domilise's | **Uptown** | __26__
Martin Wine | **Metairie** | __23__
Mike Serio's | **CBD** | __19__
Roly Poly | **multi.** | __18__
Stein's | **Lower Garden** | __23__
Z St. James Cheese | **Uptown** | __26__
Whole Foods | **multi.** | __23__

SEAFOOD

Z Acme Oyster | **multi.** | __22__
Andrea's | **Metairie** | __21__
Z Arnaud's | **French Qtr** | __25__
Austin's | **Metairie** | __-__
NEW Beebe's | **Lakefront** | __25__
Besh Steak | **CBD** | __25__
Big Al's Seafood | **multi.** | __19__
Bourbon House | **French Qtr** | __21__

Bozo's | **Metairie**	22
Bubba Gump | **French Qtr**	13
Cannon's | **Uptown**	16
Carmine's | **Metairie**	20
Casamento's | **Uptown**	25
Deanie's | **multi.**	22
Don's Seafood | **Metairie**	19
☑ Drago's | **multi.**	25
Felix's Oyster Bar | **French Qtr**	‒
Franky & Johnny's | **Uptown**	20
Galley | **Old Metairie**	24
Grand Isle | **Warehouse**	19
☑ GW Fins | **French Qtr**	26
Harbor Seafood | **Kenner**	24
Jack Dempsey's | **Bywater**	19
Landry's | **multi.**	16
Mandina's | **Mid-City**	23
☑ Martinique | **Uptown**	26
Middendorf's | **Manchac**	24
New Orleans Food | **multi.**	22
New Orleans Hamburger | **multi.**	17
Pascal's Manale | **Uptown**	23
R & O's | **Bucktown**	21
Red Fish Grill | **French Qtr**	22
Rest. des Familles | **Crown Pt**	22
☑ RioMar | **Warehouse**	26
NEW Sailor's Seafood | **Mid-City**	‒
Saltwater Grill | **Riverbend**	16
Tony Mandina's | **Gretna**	22
Trey Yuen | **multi.**	23
Two Tony's | **Bucktown**	23
Vucinovich | **New Orleans E**	‒
Zeke's | **Old Metairie**	17

SMALL PLATES

(See also Spanish tapas specialist)

NEW Arabesque | Eclectic | **Mid-City**	23
Barú Bistro | Nuevo Latino | **Uptown**	23
Cochon | Cajun | **Warehouse**	25
Delachaise | French | **Uptown**	22
☑ Herbsaint | Amer. | **Warehouse**	26

NEW Rambla | French | **CBD**	‒
Vega Tapas | Med. | **Old Metairie**	24
NEW Wolfe's | Amer. | **French Qtr**	‒

SOUL FOOD

Dooky Chase | **Treme**	24
Fiorella's Café | **French Qtr**	21
☑ Jacques-Imo's | **Carrollton**	26
Praline Connection | **Faub Marigny**	22
Willie Mae's | **Treme**	25

SOUTHERN

Bistro Daisy | **Uptown**	26
Cafe Atchafalaya | **Irish Channel**	19
Café Reconcile | **Central City**	22
Coop's Place | **French Qtr**	22
Eat | **French Qtr**	24
Elizabeth's | **Bywater**	24
NEW J'anita's | **Lower Garden**	23
Oak St. Cafe | **Carrollton**	‒
Praline Connection | **Faub Marigny**	22
Store | **CBD**	23
Ye Olde College | **Carrollton**	21

SPANISH

(* tapas specialist)

Café Granada* | **Carrollton**	22
Laurentino's* | **Metairie**	22
Lola's | **Faub St. John**	25
NEW Rambla* | **CBD**	‒
☑ RioMar* | **Warehouse**	26
NEW Stop 9 | **Lower Garden**	15

STEAKHOUSES

Besh Steak | **CBD**	25
Charlie's Steak | **Uptown**	‒
Crazy Johnnie's | **Metairie**	21
Crescent City Steak | **Mid-City**	25
☑ Dickie Brennan's | **French Qtr**	25
Fire of Brazil | **French Qtr**	21
☑ La Boca | **Warehouse**	27

Morton's | **French Qtr**	25	Coffee Rani | **multi.**	23
Mr. John's | **Lower Garden**	24	Jazmine Café | **Riverbend**	19
Outback | **Metairie**	17	Nirvana Indian | **Uptown**	21
Rib Room | **French Qtr**	25	Pho Tau Bay | **Gretna**	25
☒ Ruth's Chris | **multi.**	26	Slim Goodies | **Garden**	21
Shula's | **CBD**	20	Taj Mahal | **Old Metairie**	22
Young's | **Slidell**	24	13 Monaghan | **Faub Marigny**	19

THAI

Bangkok Thai | **Riverbend**	20
Basil Leaf | **Carrollton**	21
La Thai | **Uptown**	22
Siamese | **Metairie**	22
Singha | **CBD**	22
Sukho Thai | **Faub Marigny**	–

TUNISIAN

Jamila's Cafe | **Uptown**	24

VEGETARIAN

Angeli/Decatur | **French Qtr**	20
Apple Seed | **CBD**	22
Basil Leaf | **Carrollton**	21
Bennachin | **French Qtr**	23
Boswell's Jamaican | **Mid-City**	–
Cafe Rani | **Garden**	20

VIETNAMESE

August Moon | **Uptown**	17
Ba Mien | **New Orleans E**	–
Café Minh | **Mid-City**	25
Dong Phuong | **New Orleans E**	23
Doson's | **Mid-City**	19
Frosty's Caffe | **multi.**	25
Jazmine Café | **Riverbend**	19
Kim Son | **Gretna**	24
Nine Roses | **Gretna**	24
Pho Bang | **multi.**	21
Pho Danh 4 | **Gretna**	–
Pho Tau Bay | **Gretna**	25
Tan Dinh | **Gretna**	25

WEST AFRICAN

Bennachin | **French Qtr**	23

Dining Locations

Includes restaurant names, cuisines and Food ratings.

New Orleans

DINING

BUCKTOWN

Deanie's	*Seafood*	22
R & O's	*Italian*	21
Two Tony's	*Italian*	23

BYWATER

Bywater BBQ	*Amer./BBQ*	16
Coffea Cafe	*Coffee*	–
NEW Country Club	*Amer.*	22
Elizabeth's	*Diner*	24
Jack Dempsey's	*Seafood*	19
Joint	*BBQ*	25
Julie's Little Indian	*Creole/Indian*	18
Sugar Park	*Pizza*	25

CARROLLTON

Basil Leaf	*Thai*	21
Café Granada	*Spanish*	22
Five Happiness	*Chinese*	22
Gelato Pazzo	*Italian*	25
☑ Jacques-Imo's	*Creole/Soul*	26
Lebanon's Café	*Lebanese*	23
Maple St. Cafe	*Italian/Med.*	22
Mikimoto	*Japanese*	–
Mona's Cafe	*Mideast.*	19
NINJA	*Japanese*	24
Oak St. Cafe	*Southern*	–
Riccobono's Panola St.	*Amer.*	–
rue de la course	*Coffee*	19
Ye Olde College	*Creole/Southern*	21

CBD (CENTRAL BUSINESS DISTRICT)

Apple Seed	*Veg.*	22
☑ August	*Continental/French*	28
Besh Steak	*Seafood/Steak*	25
Bon Ton Café	*Cajun*	24

Café Adelaide	*Creole*	24
CC's Coffee	*Coffee*	19
Crystal Room	*Creole/French*	–
☑ Cuvée	*Continental/Creole*	26
☑ Drago's	*Seafood*	25
Gordon Biersch	*Amer.*	16
Horinoya	*Japanese*	24
Italian Pie	*Pizza*	17
Liborio Cuban	*Cuban*	21
Li'l Dizzy's	*Creole*	22
Lüke	*French*	23
Mike Serio's	*Po' Boys*	19
☑ MiLa	*Contemp. LA*	26
Mother's	*Amer./Cajun*	22
New Orleans Grill	*Contemp. LA*	24
P&G	*Amer.*	17
PJ's Coffee	*Coffee*	19
NEW Rambla	*French/Spanish*	–
Roly Poly	*Sandwiches*	18
☑ Ruth's Chris	*Steak*	26
Shula's	*Steak*	20
Singha	*Thai*	22
Steve's Diner	*Diner*	16
Store	*Amer.*	23
Whole Hog	*BBQ*	23
Zoë	*Contemp. LA*	22

CENTRAL CITY

Café Reconcile	*Southern*	22

CHALMETTE

Cafe Roma	*Pizza*	20
Rocky & Carlo's	*Creole/Italian*	22

FAUBOURG MARIGNY

Adolfo's	*Italian*	24
Feelings Cafe	*Amer./Creole*	21
Marigny Brass.	*Eclectic*	22

LOCATIONS

Mona's Cafe | *Mideast.* 19

NEW New Orleans Cake | *Amer.* -

Praline Connection | *Soul* 22

Sukho Thai | *Thai* -

13 Monaghan | *Eclectic/Veg.* 19

Tomatillo's | *Mex.* 16

Wasabi | *Japanese* 24

NEW Yuki Izakaya | *Japanese* -

FAUBOURG ST. JOHN

Café Degas | *French* 24

NEW Daniel's on Bayou | *Creole/Italian* -

La Vita | *Italian/Med.* 13

Liuzza's by Track | *Creole* 23

Lola's | *Spanish* 25

FRENCH QUARTER

Z Acme Oyster | *Seafood* 22

Alpine | *Cajun/Creole* 18

Angeli/Decatur | *Med./Pizza* 20

Z Antoine's | *Creole/French* 24

Z Arnaud's | *Creole* 25

Bacco | *Italian* 24

Z Bayona | *Amer.* 28

Begue's | *Creole/French* 24

Bennachin | *African/Veg.* 23

Bistro/Maison | *Creole/French* 26

Bourbon House | *Seafood* 21

Z Brennan's | *Creole* 24

Z Broussard's | *Creole/French* 25

Bubba Gump | *Amer./Seafood* 13

Café Amelie | *Contemp. LA* 23

Cafe Beignet | *Cajun* 20

Z Café Du Monde | *Coffee/Dessert* 24

Cafe Giovanni | *Italian* 24

Cafe Maspero | *Po' Boys* 19

Cafe Pontalba | *Cajun/Creole* 18

Café Sbisa | *Creole* -

CC's Coffee | *Coffee* 19

Z Central Grocery | *Sandwiches* 25

Clover Grill | *Diner* 21

Coffee Pot | *Amer./Creole* 21

Coop's Place | *Cajun/Southern* 22

Country Flame | *Cuban/Mex.* 18

Court/Sisters | *Creole* 20

Crescent City Brew | *Contemp. LA* 17

Croissant d'Or | *Bakery* 24

Deanie's | *Seafood* 22

Z Dickie Brennan's | *Steak* 25

Dominique's | *French* 25

Eat | *Southern* 24

El Gato Negro | *Mex.* 21

Felipe's Taqueria | *Mex.* -

Felix's Oyster Bar | *Creole/Seafood* -

Fiorella's Café | *Creole/Soul* 21

Fire of Brazil | *Brazilian/Steak* 21

Z Galatoire's | *Creole/French* 27

Gumbo Shop | *Creole* 21

Z GW Fins | *Seafood* 26

Hard Rock Cafe | *Amer.* 13

NEW Hostel | *French* -

Irene's Cuisine | *Italian* 26

Iris | *Amer.* 25

NEW Italian Barrel | *Italian* -

NEW Jager Haus | *German* -

Jazz Tacos | *Central Amer.* 16

Johnny's Po-Boy | *Po' Boys* -

Z K-Paul's | *Cajun* 27

Z La Divina | *Italian* 26

Landry's | *Seafood* 16

Louisiana Pizza | *Italian* 22

Meauxbar | *French* 24

Mélange | *Contemp. LA* 19

Mona Lisa | *Italian* 23

Morton's | *Steak* 25

Z Mr. B's Bistro | *Contemp. LA* 25

Z Muriel's | *Creole* 23

Napoleon House | Creole/Med. | 19

🅩 NOLA | Contemp. LA | 26

Olivier's | Creole | 21

Orleans Grapevine | French | 22

Palace Café | Creole | 24

🅩 Pelican Club | Amer. | 26

Petunia's | Cajun/Creole | 22

Port of Call | Amer. | 24

Red Fish Grill | Seafood | 22

Remoulade | Creole | 18

Rib Room | Steak | 25

Royal Blend | Coffee | 16

🅩 Stella! | Amer. | 28

Tujague's | Creole | 21

NEW Wolfe's | Contemp. LA | -

GARDEN DISTRICT

Cafe Rani | Eclectic/Veg. | 20

CC's Coffee | Coffee | 19

🅩 Commander's | Creole | 27

NEW Gott Gourmet Café | Contemp. LA | -

Grocery | Contemp. LA | -

Joey K's | Creole | 19

🅩 La Divina | Italian | 26

PJ's Coffee | Coffee | 19

Reginelli's | Pizza | 21

rue de la course | Coffee | 19

Semolina's Bistro Italia | Italian | 17

Slim Goodies | Amer. | 21

🅩 Sucré | Dessert | 25

GRETNA

Clémentine | Belgian | 24

Easy Dogs | Hot Dogs | 19

Kim Son | Chinese/Viet. | 24

Nine Roses | Chinese/Viet. | 24

O'Henry's | Amer. | 13

Pho Danh 4 | Viet. | -

Pho Tau Bay | Viet. | 25

Popeyes | Amer. | 22

Pupuseria Divino | Central Amer./Mex. | 21

Sun Ray Grill | Amer. | 21

Tan Dinh | Viet. | 25

Taqueria Sanchez | Mex. | -

Tony Mandina's | Italian/Seafood | 22

HARAHAN/ RIVER RIDGE

Hillbilly BBQ | BBQ | 23

Kyoto II | Japanese | 22

La Madeleine | Bakery | 20

Reginelli's | Pizza | 21

Smilie's | Creole/Italian | 17

Taqueria Corona | Mex. | 21

Zea | Eclectic | 23

IRISH CHANNEL

Cafe Atchafalaya | Creole/Southern | 19

Parasol's | Amer./Irish | 24

JEFFERSON

Bud's Broiler | Burgers | 20

Copeland's | Cajun/Creole | 19

🅩 Crabby Jack's | Po' Boys | 26

Italian Pie | Pizza | 17

New Orleans Hamburger | Burgers/Seafood | 17

Venezia | Italian | 22

KENNER

Brick Oven | Italian | 21

Bud's Broiler | Burgers | 20

Chateau Coffee | Coffee | 19

Come Back Inn | Amer. | 19

Fiesta Latina | Pan-Latin | -

Harbor Seafood | Seafood | 24

Imperial Garden | Chinese | -

Italian Pie | Pizza | 17

🅩 Le Parvenu | Amer./Creole | 26

O'Henry's | Amer. | 13

NEW Pellicano | Amer. | -

Reginelli's | Pizza | 21

Rist. Da Piero | *Italian* 27

Sake Cafe | *Japanese* 23

Taqueria Sanchez | *Mex.* -

Zea | *Eclectic* 23

LAKEFRONT/ LAKEVIEW

NEW Beebe's | 25
Contemp. LA/Seafood

Chateau Coffee | *Coffee* 19

NEW Lago | *Amer.* 24

NEW Lakeview Brew | *Coffee* -

Lakeview Harbor | *Pub* 20

Landry's | *Seafood* 16

Reginelli's | *Pizza* 21

Russell's Marina | *Diner* 19

Tony Angello's | *Italian* 24

LOWER GARDEN DISTRICT

Big Al's Seafood | 19
Cajun/Seafood

Blue Plate Cafe | *Amer.* 22

Cafe Roma | *Pizza* 20

Copeland's Cheesecake | *Amer.* 19

Eleven 79 | *Creole/Italian* 25

Z Emeril's Delmonico | *Creole* 26

NEW Hoshun | 23
Chinese/Japanese

Houston's | *Amer.* 22

NEW J'anita's | *BBQ/Southern* 23

Le Citron | *Creole/Italian* 23

Mayas | *Pan-Latin* -

Melting Pot | *Fondue* 19

Miyako | *Japanese* 21

Mr. John's | *Steak* 24

Popeyes | *Amer.* 22

Slice | *Pizza* 23

Stein's | *Deli* 23

NEW Stop 9 | *Eclectic* 15

Surrey's Juice | *Amer.* 25

Sushi Brothers | *Japanese* 25

Trolley Stop | *Diner* 20

Voodoo BBQ | *BBQ* 20

NEW West Indies | *Pan-Latin* -

Zea | *Eclectic* 23

METAIRIE

Z Acme Oyster | *Seafood* 22

Acropolis | *Med.* 24

Andrea's | *Italian/Seafood* 21

Anselmo's | *Italian* 19

Austin's | *Creole/Seafood* -

Bozo's | *Seafood* 22

Bravo! | *Italian* 20

Bud's Broiler | *Burgers* 20

Byblos | *Mideast.* 22

Z Café East | *Chinese* 22

Caffe! Caffe! | *Coffee* 22

Carmine's | *Italian* 20

Carreta's Grill | *Mex.* 19

Casablanca | *Moroccan* 21

Casa Garcia | *Mex.* 20

CC's Coffee | *Coffee* 19

Chad's Bistro | *Amer.* 18

Chateau Coffee | *Coffee* 19

Churros Café | *Coffee/Cuban* -

Come Back Inn | *Amer.* 19

Copeland's Cheesecake | *Amer.* 19

NEW Copeland's Social | *Amer.* -

Corky's BBQ | *BBQ* 19

Crazy Johnnie's | *Steak* 21

Z Cypress | *Creole* 27

Don's Seafood | *Seafood* 19

Z Drago's | *Seafood* 25

Fausto's Bistro | *Italian* 22

Frosty's Caffe | *Viet.* 25

Fury's | *Creole/Italian* 23

NEW Gimchi | *Japanese/Korean* 19

Houston's | *Amer.* 22

Impastato's | *Creole/Italian* 23

Italian Pie | *Pizza* 17

Kanno | *Japanese* 28

Korea House | *Korean* 24

Kosher Cajun Deli	*Deli*	21
NEW La Famiglia	*Creole/Italian*	–
La Madeleine	*Bakery*	20
Laurentino's	*Italian/Spanish*	22
Lee's Hamburgers	*Burgers*	20
Little Tokyo	*Japanese*	24
Martin Wine	*Sandwiches*	23
Morning Call	*Coffee*	25
Mr. Ed's	*Creole*	20
Mr. Gyros	*Greek*	24
Nacho Mama's	*Mex.*	15
New City Grille	*Contemp. LA*	22
New Orleans Hamburger	*Burgers/Seafood*	17
Outback	*Steak*	17
P.F. Chang's	*Chinese*	20
Pho Bang	*Viet.*	21
PJ's Coffee	*Coffee*	19
Popeyes	*Amer.*	22
Pupuseria Macarena	*Pan-Latin*	–
Raising Cane's	*Amer./Chicken*	18
Riccobono's	*Creole/Italian*	21
Rist. Filippo	*Italian*	24
Roly Poly	*Sandwiches*	18
Royal Blend	*Coffee*	16
Royal China	*Chinese*	24
Russell's Short Stop	*Po' Boys*	20
Z Ruth's Chris	*Steak*	26
Sake Cafe	*Japanese*	23
Semolina	*Eclectic/Italian*	17
Serranos Salsa Co.	*Nuevo Latino*	18
Shogun	*Japanese*	24
Siamese	*Thai*	22
Sun Ray Grill	*Amer.*	21
Taco San Miguel	*Mex.*	17
Taqueria Corona	*Mex.*	21
Taqueria Sanchez	*Mex.*	–
Tower of Pizza	*Pizza*	–
Vincent's	*Italian*	24
Whole Foods	*Eclectic*	23
Zea	*Eclectic*	23

MID-CITY

Z Angelo Brocato	*Dessert*	28
NEW Arabesque	*Eclectic*	23
Beachcorner	*Pub*	21
Betsy's Pancake	*Amer.*	22
Boswell's Jamaican	*Jamaican*	–
Café Minh	*French/Viet.*	25
CC's Coffee	*Coffee*	19
Crescent City Steak	*Steak*	25
Doson's	*Chinese/Viet.*	19
Fellini's	*Italian/Med.*	20
Islas Roatan	*Honduran*	–
Italian Pie	*Pizza*	17
Juan's Burrito	*Mex.*	21
Li'l Dizzy's	*Creole*	22
Little Tokyo	*Japanese*	24
Liuzza's Rest.	*Creole/Italian*	21
Mandina's	*Creole*	23
Mona's Cafe	*Mideast.*	19
Parkway Bakery	*Po' Boys*	25
PJ's Coffee	*Coffee*	19
Popeyes	*Amer.*	22
Z Ralph's/Park	*Contemp. LA*	25
NEW Ruby Slipper	*Amer.*	23
NEW Sailor's Seafood	*Seafood*	–
Taco San Miguel	*Mex.*	17
Taqueria Guerrero	*Mex.*	–
Venezia	*Italian*	22

NEW ORLEANS EAST

Ba Mien	*Viet.*	–
Dong Phuong	*Viet.*	23
Pho Bang	*Viet.*	21
Vucinovich	*Seafood*	–
Walker BBQ	*BBQ*	25

OLD METAIRIE

Byblos	*Mideast.*	22
Chateau du Lac	*French*	25
Galley	*Po' Boys/Seafood*	24
Great Wall	*Chinese*	22
Lee's Hamburgers	*Burgers*	20

DINING

LOCATIONS

Mark Twain's	*Pizza*	22
Oscar's	*Amer.*	19
Taj Mahal	*Indian/Veg.*	22
Vega Tapas	*Med.*	24
Zeke's	*Seafood*	17

RIVERBEND

Bangkok Thai	*Thai*	20
☒ Brigtsen's	*Contemp. LA*	28
Camellia Grill	*Amer.*	23
Dante's Kitchen	*Contemp. LA/Creole*	25
GB's Patio B&G	*Amer.*	17
Hana Japanese	*Japanese*	21
Jazmine Café	*Viet.*	19
La Madeleine	*Bakery*	20
Louisiana Pizza	*Italian*	22
Mat & Naddie's	*Contemp. LA*	23
O'Henry's	*Amer.*	13
One Rest.	*Amer.*	25
Refuel	*Eclectic*	22
Saltwater Grill	*Seafood*	16
Sara's	*Asian/Creole*	24

TREME

Dooky Chase	*Creole/Soul*	24
Willie Mae's	*Soul*	25

UPTOWN

Audubon Park	*Sandwiches*	15
August Moon	*Chinese/Viet.*	17
Babylon Café	*Mideast.*	21
Barú Bistro	*Nuevo Latino*	23
Bistro Daisy	*Amer./Southern*	26
Bluebird Cafe	*Diner*	22
Bud's Broiler	*Burgers*	20
Byblos	*Mideast.*	22
Cannon's	*Amer./Seafood*	16
Casamento's	*Seafood*	25
CC's Coffee	*Coffee*	19
Charlie's Steak	*Steak*	-
Ciro's Côté Sud	*French*	-
☒ Clancy's	*Creole*	27
Crêpes à la Cart	*French*	25
Delachaise	*French*	22
☒ Dick & Jenny's	*Creole/Eclectic*	26
☒ Domilise's	*Cajun/Creole*	26
Dunbar's Creole	*Creole*	25
Felipe's Taqueria	*Mex.*	-
Flaming Torch	*Continental/French*	23
Franky & Johnny's	*Cajun*	20
Fresco Cafe	*Med./Pizza*	19
☒ Gautreau's	*Amer./French*	28
☒ Hansen's Sno-Bliz	*Dessert*	28
Ignatius Eatery	*Creole/Po' Boys*	21
NEW Il Posto Café	*Italian*	24
Jamila's Cafe	*Med./Tunisian*	24
Juan's Burrito	*Mex.*	21
Kyoto	*Japanese*	24
☒ La Boulangerie	*Bakery*	28
La Crêpe Nanou	*French*	24
☒ La Petite Grocery	*Contemp. LA/French*	26
La Thai	*Cajun/Thai*	22
☒ Lilette	*French*	26
NEW Mahony's	*Po' Boys*	-
☒ Martinique	*French*	26
Mona's Cafe	*Mideast.*	19
Nacho Mama's	*Mex.*	15
New York Pizza	*Pizza*	21
Nirvana Indian	*Indian*	21
Pascal's Manale	*Italian*	23
Patois	*Amer./French*	25
PJ's Coffee	*Coffee*	19
Popeyes	*Amer.*	22
Reginelli's	*Pizza*	21
Roly Poly	*Sandwiches*	18
Sake Cafe	*Japanese*	23
St. Charles Tav.	*Amer.*	14
☒ St. James Cheese	*Continental*	26
Superior Grill	*Mex.*	20
Taqueria Corona	*Mex.*	21

Theo's | *Pizza* — 24

🔄 Upperline | *Contemp. LA* — 26

Vincent's | *Italian* — 24

🔄 Vizard's | *Contemp. LA* — 26

Whole Foods | *Eclectic* — 23

WAREHOUSE DISTRICT

Cochon | *Cajun* — 25

NEW Creole Skillet | *Contemp. LA* — ⌐

🔄 Emeril's | *Contemp. LA* — 25

Ernst Cafe | *Amer.* — 16

Grand Isle | *Creole* — 19

🔄 Herbsaint | *Amer./French* — 26

Hipstix | *Asian Fusion* — 21

🔄 La Boca | *Argent./Steak* — 27

La Côte | *Contemp. LA* — 22

Leonardo Tratt. | *Italian* — ⌐

Lucy's Surfer's | *Cal./Mex.* — 14

Mulate's | *Cajun* — 19

🔄 RioMar | *Seafood* — 26

Rock-n-Sake | *Japanese* — 23

7 on Fulton | *Contemp. LA* — 22

Sun Ray Grill | *Amer.* — 21

Tommy's Cuisine | *Creole/Italian* — 25

Ugly Dog | *BBQ* — 20

Wolfe's/Warehouse | *Creole* — 21

WEST BANK

NEW Alligator Pear | *Contemp. LA* — ⌐

Bud's Broiler | *Burgers* — 20

Cafe DiBlasi | *Italian* — 21

China Doll | *Chinese* — 22

Copeland's | *Cajun/Creole* — 19

DiMartino's | *Sandwiches* — 22

Frosty's Caffe | *Viet.* — 25

Italian Pie | *Pizza* — 17

New Orleans Food | *Cajun/Seafood* — 22

Pho Bang | *Viet.* — 21

PJ's Coffee | *Coffee* — 19

Popeyes | *Amer.* — 22

Rest. des Familles | *Cajun/Seafood* — 22

NEW Shane's Rib Shack | *BBQ* — 18

Zea | *Eclectic* — 23

Beyond New Orleans

ABITA SPRINGS/ COVINGTON

Abita Brew | *Creole/Eclectic* — 19

🔄 Acme Oyster | *Seafood* — 22

Coffee Rani | *Diner* — 23

Copeland's | *Cajun/Creole* — 19

🔄 Dakota | *Amer./Contemp. LA* — 28

Etoile | *Amer./French* — 22

New Orleans Food | *Cajun/Seafood* — 22

🔄 Rist. del Porto | *Italian* — 26

AVONDALE

🔄 Mosca's | *Italian* — 26

HOUMA

Big Al's Seafood | *Cajun/Seafood* — 19

Copeland's | *Cajun/Creole* — 19

New Orleans Hamburger | *Burgers/Seafood* — 17

LACOMBE

🔄 La Provence | *Creole/French* — 27

Sal & Judy's | *Creole/Italian* — 26

MANCHAC

Middendorf's | *Seafood* — 24

MANDEVILLE/ HAMMOND

Caffe! Caffe! | *Coffee* — 22

Coffee Rani | *Diner* — 23

Fazzio's | *Italian* — 20

Italian Pie | *Pizza* — 17

La Madeleine | *Bakery* — 20

Little Tokyo | *Japanese* — 24

Lucy's Surfer's | *Cal./Mex.* — 14

Mandina's | *Creole* | 23
New Orleans Hamburger |
  Burgers/Seafood | 17
Nuvolari's | *Italian* | 24
PJ's Coffee | *Coffee* | 19
Roly Poly | *Sandwiches* | 18
Semolina | *Eclectic/Italian* | 17
Trey Yuen | *Chinese/Seafood* | 23

SLIDELL

Carreta's Grill | *Mex.* | 19
Italian Pie | *Pizza* | 17
Young's | *Steak* | 24

ST. ROSE

Voodoo BBQ | *BBQ* | 20

VACHERIE

Oak Alley | *Cajun/Creole* | 19

Dining Special Features

Listings cover the best in each category and include names, locations and Food ratings. Multi-location restaurants' features may vary by branch.

BREAKFAST

(See also Hotel Dining)

Alpine | French Qtr	18
Audubon Park | Uptown	15
Betsy's Pancake | Mid-City	22
Bluebird Cafe | Uptown	22
Blue Plate Cafe | Lower Garden	22
⚡ Brennan's | French Qtr	24
⚡ Café Du Monde | French Qtr	24
Caffe! Caffe! | multi.	22
CC's Coffee | Garden	19
Chateau Coffee | Kenner	19
Clover Grill | French Qtr	21
Coffee Pot | French Qtr	21
Coffee Rani | multi.	23
Croissant d'Or | French Qtr	24
Elizabeth's | Bywater	24
La Madeleine | multi.	20
Mike Serio's | CBD	19
Morning Call | Metairie	25
Mother's | CBD	22
NEW New Orleans Cake | Faub Marigny	-
Nine Roses | Gretna	24
Petunia's | French Qtr	22
Pho Tau Bay | Gretna	25
PJ's Coffee | Uptown	19
Riccobono's | Metairie	21
Royal Blend | multi.	16
NEW Ruby Slipper | Mid-City	23
rue de la course | multi.	19
Russell's Marina | Lakefront	19
Slim Goodies | Garden	21
St. Charles Tav. | Uptown	14
Surrey's Juice | Lower Garden	25
Trolley Stop | Lower Garden	20
Whole Foods | Metairie	23

BRUNCH

Andrea's | Metairie	21
⚡ Antoine's | French Qtr	24
⚡ Arnaud's | French Qtr	25
Audubon Park | Uptown	15
Begue's | French Qtr	24
Blue Plate Cafe | Lower Garden	22
⚡ Brennan's | French Qtr	24
Bywater BBQ | Bywater	16
Cafe Atchafalaya | Irish Channel	19
Café Degas | Faub St. John	24
Cafe Rani | Garden	20
Coffee Rani | multi.	23
⚡ Commander's | Garden	27
Copeland's | multi.	19
Court/Sisters | French Qtr	20
Dante's Kitchen | Riverbend	25
Eat | French Qtr	24
Elizabeth's | Bywater	24
Feelings Cafe | Faub Marigny	21
Flaming Torch | Uptown	23
La Côte | Warehouse	22
⚡ La Provence | Lacombe	27
Marigny Brass. | Faub Marigny	22
Martin Wine | Metairie	23
⚡ Muriel's | French Qtr	23
Palace Café | French Qtr	24
Patois | Uptown	25
⚡ Ralph's/Park | Mid-City	25
Rest. des Familles | Crown Pt	22
Rib Room | French Qtr	25
Slim Goodies | Garden	21
Smilie's | Harahan	17

BUFFET

(Check availability)

Boswell's Jamaican | Mid-City	-
Court/Sisters | French Qtr	20

Crystal Room | **CBD**	–
Fire of Brazil | **French Qtr**	21
La Côte | **Warehouse**	22
NEW Lago | **Lakeview**	24
Li'l Dizzy's | **CBD**	22
Mat & Naddie's | **Riverbend**	23
Nirvana Indian | **Uptown**	21
Smilie's | **Harahan**	17
Taj Mahal | **Old Metairie**	22

BUSINESS DINING

Andrea's | **Metairie**	21
Z Antoine's | **French Qtr**	24
Z Arnaud's | **French Qtr**	25
Z August | **CBD**	28
Bacco | **French Qtr**	24
Bon Ton Café | **CBD**	24
Z Brennan's | **French Qtr**	24
Café Adelaide | **CBD**	24
Z Commander's | **Garden**	27
NEW Creole Skillet | **Warehouse**	–
Crystal Room | **CBD**	–
Z Cuvée | **CBD**	26
Z Dickie Brennan's | **French Qtr**	25
Z Emeril's | **Warehouse**	25
Z Emeril's Delmonico | **Lower Garden**	26
Z Galatoire's | **French Qtr**	27
Z Gautreau's | **Uptown**	28
Gordon Biersch | **CBD**	16
Z GW Fins | **French Qtr**	26
Z Herbsaint | **Warehouse**	26
Z La Petite Grocery | **Uptown**	26
Lüke | **CBD**	23
Morton's | **French Qtr**	25
Z Mr. B's Bistro | **French Qtr**	25
Z Muriel's | **French Qtr**	23
New City Grille | **Metairie**	22
New Orleans Grill | **CBD**	24
Z NOLA | **French Qtr**	26
Palace Café | **French Qtr**	24
Z Pelican Club | **French Qtr**	26

Z Ralph's/Park | **Mid-City**	25
Red Fish Grill | **French Qtr**	22
Rib Room | **French Qtr**	25
Z Ruth's Chris | **Metairie**	26
NEW Wolfe's | **French Qtr**	–
Zoë | **CBD**	22

BYO

Babylon Café | **Uptown**	21
Barú Bistro | **Uptown**	23
Bennachin | **French Qtr**	23
Café Minh | **Mid-City**	25
Café Sbisa | **French Qtr**	–
Charlie's Steak | **Uptown**	–
Chateau Coffee | **Lakeview**	19
Coffea Cafe | **Bywater**	–
Z Crabby Jack's | **Jefferson**	26
Z Cypress | **Metairie**	27
Eat | **French Qtr**	24
Fire of Brazil | **French Qtr**	21
Z Gautreau's | **Uptown**	28
Gelato Pazzo | **Carrollton**	25
NEW Gott Gourmet Café | **Garden**	–
Hillbilly BBQ | **River Ridge**	23
Jazmine Café | **Riverbend**	19
Julie's Little Indian | **Bywater**	18
Z K-Paul's | **French Qtr**	27
La Crêpe Nanou | **Uptown**	24
Z La Petite Grocery | **Uptown**	26
Laurentino's | **Metairie**	22
Lebanon's Café | **Carrollton**	23
Lola's | **Faub St. John**	25
Louisiana Pizza | **French Qtr**	22
Lüke | **CBD**	23
Mandina's | **Mid-City**	23
Maple St. Cafe | **Carrollton**	22
Marigny Brass. | **Faub Marigny**	22
Z Martinique | **Uptown**	26
Mat & Naddie's | **Riverbend**	23
Melting Pot | **Lower Garden**	19
Miyako | **Lower Garden**	21

Mona Lisa | **French Qtr**	23
Mona's Cafe | **multi.**	19
Morton's | **French Qtr**	25
☑ Mosca's | **Avondale**	26
☑ Mr. B's Bistro | **French Qtr**	25
☑ Muriel's | **French Qtr**	23
New City Grille | **Metairie**	22
Nuvolari's | **Mandeville**	24
Oak St. Cafe | **Carrollton**	-
Orleans Grapevine | **French Qtr**	22
Palace Café | **French Qtr**	24
Parkway Bakery | **Mid-City**	25
Pascal's Manale | **Uptown**	23
☑ Pelican Club | **French Qtr**	26
NEW Pellicano | **Kenner**	-
Pho Tau Bay | **Gretna**	25
Praline Connection | **Faub Marigny**	22
☑ Ralph's/Park | **Mid-City**	25
Red Fish Grill | **French Qtr**	22
Refuel | **Riverbend**	22
Reginelli's | **multi.**	21
Remoulade | **French Qtr**	18
Rest. des Familles | **Crown Pt**	22
Rib Room | **French Qtr**	25
☑ RioMar | **Warehouse**	26
Rist. Da Piero | **Kenner**	27
☑ Rist. del Porto | **Covington**	26
Rist. Filippo | **Metairie**	24
Rock-n-Sake | **Warehouse**	23
☑ Ruth's Chris | **Metairie**	26
Sake Cafe | **multi.**	23
Sal & Judy's | **Lacombe**	26
Sara's | **Riverbend**	24
Slim Goodies | **Garden**	21
☑ St. James Cheese | **Uptown**	26
Sukho Thai | **Faub Marigny**	-
Taco San Miguel | **multi.**	17
Taqueria Guerrero | **Mid-City**	-
Tony Angello's | **Lakeview**	24
☑ Upperline | **Uptown**	26
Vucinovich | **New Orleans E**	-

☑ August | *John Besh* | **CBD**	28
☑ Bayona | *Susan Spicer* | **French Qtr**	28
Besh Steak | *John Besh* | **CBD**	25
☑ Brigtsens | *Frank Brigtsen* | **Riverbend**	28
Cochon | *Donald Link* | **Warehouse**	25
☑ Commander's | *Tory McPhail* | **Garden**	27
☑ Cuvée | *Robert Iacovone* | **CBD**	26
Dominique's | *Dominique Macquet* | **French Qtr**	25
☑ Emeril's | *Emeril Lagasse* | **Warehouse**	25
☑ Emeril's Delmonico | *Emeril Lagasse* | **Lower Garden**	26
☑ Herbsaint | *Donald Link* | **Warehouse**	26
☑ K-Paul's | *Paul Prudhomme* | **French Qtr**	27
☑ La Provence | *John Besh* | **Lacombe**	27
☑ Lilette | *John Harris* | **Uptown**	26
Lüke | *John Besh* | **CBD**	23
☑ MiLa | *Allison Vines-Rushing/ Slade Rushing* | **CBD**	26
☑ NOLA | *Emeril Lagasse* | **French Qtr**	26
☑ Stella! | *Scott Boswell* | **French Qtr**	28
☑ Upperline | *Ken Smith* | **Uptown**	26
☑ Vizard's | *Kevin Vizard* | **Uptown**	26
NEW Wolfe's | *Tom Wolfe* | **French Qtr**	-
Wolfe's/Warehouse | *Tom Wolfe* | **Warehouse**	21

CHILD-FRIENDLY

(Alternatives to the usual fast-food places; * children's menu available)

☑ Acme Oyster | **multi.**	22
Acropolis* | **Metairie**	24
Andrea's* | **Metairie**	21

Anselmo's* | **Metairie**	19	Country Flame | **French Qtr**	18
August Moon | **Uptown**	17	Crazy Johnnie's | **Metairie**	21
Bacco | **French Qtr**	24	Crescent City Brew* | **French Qtr**	17
Bangkok Thai | **Riverbend**	20	Crescent City Steak | **Mid-City**	25
Basil Leaf | **Carrollton**	21	Crystal Room* | **CBD**	-
Begue's | **French Qtr**	24	☑ Dakota* | **Covington**	28
Bennachin | **French Qtr**	23	Dante's Kitchen | **Riverbend**	25
Betsy's Pancake* | **Mid-City**	22	Deanie's* | **multi.**	22
Bon Ton Café | **CBD**	24	DiMartino's* | **Algiers**	22
Bourbon House | **French Qtr**	21	☑ Domilise's | **Uptown**	26
Bozo's* | **Metairie**	22	Don's Seafood* | **Metairie**	19
Bravo!* | **Metairie**	20	☑ Drago's* | **Metairie**	25
☑ Brennan's* | **French Qtr**	24	Elizabeth's | **Bywater**	24
Brick Oven | **Kenner**	21	Fausto's Bistro* | **Metairie**	22
☑ Broussard's | **French Qtr**	25	Fazzio's* | **Mandeville**	20
Bubba Gump* | **French Qtr**	13	Felix's Oyster Bar* | **French Qtr**	-
Byblos | **Old Metairie**	22	Fellini's* | **Mid-City**	20
Cafe Atchafalaya | **Irish Channel**	19	Fiorella's Café | **French Qtr**	21
Café Degas | **Faub St. John**	24	Five Happiness | **Carrollton**	22
Cafe DiBlasi* | **Terrytown**	21	Franky & Johnny's* | **Uptown**	20
☑ Café Du Monde | **French Qtr**	24	Frosty's Caffe | **Metairie**	25
Cafe Giovanni | **French Qtr**	24	Fury's* | **Metairie**	23
Cafe Maspero | **French Qtr**	19	Galley* | **Old Metairie**	24
Cafe Pontalba* | **French Qtr**	18	GB's Patio B&G* | **Riverbend**	17
Cafe Rani* | **Garden**	20	Harbor Seafood* | **Kenner**	24
Café Reconcile | **Central City**	22	Hard Rock Cafe* | **French Qtr**	13
Caffe! Caffe!* | **multi.**	22	Houston's* | **Metairie**	22
Cannon's* | **Uptown**	16	Impastato's | **Metairie**	23
Carreta's Grill* | **Metairie**	19	Joey K's* | **Garden**	19
Casablanca | **Metairie**	21	Kim Son | **Gretna**	24
Chateau Coffee* | **multi.**	19	Kyoto II* | **Harahan**	22
China Doll | **Harvey**	22	La Madeleine* | **multi.**	20
Churros Café | **Metairie**	-	Landry's* | **French Qtr**	16
Ciro's Côté Sud | **Uptown**	-	Liuzza's by Track | **Faub St. John**	23
Coffee Pot | **French Qtr**	21	Louisiana Pizza* | **multi.**	22
Coffee Rani* | **multi.**	23	Lucy's Surfer's* | **Warehouse**	14
Come Back Inn* | **multi.**	19	Mandina's* | **Mid-City**	23
Copeland's* | **multi.**	19	Middendorf's* | **Manchac**	24
Copeland's Cheesecake* | **Metairie**	19	Mike Serio's | **CBD**	19
		Mona's Cafe* | **multi.**	19
Corky's BBQ* | **Metairie**	19	☑ Mosca's | **Avondale**	26

Mother's* | **CBD**	22
Mr. Ed's* | **Metairie**	20
Mr. Gyros* | **Metairie**	24
Mulate's* | **Warehouse**	19
New Orleans Food* | **multi.**	22
New Orleans Hamburger* | **Metairie**	17
NINJA | **Carrollton**	24
Nuvolari's* | **Mandeville**	24
Oak Alley* | **Vacherie**	19
Olivier's | **French Qtr**	21
Palace Café* | **French Qtr**	24
Pascal's Manale | **Uptown**	23
Z Pelican Club* | **French Qtr**	26
Pupuseria Divino* | **Gretna**	21
R & O's* | **Bucktown**	21
Red Fish Grill* | **French Qtr**	22
Reginelli's | **Uptown**	21
Remoulade | **French Qtr**	18
Rest. des Familles* | **Crown Pt**	22
Rib Room* | **French Qtr**	25
Riccobono's* | **Metairie**	21
Rocky & Carlo's* | **Chalmette**	22
Royal China | **Metairie**	24
rue de la course | **Carrollton**	19
Russell's Marina* | **Lakefront**	19
Russell's Short Stop | **Metairie**	20
Sake Cafe* | **multi.**	23
Sal & Judy's* | **Lacombe**	26
Saltwater Grill* | **Riverbend**	16
Semolina* | **Metairie**	17
Semolina's Bistro Italia* | **Garden**	17
Serranos Salsa Co.* | **Metairie**	18
Shogun* | **Metairie**	24
Siamese | **Metairie**	22
Smilie's* | **Harahan**	17
Steve's Diner* | **CBD**	16
Sun Ray Grill* | **multi.**	21
Tan Dinh | **Gretna**	25
Taqueria Corona* | **multi.**	21
Tony Angello's | **Lakeview**	24

Tony Mandina's* | **Gretna**	22
Trey Yuen* | **multi.**	23
Two Tony's* | **Bucktown**	23
Venezia* | **multi.**	22
Vincent's* | **multi.**	24
Voodoo BBQ* | **multi.**	20
Whole Foods | **Uptown**	23
Ye Olde College* | **Carrollton**	21
Young's* | **Slidell**	24
Zea* | **multi.**	23
Zeke's* | **Old Metairie**	17

CONVENTION CENTER CONVENIENCE

Besh Steak | **CBD**	25
Café Adelaide | **CBD**	24
Z Drago's | **CBD**	25
Eleven 79 | **Lower Garden**	25
Z Emeril's | **Warehouse**	25
Gordon Biersch | **CBD**	16
Grand Isle | **Warehouse**	19
Z La Boca | **Warehouse**	27
La Côte | **Warehouse**	22
Morton's | **French Qtr**	25
Mulate's | **Warehouse**	19
New Orleans Grill | **CBD**	24
Z RioMar | **Warehouse**	26
Rock-n-Sake | **Warehouse**	23
7 on Fulton | **Warehouse**	22
Tommy's Cuisine | **Warehouse**	25
Wolfe's/Warehouse | **Warehouse**	21

DINING ALONE

(Other than hotels and places with counter service)

Blue Plate Cafe | **Lower Garden**	22
Byblos | **multi.**	22
Cafe Atchafalaya | **Irish Channel**	19
Cafe Maspero | **French Qtr**	19
Cafe Pontalba | **French Qtr**	18
Cafe Rani | **Garden**	20
Caffe! Caffe! | **Metairie**	22

Ciro's Côté Sud | **Uptown**	‑
Cochon | **Warehouse**	25
ⓩ Domilise's | **Uptown**	26
Fire of Brazil | **French Qtr**	21
Hana Japanese | **Riverbend**	21
Jazmine Café | **Riverbend**	19
Joey K's | **Garden**	19
Kyoto | **Uptown**	24
Landry's | **Lakefront**	16
Lebanon's Café | **Carrollton**	23
Li'l Dizzy's | **Mid-City**	22
ⓩ Lilette | **Uptown**	26
Mandina's | **Mid-City**	23
Maple St. Cafe | **Carrollton**	22
Marigny Brass. | **Faub Marigny**	22
ⓩ Mr. B's Bistro | **French Qtr**	25
Napoleon House | **French Qtr**	19
Nine Roses | **Gretna**	24
ⓩ NOLA | **French Qtr**	26
Pascal's Manale | **Uptown**	23
ⓩ Pelican Club | **French Qtr**	26
Port of Call | **French Qtr**	24
Sake Cafe | **multi.**	23
Saltwater Grill | **Riverbend**	16
Taj Mahal | **Old Metairie**	22
Taqueria Corona | **multi.**	21
Taqueria Guerrero | **Mid-City**	‑
Tujague's | **French Qtr**	21
ⓩ Upperline | **Uptown**	26

ENTERTAINMENT

(Call for days and
times of performances)

Andrea's | piano | **Metairie**	21
NEW Beebe's | jazz | **Lakefront**	25
Begue's | piano | **French Qtr**	24
ⓩ Broussard's | piano | **French Qtr**	25
Cafe Beignet | jazz | **French Qtr**	20
Cafe Giovanni | opera singer/pianist | **French Qtr**	24
Café Granada | guitar | **Carrollton**	22
Carreta's Grill | bands/magician | **Metairie**	19
ⓩ Commander's | jazz | **Garden**	27
NEW Copeland's Social | varies | **Metairie**	‑
Court/Sisters | jazz | **French Qtr**	20
Hard Rock Cafe | bands | **French Qtr**	13
Houston's | jazz | **Lower Garden**	22
Impastato's | vocals | **Metairie**	23
Irene's Cuisine | piano | **French Qtr**	26
Jamila's Cafe | belly dancer | **Uptown**	24
Landry's | varies | **French Qtr**	16
ⓩ La Provence | piano | **Lacombe**	27
Marigny Brass. | jazz | **Faub Marigny**	22
Mat & Naddie's | jazz | **Riverbend**	23
Mulate's | Cajun | **Warehouse**	19
ⓩ Muriel's | jazz | **French Qtr**	23
Palace Café | jazz | **French Qtr**	24
ⓩ Pelican Club | piano | **French Qtr**	26
ⓩ Ralph's/Park | piano | **Mid-City**	25
Rib Room | jazz | **French Qtr**	25
Saltwater Grill | jazz | **Riverbend**	16
Tommy's Cuisine | piano | **Warehouse**	25
Tony Mandina's | piano | **Gretna**	22
NEW West Indies | jazz | **Lower Garden**	‑

FAMILY-STYLE

Anselmo's | **Metairie**	19
Bubba Gump | **French Qtr**	13
Charlie's Steak | **Uptown**	‑
Deanie's | **multi.**	22
DiMartino's | **multi.**	22
Dong Phuong | **New Orleans E**	23
Fausto's Bistro | **Metairie**	22
Fury's | **Metairie**	23
Great Wall | **Old Metairie**	22
Jack Dempsey's | **Bywater**	19
Jamila's Cafe | **Uptown**	24
Kim Son | **Gretna**	24

Mosca's | **Avondale**	26
Mother's | **CBD**	22
New Orleans Food | **Harvey**	22
Royal China | **Metairie**	24
Shogun | **Metairie**	24
Sun Ray Grill | **Gretna**	21
Two Tony's | **Bucktown**	23

FIREPLACES

Andrea's | **Metairie**	21
Court/Sisters | **French Qtr**	20
Crystal Room | **CBD**	-
La Provence | **Lacombe**	27
Le Citron | **Lower Garden**	23
Orleans Grapevine | **French Qtr**	22
Rest. des Familles | **Crown Pt**	22
Stella! | **French Qtr**	28

GAME IN SEASON

Andrea's | **Metairie**	21
August | **CBD**	28
Bacco | **French Qtr**	24
Bistro/Maison | **French Qtr**	26
Bistro Daisy | **Uptown**	26
Brigtsen's | **Riverbend**	28
Cafe Atchafalaya | **Irish Channel**	19
Café Sbisa | **French Qtr**	-
Commander's | **Garden**	27
NEW Creole Skillet | **Warehouse**	-
Cuvée | **CBD**	26
Cypress | **Metairie**	27
Dakota | **Covington**	28
Delachaise | **Uptown**	22
Dick & Jenny's | **Uptown**	26
Feelings Cafe | **Faub Marigny**	21
Five Happiness | **Carrollton**	22
Gautreau's | **Uptown**	28
NEW Hostel | **French Qtr**	-
Iris | **French Qtr**	25
Jacques-Imo's | **Carrollton**	26
La Petite Grocery | **Uptown**	26
La Provence | **Lacombe**	27

Lola's | **Faub St. John**	25
Lüke | **CBD**	23
Maple St. Cafe | **Carrollton**	22
Marigny Brass. | **Faub Marigny**	22
Martinique | **Uptown**	26
Mat & Naddie's | **Riverbend**	23
Meauxbar | **French Qtr**	24
Mélange | **French Qtr**	19
MiLa | **CBD**	26
Mr. Ed's | **Metairie**	20
New Orleans Grill | **CBD**	24
Oak St. Cafe | **Carrollton**	-
Olivier's | **French Qtr**	21
Orleans Grapevine | **French Qtr**	22
Palace Café | **French Qtr**	24
NEW Pellicano | **Kenner**	-
Rist. del Porto | **Covington**	26
7 on Fulton | **Warehouse**	22
St. James Cheese | **Uptown**	26
Upperline | **Uptown**	26
NEW Wolfe's | **French Qtr**	-

HISTORIC PLACES

(Year opened; * building)

1726 | Le Citron* | **Lower Garden**	23
1750 | Alpine* | **French Qtr**	18
1794 | Crescent City Brew* | **French Qtr**	17
1795 | Feelings Cafe* | **Faub Marigny**	21
1795 | Gumbo Shop* | **French Qtr**	21
1797 | Napoleon House* | **French Qtr**	19
1800 | Bayona* | **French Qtr**	28
1800 | Grocery* | **Garden**	-
1800 | 7 on Fulton* | **Warehouse**	22
1830 | Petunia's* | **French Qtr**	22
1831 | Broussard's* | **French Qtr**	25
1832 | Court/Sisters* | **French Qtr**	20
1839 | Oak Alley* | **Vacherie**	19
1840 | Antoine's | **French Qtr**	24
1840 | Eat* | **French Qtr**	24

DINING

SPECIAL FEATURES

Year	Restaurant	Location	Rating
1853	Begue's	French Qtr	24
1856	Tujague's	French Qtr	21
1862	Café Du Monde	French Qtr	24
1870	Morning Call	Metairie	25
1877	Upperline*	Uptown	26
1879	Sun Ray Grill*	Warehouse	21
1880	Commander's	Garden	27
1890	Brigtsen's*	Riverbend	28
1890	La Petite Grocery*	Uptown	26
1893	Whole Foods*	Uptown	23
1894	Coffee Pot*	French Qtr	21
1899	Café Sbisa	French Qtr	–
1899	Julie's Little Indian*	Bywater	18
1900	Felix's Oyster Bar*	French Qtr	–
1900	Mat & Naddie's*	Riverbend	23
1902	Ernst Cafe*	Warehouse	16
1905	Angelo Brocato	Mid-City	28
1905	Galatoire's	French Qtr	27
1906	Central Grocery	French Qtr	25
1907	Crystal Room	CBD	–
1910	Acme Oyster	French Qtr	22
1913	Pascal's Manale	Uptown	23
1916	Liuzza's by Track	Faub St. John	23
1918	Arnaud's	French Qtr	25
1919	Casamento's	Uptown	25
1919	CC's Coffee	multi.	19
1920	Iris*	French Qtr	25
1924	Domilise's	Uptown	26
1928	Bozo's	Metairie	22
1929	Ye Olde College*	Carrollton	21
1930	Arabesque*	Mid-City	23
1931	St. Charles Tav.	Uptown	14
1932	Charlie's Steak	Uptown	–
1932	Mandina's	Mid-City	23
1934	Crescent City Steak	Mid-City	25
1934	Middendorf's	Manchac	24
1937	Fiorella's Café	French Qtr	21
1937	Nuvolari's*	Mandeville	24
1938	Mother's	CBD	22
1939	Hansen's Sno-Bliz	Uptown	28
1940	Dooky Chase	Treme	24
1942	Franky & Johnny's	Uptown	20
1946	Brennan's	French Qtr	24
1946	Camellia Grill	Riverbend	23
1946	Mosca's	Avondale	26
1947	Liuzza's Rest.	Mid-City	21
1950	Clover Grill	French Qtr	21
1950	Johnny's Po-Boy	French Qtr	–
1952	Parasol's	Irish Channel	24
1953	Bon Ton Café	CBD	24
1957	Venezia	Mid-City	22
1957	Willie Mae's	Treme	25
1958	Mike Serio's	CBD	19

HOTEL DINING

		Rating
Astor Crowne Plaza Hotel		
Bourbon House	French Qtr	21
Bienville House		
Iris	French Qtr	25
Harrah's Hotel		
🇿 Ruth's Chris	CBD	26
Hilton New Orleans Riverside		
🇿 Drago's	CBD	25
International House Hotel		
NEW Rambla	CBD	–
JW Marriott		
Shula's	CBD	20
Le Pavillon Hotel		
Crystal Room	CBD	–
Loews		
Café Adelaide	CBD	24
Maison de Ville, Hotel		
Bistro/Maison	French Qtr	26
Maison Dupuy		
Dominique's	French Qtr	25
Marriott at Convention Center		
Wolfe's/Warehouse	Warehouse	21

Omni Royal Orleans
   Rib Room | **French Qtr** — 25

Provincial, Hotel
   Z Stella! | **French Qtr** — 28

Renaissance Arts Hotel
   La Côte | **Warehouse** — 22

Renaissance Pere Marquette
   Z MiLa | **CBD** — 26

Ritz-Carlton
   Mélange | **French Qtr** — 19

Royal Sonesta Hotel
   Begue's | **French Qtr** — 24

St. James Hotel
   Z Cuvée | **CBD** — 26

W French Quarter
   Bacco | **French Qtr** — 24

Whitney
   Li'l Dizzy's | **CBD** — 22

Windsor Court Hotel
   New Orleans Grill | **CBD** — 24

W New Orleans
   Zoë | **CBD** — 22

Wyndham Riverfront
   7 on Fulton | **Warehouse** — 22

LATE DINING

(Weekday closing hour)

Angeli/Decatur | 2 AM | **French Qtr** — 20

Beachcorner | 1 AM | **Mid-City** — 21

Bud's Broiler | 24 hrs. | **Metairie** — 20

Z Café Du Monde | 24 hrs. | **French Qtr** — 24

Cafe Roma | 12 AM | **Lower Garden** — 20

Clover Grill | 24 hrs. | **French Qtr** — 21

Coop's Place | 2 AM | **French Qtr** — 22

Crêpes à la Cart | 12 AM | **Uptown** — 25

Delachaise | 2 AM | **Uptown** — 22

Ernst Cafe | 12 AM | **Warehouse** — 16

Gordon Biersch | 12 AM | **CBD** — 16

NEW Hoshun | 2 AM | **Lower Garden** — 23

Morning Call | 24 hrs. | **Metairie** — 25

O'Henry's | 12 AM | **multi.** — 13

Oscar's | 12 AM | **Old Metairie** — 19

Port of Call | 12 AM | **French Qtr** — 24

Remoulade | 12 AM | **French Qtr** — 18

rue de la course | 12 AM | **multi.** — 19

St. Charles Tav. | 24 hrs. | **Uptown** — 14

13 Monaghan | 4 AM | **Faub Marigny** — 19

NEW Yuki Izakaya | 12 AM | **Faub Marigny** — –

LOCAL FAVORITES

Bistro/Maison | **French Qtr** — 26

Bon Ton Café | **CBD** — 24

Bozo's | **Metairie** — 22

Byblos | **Uptown** — 22

Café Degas | **Faub St. John** — 24

Cafe Rani | **Garden** — 20

Camellia Grill | **Riverbend** — 23

Z Crabby Jack's | **Jefferson** — 26

Crescent City Steak | **Mid-City** — 25

Croissant d'Or | **French Qtr** — 24

Z Cypress | **Metairie** — 27

Dante's Kitchen | **Riverbend** — 25

Deanie's | **Bucktown** — 22

Dooky Chase | **Treme** — 24

Z Drago's | **Metairie** — 25

Elizabeth's | **Bywater** — 24

Z Gautreau's | **Uptown** — 28

Z Hansen's Sno-Bliz | **Uptown** — 28

Jack Dempsey's | **Bywater** — 19

Z Jacques-Imo's | **Carrollton** — 26

Z K-Paul's | **French Qtr** — 27

Landry's | **Lakefront** — 16

Li'l Dizzy's | **Mid-City** — 22

Liuzza's by Track | **Faub St. John** — 23

Liuzza's Rest. | **Mid-City** — 21

Mandina's | **Mid-City** — 23

Z Martinique | **Uptown** — 26

Middendorf's | **Manchac** — 24

☑ Mr. B's Bistro	**French Qtr**	25
Napoleon House	**French Qtr**	19
Petunia's	**French Qtr**	22
R & O's	**Bucktown**	21
Tony Angello's	**Lakeview**	24
Ye Olde College	**Carrollton**	21

MEET FOR A DRINK

Abita Brew	**Abita Springs**	19
☑ Arnaud's	**French Qtr**	25
Crescent City Brew	**French Qtr**	17
☑ Cypress	**Metairie**	27
NEW Daniel's on Bayou	**Faub St. John**	–
Ernst Cafe	**Warehouse**	16
Gordon Biersch	**CBD**	16
Grand Isle	**Warehouse**	19
☑ GW Fins	**French Qtr**	26
☑ Herbsaint	**Warehouse**	26
NEW Hostel	**French Qtr**	–
Houston's	**Metairie**	22
Iris	**French Qtr**	25
NEW Italian Barrel	**French Qtr**	–
NEW Jager Haus	**French Qtr**	–
NEW Lago	**Lakeview**	24
Landry's	**Lakefront**	16
Mélange	**French Qtr**	19
☑ Muriel's	**French Qtr**	23
☑ Pelican Club	**French Qtr**	26
Red Fish Grill	**French Qtr**	22
NEW Yuki Izakaya	**Faub Marigny**	–

NATURAL/ORGANIC

Apple Seed	**CBD**	22
Café Sbisa	**French Qtr**	–
☑ Dakota	**Covington**	28
Dante's Kitchen	**Riverbend**	25
☑ La Petite Grocery	**Uptown**	26
Orleans Grapevine	**French Qtr**	22
☑ Rist. del Porto	**Covington**	26
NEW Stop 9	**Lower Garden**	15
☑ Sucré	**Garden**	25

NOTEWORTHY NEWCOMERS

Alligator Pear	**Harvey**	–
Arabesque	**Mid-City**	23
Beebe's	**Lakefront**	25
Big Al's Seafood	**Lower Garden**	19
Copeland's Social	**Metairie**	–
Country Club	**Bywater**	22
Creole Skillet	**Warehouse**	–
Daniel's on Bayou	**Faub St. John**	–
Felipe's Taqueria	**French Qtr**	–
Gimchi	**Metairie**	19
Gott Gourmet Café	**Garden**	–
Hoshun	**Lower Garden**	23
Hostel	**French Qtr**	–
Il Posto Café	**Uptown**	24
Italian Barrel	**French Qtr**	–
Jager Haus	**French Qtr**	–
J'anita's	**Lower Garden**	23
☑ La Divina	**French Qtr**	26
La Famiglia	**Metairie**	–
Lago	**Lakeview**	24
Lakeview Brew	**Lakeview**	–
Mahony's	**Uptown**	–
New Orleans Cake	**Faub Marigny**	–
Pellicano	**Kenner**	–
Rambla	**CBD**	–
Ruby Slipper	**Mid-City**	23
☑ Ruth's Chris	**CBD**	26
Sailor's Seafood	**Mid-City**	–
Shane's Rib Shack	**Marrero**	18
Stop 9	**Lower Garden**	15
West Indies	**Lower Garden**	–
Wolfe's	**French Qtr**	–
Yuki Izakaya	**Faub Marigny**	–

OFFBEAT

Adolfo's	**Faub Marigny**	24
Byblos	**Old Metairie**	22
Café Degas	**Faub St. John**	24
☑ Central Grocery	**French Qtr**	25
Coffea Cafe	**Bywater**	–

NEW Country Club | **Bywater**	22
Country Flame | **French Qtr**	18
Delachaise | **Uptown**	22
Z Dick & Jenny's | **Uptown**	26
Easy Dogs | **Gretna**	19
Eleven 79 | **Lower Garden**	25
Fausto's Bistro | **Metairie**	22
Z Jacques-Imo's | **Carrollton**	26
Le Citron | **Lower Garden**	23
Mat & Naddie's | **Riverbend**	23
Mother's | **CBD**	22
Parasol's | **Irish Channel**	24
Port of Call | **French Qtr**	24
Praline Connection | **Faub Marigny**	22
Pupuseria Divino | **Gretna**	21
Rocky & Carlo's | **Chalmette**	22
Slim Goodies | **Garden**	21
NEW Yuki Izakaya | **Faub Marigny**	-

OUTDOOR DINING

(G=garden; P=patio; S=sidewalk; T=terrace)

Abita Brew | G, P | **Abita Springs**	19
Alpine | G | **French Qtr**	18
Audubon Park | T | **Uptown**	15
Babylon Café | S | **Uptown**	21
Barú Bistro | S | **Uptown**	23
Basil Leaf | S | **Carrollton**	21
Z Bayona | P | **French Qtr**	28
Beachcorner | P | **Mid-City**	21
Z Brennan's | G | **French Qtr**	24
Brick Oven | P | **Kenner**	21
Z Broussard's | P | **French Qtr**	25
Bubba Gump | P, T | **French Qtr**	13
Bywater BBQ | P | **Bywater**	16
Café Amelie | G | **French Qtr**	23
Cafe Atchafalaya | S | **Irish Channel**	19
Cafe Beignet | P | **French Qtr**	20
Z Café Du Monde | P | **French Qtr**	24
Cafe Rani | P | **Garden**	20
Caffe! Caffe! | P, S | **multi.**	22
CC's Coffee | P | **Garden**	19

Chateau Coffee | S | **Kenner**	19
Coffea Cafe | G | **Bywater**	-
Coffee Pot | P | **French Qtr**	21
Coffee Rani | P, S | **multi.**	23
Z Commander's | P | **Garden**	27
Court/Sisters | P | **French Qtr**	20
Crazy Johnnie's | T | **Metairie**	21
Crescent City Brew | P, T | **French Qtr**	17
Croissant d'Or | P | **French Qtr**	24
Dante's Kitchen | P | **Riverbend**	25
Z Dick & Jenny's | P | **Uptown**	26
Dominique's | P | **French Qtr**	25
Feelings Cafe | P | **Faub Marigny**	21
Fellini's | S | **Mid-City**	20
Flaming Torch | S | **Uptown**	23
Fresco Cafe | T | **Uptown**	19
Galley | P | **Old Metairie**	24
GB's Patio B&G | P | **Riverbend**	17
Gordon Biersch | P | **CBD**	16
Gumbo Shop | P | **French Qtr**	21
Hard Rock Cafe | T | **French Qtr**	13
Z Herbsaint | S | **Warehouse**	26
Ignatius Eatery | S | **Uptown**	21
Iris | P | **French Qtr**	25
Z Jacques-Imo's | P | **Carrollton**	26
Jamila's Cafe | T | **Uptown**	24
Jazz Tacos | S | **French Qtr**	16
Joint | G | **Bywater**	25
Julie's Little Indian | P | **Bywater**	18
Z K-Paul's | T | **French Qtr**	27
La Crêpe Nanou | S | **Uptown**	24
La Madeleine | P, S | **multi.**	20
Lebanon's Café | P | **Carrollton**	23
Le Citron | P | **Lower Garden**	23
Z Le Parvenu | P | **Kenner**	26
Z Lilette | P | **Uptown**	26
Louisiana Pizza | S | **French Qtr**	22
Lucy's Surfer's | S | **Warehouse**	14
Maple St. Cafe | P | **Carrollton**	22
Z Martinique | G, P | **Uptown**	26

Martin Wine | P | **Metairie** 23

Mat & Naddie's | P | **Riverbend** 23

Mona's Cafe | P, S | **multi.** 19

Nacho Mama's | P | **Uptown** 15

Napoleon House | P | **French Qtr** 19

New Orleans Food | P | **Covington** 22

New York Pizza | S | **Uptown** 21

Nirvana Indian | P | **Uptown** 21

Oak Alley | P | **Vacherie** 19

O'Henry's | S, T | **multi.** 13

Parkway Bakery | P, W | **Mid-City** 25

Z Pelican Club | S | **French Qtr** 26

PJ's Coffee | P | **multi.** 19

Roly Poly | S | **Uptown** 18

Royal Blend | G, P | **multi.** 16

rue de la course | S | **multi.** 19

Russell's Marina | P | **Lakefront** 19

Saltwater Grill | P | **Riverbend** 16

Semolina | P | **Metairie** 17

Serranos Salsa Co. | P | **Metairie** 18

Slice | S | **Lower Garden** 23

Slim Goodies | G | **Garden** 21

Sun Ray Grill | P | **Warehouse** 21

Superior Grill | P | **Uptown** 20

Taqueria Corona | S | **Harahan** 21

Theo's | S | **Uptown** 24

Ugly Dog | P | **Warehouse** 20

Voodoo BBQ | P | **Lower Garden** 20

Whole Foods | P | **multi.** 23

PARKING

(V=valet, *=validated)

Bacco* | **French Qtr** 24

Z Bayona* | **French Qtr** 28

Begue's | V* | **French Qtr** 24

Besh Steak* | **CBD** 25

Bon Ton Café* | **CBD** 24

Z Brennan's* | **French Qtr** 24

Café Adelaide | V | **CBD** 24

Cafe Giovanni* | **French Qtr** 24

Cochon* | **Warehouse** 25

Z Commander's | V | **Garden** 27

Copeland's Cheesecake | V | **multi.** 19

Z Cuvée | V | **CBD** 26

Z Dickie Brennan's | V* | **French Qtr** 25

Dominique's | V* | **French Qtr** 25

Z Drago's* | **CBD** 25

Z Emeril's | V | **Warehouse** 25

Z Emeril's Delmonico | V | **Lower Garden** 26

Gordon Biersch* | **CBD** 16

Grand Isle* | **Warehouse** 19

Z GW Fins* | **French Qtr** 26

Z K-Paul's* | **French Qtr** 27

La Côte | V | **Warehouse** 22

Mélange | V | **French Qtr** 19

Z MiLa | V | **CBD** 26

Morton's* | **French Qtr** 25

Z Mr. B's Bistro* | **French Qtr** 25

Mr. John's | V | **Lower Garden** 24

Z Muriel's* | **French Qtr** 23

New City Grille | V | **Metairie** 22

New Orleans Grill | V* | **CBD** 24

Z NOLA* | **French Qtr** 26

Palace Café* | **French Qtr** 24

Z Pelican Club* | **French Qtr** 26

Z Ralph's/Park | V | **Mid-City** 25

Rib Room* | **French Qtr** 25

Z RioMar* | **Warehouse** 26

Z Ruth's Chris | V* | **multi.** 26

7 on Fulton | V | **Warehouse** 22

Shula's | V | **CBD** 20

Z Stella! | V | **French Qtr** 28

Z Vizard's | V | **Uptown** 26

Wolfe's/Warehouse | V | **Warehouse** 21

Zea | V | **Lower Garden** 23

Zoë | V | **CBD** 22

PEOPLE-WATCHING

Z Antoine's | **French Qtr** 24

Z Arnaud's | **French Qtr** 25

Bacco | **French Qtr** 24

Ⓩ Bayona | **French Qtr** 28

Ⓩ Brennan's | **French Qtr** 24

Ⓩ Brigtsen's | **Riverbend** 28

Café Adelaide | **CBD** 24

Ⓩ Café Du Monde | **French Qtr** 24

Ⓩ Café East | **Metairie** 22

Cafe Maspero | **French Qtr** 19

Cafe Pontalba | **French Qtr** 18

Ⓩ Clancy's | **Uptown** 27

Clover Grill | **French Qtr** 21

Coffee Pot | **French Qtr** 21

Ⓩ Commander's | **Garden** 27

Delachaise | **Uptown** 22

Ⓩ Dickie Brennan's | **French Qtr** 25

Ⓩ Emeril's | **Warehouse** 25

Ⓩ Emeril's Delmonico | 26
Lower Garden

Ⓩ Galatoire's | **French Qtr** 27

Ⓩ Gautreau's | **Uptown** 28

Gumbo Shop | **French Qtr** 21

Irene's Cuisine | **French Qtr** 26

Ⓩ K-Paul's | **French Qtr** 27

La Crêpe Nanou | **Uptown** 24

Ⓩ La Petite Grocery | **Uptown** 26

Ⓩ Le Parvenu | **Kenner** 26

Liborio Cuban | **CBD** 21

Li'l Dizzy's | **multi.** 22

Lüke | **CBD** 23

Mother's | **CBD** 22

Ⓩ Mr. B's Bistro | **French Qtr** 25

Ⓩ Muriel's | **French Qtr** 23

New City Grille | **Metairie** 22

New Orleans Grill | **CBD** 24

Ⓩ NOLA | **French Qtr** 26

Palace Café | **French Qtr** 24

Parasol's | **Irish Channel** 24

Parkway Bakery | **Mid-City** 25

Patois | **Uptown** 25

Ⓩ Pelican Club | **French Qtr** 26

Ⓩ Ralph's/Park | **Mid-City** 25

Rib Room | **French Qtr** 25

Ⓩ Rist. del Porto | **Covington** 26

Ⓩ Ruth's Chris | **Metairie** 26

St. Charles Tav. | **Uptown** 14

Tommy's Cuisine | **Warehouse** 25

Trey Yuen | **multi.** 23

Ⓩ Upperline | **Uptown** 26

🆕 Wolfe's | **French Qtr** -

POWER SCENES

Andrea's | **Metairie** 21

Ⓩ Antoine's | **French Qtr** 24

Ⓩ Arnaud's | **French Qtr** 25

Ⓩ August | **CBD** 28

Bistro/Maison | **French Qtr** 26

Boswell's Jamaican | **Mid-City** -

Ⓩ Brennan's | **French Qtr** 24

Café Adelaide | **CBD** 24

Ⓩ Commander's | **Garden** 27

Ⓩ Emeril's | **Warehouse** 25

Ⓩ Emeril's Delmonico | 26
Lower Garden

Ⓩ Galatoire's | **French Qtr** 27

Ⓩ Gautreau's | **Uptown** 28

Ⓩ La Petite Grocery | **Uptown** 26

Ⓩ Lilette | **Uptown** 26

Morton's | **French Qtr** 25

Ⓩ Mr. B's Bistro | **French Qtr** 25

New Orleans Grill | **CBD** 24

Ⓩ Ralph's/Park | **Mid-City** 25

Rib Room | **French Qtr** 25

Ⓩ Ruth's Chris | **Metairie** 26

PRIX FIXE MENUS

(Call for prices and times)

Acropolis | **Metairie** 24

Ⓩ Arnaud's | **French Qtr** 25

Ⓩ Bayona | **French Qtr** 28

Ⓩ Brennan's | **French Qtr** 24

Cafe Giovanni | **French Qtr** 24

Carmine's | **Metairie** 20

Court/Sisters | **French Qtr** 20

Ⓩ Cuvée | **CBD** 26

Z Emeril's | **Warehouse**	25
Impastato's | **Metairie**	23
Z La Provence | **Lacombe**	27
La Thai | **Uptown**	22
Z Martinique | **Uptown**	26
Z NOLA | **French Qtr**	26
Palace Café | **French Qtr**	24
Rest. des Familles | **Crown Pt**	22
Rib Room | **French Qtr**	25
Sake Cafe | **Metairie**	23
Z Stella! | **French Qtr**	28
Tujague's | **French Qtr**	21
Z Upperline | **Uptown**	26
Vega Tapas | **Old Metairie**	24
Z Vizard's | **Uptown**	26

QUICK BITES

(Besides fast food and diners)

Adolfo's | **Faub Marigny**	24
Angeli/Decatur | **French Qtr**	20
Apple Seed | **CBD**	22
Audubon Park | **Uptown**	15
Babylon Café | **Uptown**	21
Beachcorner | **Mid-City**	21
Coffee Pot | **French Qtr**	21
Z Crabby Jack's | **Jefferson**	26
Crazy Johnnie's | **Metairie**	21
NEW Daniel's on Bayou | **Faub St. John**	-
DiMartino's | **Algiers**	22
Fiorella's Café | **French Qtr**	21
Gelato Pazzo | **Carrollton**	25
Grocery | **Garden**	-
NEW Italian Barrel | **French Qtr**	-
NEW Jager Haus | **French Qtr**	-
Joey K's | **Garden**	19
Johnny's Po-Boy | **French Qtr**	-
NEW Mahony's | **Uptown**	-
Marigny Brass. | **Faub Marigny**	22
Martin Wine | **Metairie**	23
Oscar's | **Old Metairie**	19
Parasol's | **Irish Channel**	24

Riccobono's Panola St. | **Carrollton**	-
Store | **CBD**	23
Taqueria Guerrero | **Mid-City**	-
Whole Hog | **CBD**	23

QUIET CONVERSATION

Z Antoine's | **French Qtr**	24
Z Broussard's | **French Qtr**	25
Cafe Giovanni | **French Qtr**	24
Z Cuvée | **CBD**	26
Feelings Cafe | **Faub Marigny**	21
Flaming Torch | **Uptown**	23
Grand Isle | **Warehouse**	19
Horinoya | **CBD**	24
Imperial Garden | **Kenner**	-
La Côte | **Warehouse**	22
NEW La Famiglia | **Metairie**	-
Z La Provence | **Lacombe**	27
La Vita | **Faub St. John**	13
Leonardo Tratt. | **Warehouse**	-
Z Le Parvenu | **Kenner**	26
NEW New Orleans Cake | **Faub Marigny**	-
New Orleans Grill | **CBD**	24
Taj Mahal | **Old Metairie**	22
Tomatillo's | **Faub Marigny**	16
NEW West Indies | **Lower Garden**	-
Zoë | **CBD**	22

RAW BARS

Z Acme Oyster | **multi.**	22
Bourbon House | **French Qtr**	21
Bozo's | **Metairie**	22
Casamento's | **Uptown**	25
Crescent City Brew | **French Qtr**	17
Deanie's | **French Qtr**	22
Z Drago's | **multi.**	25
Felix's Oyster Bar | **French Qtr**	-
Grand Isle | **Warehouse**	19
Harbor Seafood | **Kenner**	24
Landry's | **French Qtr**	16
Pascal's Manale | **Uptown**	23

Red Fish Grill | **French Qtr** 22

Remoulade | **French Qtr** 18

NEW Sailor's Seafood | **Mid-City** -

Saltwater Grill | **Riverbend** 16

Zeke's | **Old Metairie** 17

ROMANTIC PLACES

Andrea's | **Metairie** 21

🆉 Antoine's | **French Qtr** 24

🆉 Arnaud's | **French Qtr** 25

🆉 August | **CBD** 28

Bacco | **French Qtr** 24

🆉 Bayona | **French Qtr** 28

Bistro/Maison | **French Qtr** 26

🆉 Brennan's | **French Qtr** 24

🆉 Broussard's | **French Qtr** 25

Café Amelie | **French Qtr** 23

Café Degas | **Faub St. John** 24

Cafe Giovanni | **French Qtr** 24

🆉 Commander's | **Garden** 27

Crystal Room | **CBD** -

🆉 Cuvée | **CBD** 26

NEW Daniel's on Bayou | **Faub St. John** -

🆉 Emeril's | **Warehouse** 25

🆉 Emeril's Delmonico | **Lower Garden** 26

Feelings Cafe | **Faub Marigny** 21

Irene's Cuisine | **French Qtr** 26

Iris | **French Qtr** 25

La Crêpe Nanou | **Uptown** 24

🆉 La Provence | **Lacombe** 27

🆉 Lilette | **Uptown** 26

New Orleans Grill | **CBD** 24

Rib Room | **French Qtr** 25

Sara's | **Riverbend** 24

🆉 Stella! | **French Qtr** 28

🆉 Upperline | **Uptown** 26

NEW West Indies | **Lower Garden** -

SENIOR APPEAL

Anselmo's | **Metairie** 19

Austin's | **Metairie** -

Betsy's Pancake | **Mid-City** 22

Bon Ton Café | **CBD** 24

Bozo's | **Metairie** 22

Bravo! | **Metairie** 20

Brick Oven | **Kenner** 21

Cafe DiBlasi | **Terrytown** 21

Cannon's | **Uptown** 16

Casamento's | **Uptown** 25

Charlie's Steak | **Uptown** -

Chateau Coffee | **Kenner** 19

🆉 Drago's | **Metairie** 25

Fausto's Bistro | **Metairie** 22

Fury's | **Metairie** 23

Great Wall | **Old Metairie** 22

Gumbo Shop | **French Qtr** 21

Impastato's | **Metairie** 23

Jack Dempsey's | **Bywater** 19

Joey K's | **Garden** 19

Kosher Cajun Deli | **Metairie** 21

NEW La Famiglia | **Metairie** -

🆉 La Provence | **Lacombe** 27

Mr. John's | **Lower Garden** 24

New City Grille | **Metairie** 22

NEW New Orleans Cake | **Faub Marigny** -

New Orleans Hamburger | **Metairie** 17

Riccobono's Panola St. | **Carrollton** -

Riccobono's | **Metairie** 21

Russell's Marina | **Lakefront** 19

Saltwater Grill | **Riverbend** 16

Stein's | **Lower Garden** 23

Tony Angello's | **Lakeview** 24

Venezia | **Mid-City** 22

Vincent's | **multi.** 24

Ye Olde College | **Carrollton** 21

SINGLES SCENES

Abita Brew | **Abita Springs** 19

🆉 Acme Oyster | **multi.** 22

Cafe Atchafalaya | **Irish Channel** 19

🆉 Café East | **Metairie** 22

Cafe Maspero	French Qtr	19
Cafe Rani	Garden	20
Ernst Cafe	Warehouse	16
Franky & Johnny's	Uptown	20
GB's Patio B&G	Riverbend	17
Gumbo Shop	French Qtr	21
Hana Japanese	Riverbend	21
Kyoto	Uptown	24
Lola's	Faub St. John	25
Louisiana Pizza	Riverbend	22
Lucy's Surfer's	Warehouse	14
Mat & Naddie's	Riverbend	23
Morning Call	Metairie	25
Napoleon House	French Qtr	19
Parasol's	Irish Channel	24
PJ's Coffee	CBD	19
Port of Call	French Qtr	24
NEW Rambla	CBD	-
Reginelli's	multi.	21
Remoulade	French Qtr	18
Rock-n-Sake	Warehouse	23
Royal Blend	Metairie	16
Semolina's Bistro Italia	Garden	17
Slim Goodies	Garden	21
Superior Grill	Uptown	20
13 Monaghan	Faub Marigny	19
Ugly Dog	Warehouse	20
Zea	Harahan	23

SLEEPERS

(Good to excellent food,
but little known)

Apple Seed	CBD	22
NEW Arabesque	Mid-City	23
NEW Beebe's	Lakefront	25
Bennachin	French Qtr	23
Café Granada	Carrollton	22
China Doll	Harvey	22
Clémentine	Gretna	24
NEW Country Club	Bywater	22
Crêpes à la Cart	Uptown	25
Z Cypress	Metairie	27

Dominique's	French Qtr	25
Dong Phuong	New Orleans E	23
Dunbar's Creole	Uptown	25
Eat	French Qtr	24
Etoile	Covington	22
Frosty's Caffe	multi.	25
Gelato Pazzo	Carrollton	25
Great Wall	Old Metairie	22
Hillbilly BBQ	River Ridge	23
Horinoya	CBD	24
NEW Hoshun	Lower Garden	23
NEW Il Posto Café	Uptown	24
Jamila's Cafe	Uptown	24
NEW J'anita's	Lower Garden	23
Kanno	Metairie	28
Korea House	Metairie	24
Kyoto II	Harahan	22
La Côte	Warehouse	22
NEW Lago	Lakeview	24
Laurentino's	Metairie	22
Le Citron	Lower Garden	23
Meauxbar	French Qtr	24
Mona Lisa	French Qtr	23
Mr. Gyros	Metairie	24
Nine Roses	Gretna	24
Nuvolari's	Mandeville	24
Orleans Grapevine	French Qtr	22
Refuel	Riverbend	22
Rest. des Familles	Crown Pt	22
Rist. Da Piero	Kenner	27
Z Rist. del Porto	Covington	26
Rist. Filippo	Metairie	24
Royal China	Metairie	24
NEW Ruby Slipper	Mid-City	23
Sara's	Riverbend	24
Siamese	Metairie	22
Singha	CBD	22
Store	CBD	23
Sugar Park	Bywater	25
Surrey's Juice	Lower Garden	25
Sushi Brothers	Lower Garden	25

Taj Mahal	**Old Metairie**	22
Tan Dinh	**Gretna**	25
Two Tony's	**Bucktown**	23
Walker BBQ	**New Orleans E**	25
Wasabi	**Faub Marigny**	24
Whole Hog	**CBD**	23
Young's	**Slidell**	24
Zoë	**CBD**	22

SPECIAL OCCASIONS

☑ Antoine's	**French Qtr**	24
☑ Arnaud's	**French Qtr**	25
☑ August	**CBD**	28
☑ Bayona	**French Qtr**	28
Bistro/Maison	**French Qtr**	26
Café Adelaide	**CBD**	24
☑ Commander's	**Garden**	27
☑ Cuvée	**CBD**	26
☑ Emeril's	**Warehouse**	25
Fire of Brazil	**French Qtr**	21
☑ Galatoire's	**French Qtr**	27
Mélange	**French Qtr**	19
New Orleans Grill	**CBD**	24
☑ Pelican Club	**French Qtr**	26
☑ Ralph's/Park	**Mid-City**	25
☑ Stella!	**French Qtr**	28
☑ Upperline	**Uptown**	26

TAKEOUT

Andrea's	**Metairie**	21
☑ Angelo Brocato	**Mid-City**	28
Bozo's	**Metairie**	22
☑ Brigtsen's	**Riverbend**	28
Byblos	**multi.**	22
Bywater BBQ	**Bywater**	16
Café Degas	**Faub St. John**	24
☑ Café Du Monde	**French Qtr**	24
Cafe Rani	**Garden**	20
Cafe Roma	**Lower Garden**	20
Carreta's Grill	**Metairie**	19
Casamento's	**Uptown**	25
☑ Central Grocery	**French Qtr**	25
Coffee Rani	**multi.**	23

Copeland's	**multi.**	19
Corky's BBQ	**Metairie**	19
Croissant d'Or	**French Qtr**	24
Dante's Kitchen	**Riverbend**	25
Deanie's	**Bucktown**	22
DiMartino's	**multi.**	22
☑ Domilise's	**Uptown**	26
Fellini's	**Mid-City**	20
Five Happiness	**Carrollton**	22
Franky & Johnny's	**Uptown**	20
Fury's	**Metairie**	23
Galley	**Old Metairie**	24
Italian Pie	**multi.**	17
☑ Jacques-Imo's	**Carrollton**	26
Joey K's	**Garden**	19
Joint	**Bywater**	25
Juan's Burrito	**multi.**	21
☑ La Boulangerie	**Uptown**	28
La Madeleine	**multi.**	20
Lee's Hamburgers	**Metairie**	20
Liborio Cuban	**CBD**	21
Liuzza's by Track	**Faub St. John**	23
Louisiana Pizza	**multi.**	22
Lucy's Surfer's	**Warehouse**	14
Mark Twain's	**Old Metairie**	22
Martin Wine	**Metairie**	23
Mat & Naddie's	**Riverbend**	23
Mona's Cafe	**multi.**	19
Mother's	**CBD**	22
Mr. Ed's	**Metairie**	20
New Orleans Food	**multi.**	22
New Orleans Hamburger	**Metairie**	17
New York Pizza	**Uptown**	21
Nine Roses	**Gretna**	24
NINJA	**Carrollton**	24
Nirvana Indian	**Uptown**	21
Nuvolari's	**Mandeville**	24
O'Henry's	**multi.**	13
P.F. Chang's	**Metairie**	20
PJ's Coffee	**multi.**	19

Popeyes | **Algiers**	22
Port of Call | **French Qtr**	24
Praline Connection | **Faub Marigny**	22
R & O's | **Bucktown**	21
Roly Poly | **multi.**	18
Royal Blend | **multi.**	16
Russell's Marina | **Lakefront**	19
Saltwater Grill | **Riverbend**	16
Semolina | **multi.**	17
Slice | **Lower Garden**	23
Slim Goodies | **Garden**	21
Smilie's | **Harahan**	17
Sun Ray Grill | **multi.**	21
Taqueria Corona | **multi.**	21
Theo's | **Uptown**	24
Trolley Stop | **Lower Garden**	20
Voodoo BBQ | **multi.**	20
Whole Foods | **multi.**	23
Ye Olde College | **Carrollton**	21
Zea | **multi.**	23

TEEN APPEAL

Bozo's | **Metairie**	22
Bravo! | **Metairie**	20
Cafe Roma | **Lower Garden**	20
Café Sbisa | **French Qtr**	-
Cannon's | **Uptown**	16
Coffee Rani | **multi.**	23
☑ Domilise's | **Uptown**	26
Franky & Johnny's | **Uptown**	20
Gelato Pazzo | **Carrollton**	25
Hana Japanese | **Riverbend**	21
Harbor Seafood | **Kenner**	24
Hard Rock Cafe | **French Qtr**	13
Houston's | **Metairie**	22
☑ Jacques-Imo's | **Carrollton**	26
Jamila's Cafe | **Uptown**	24
Jazmine Café | **Riverbend**	19
Juan's Burrito | **Uptown**	21
Kyoto | **Uptown**	24
Louisiana Pizza | **Riverbend**	22

Mark Twain's | **Old Metairie**	22
Mat & Naddie's | **Riverbend**	23
Mona Lisa | **French Qtr**	23
New York Pizza | **Uptown**	21
NINJA | **Carrollton**	24
O'Henry's | **Riverbend**	13
R & O's | **Bucktown**	21
Reginelli's | **multi.**	21
Remoulade | **French Qtr**	18
Royal Blend | **Metairie**	16
Russell's Marina | **Lakefront**	19
Semolina's Bistro Italia | **Garden**	17
Shogun | **Metairie**	24
Sun Ray Grill | **Warehouse**	21
Superior Grill | **Uptown**	20
Taqueria Corona | **multi.**	21
Trolley Stop | **Lower Garden**	20
Zea | **Harahan**	23

TRENDY

Barú Bistro | **Uptown**	23
Bistro Daisy | **Uptown**	26
Café Minh | **Mid-City**	25
Cochon | **Warehouse**	25
Delachaise | **Uptown**	22
Iris | **French Qtr**	25
☑ La Boca | **Warehouse**	27
Lüke | **CBD**	23
Meauxbar | **French Qtr**	24
☑ MiLa | **CBD**	26
Patois | **Uptown**	25
NEW Rambla | **CBD**	-
☑ Sucré | **Garden**	25
Sukho Thai | **Faub Marigny**	-
Tomatillo's | **Faub Marigny**	16
NEW Yuki Izakaya | **Faub Marigny**	-

VIEWS

Audubon Park | **Uptown**	15
Begue's | **French Qtr**	24
☑ Café Du Monde | **French Qtr**	24
Cafe Pontalba | **French Qtr**	18

DINING

SPECIAL FEATURES

Nightlife Locations

Includes venue names and Appeal ratings.

BUCKTOWN

NEW Live Bait — |

BYWATER

Markey's Bar	23
Saturn Bar	22
Z Vaughan's Lounge	27

CARROLLTON

Carrollton Station	22
Cooter Brown's	21
Madigans	19
Maple Leaf	25

CBD (CENTRAL BUSINESS DISTRICT)

Ampersand	19
NEW Bar UnCommon	—
Handsome Willy's	16
Le Phare Bar	22
Z Loa	24
Ohm Lounge	—
Z Polo Lounge	27
Z Swizzle Stick	26
Whiskey Blue	23

CENTRAL CITY

Big Top Gallery	20

FAUBOURG MARIGNY

Apple Barrel	21
Blue Nile	23
d.b.a.	24
Dragon's Den	22
Hi Ho Lounge	17
Hookah Café	21
Mimi's	24
Phoenix	—
Ray's Room	20
R Bar	19
Snug Harbor	26
Spotted Cat	25

FAUBOURG ST. JOHN

Pal's Lounge	—

FRENCH QUARTER

Abbey	15
Balcony Music	18
NEW Bar Tonique	—
Bombay Club	25
Bourbon Pub	24
Bourbon St. Blues	21
Cafe Lafitte	21
Cajun Cabin	20
Carousel Bar	26
Cat's Meow	20
Checkpoint	17
Corner Pocket	—
Coyote Ugly	16
Donna's B&G	25
Dungeon	22
Famous Door	19
French 75	25
Fritzel's Jazz	23
Funky Pirate	21
Gold Mine	20
Good Friends	21
House of Blues	23
Jimmy Buffett's	20
Johnny White's	21
Kerry Irish Pub	20
Z Lafitte's	26
Maison Bourbon	26
Molly's at Market	21
Old Absinthe Hse.	23
One Eyed Jacks	23
Oz	21
Z Pat O'Brien's	25
NEW Pravda	22
Z Preservation Hall	28
Rawhide 2010	25

| Razzoo | 18 |
| Tropical Isle | 20 |

JEFFERSON
| Rivershack Tav. | 22 |

LOWER GARDEN DISTRICT
Avenue Pub	20
Bridge Lounge	21
NEW Garden District Pub	19
Igor's B&G	19

METAIRIE
| Red Eye B&G | 15 |

MID-CITY
Banks St.	22
Bulldog	24
Chocolate Bar	-
Finn McCool's	22
Z Mid-City Lanes	26

UPTOWN
Balcony Bar	20
Boot	14
Bruno's	20
Bulldog	24
Z Columns Hotel	27
Dos Jefes Cigar	23

F&M Patio Bar	21
Fat Harry's	17
Z 45 Tchoup	21
Kingpin	22
La Nuit/Box Office	-
Le Bon Temps	22
Mayfair	22
Milan Lounge	17
Monkey Hill	21
Ms. Mae's	17
Neutral Ground	19
Snake & Jake's	23
St. Joe's Bar	20
Z Tipitina's	27

WAREHOUSE DISTRICT
Circle Bar	22
Howlin' Wolf	20
Z Le Chat Noir	26
Red Eye B&G	15
Republic	16
Rusty Nail	22
Tommy's Wine	24
NEW W.I.N.O.	24

WEST BANK
| Old Point Bar | 23 |

Nightlife Special Appeals

Listings cover the best in each category and include venue names, locations and Appeal ratings. Multi-location nightspots' features may vary by branch.

AFTER WORK

Bridge Lounge | **Lower Garden**	21
Bulldog | **multi.**	24
Z Columns Hotel | **Uptown**	27
Dos Jefes Cigar | **Uptown**	23
Fat Harry's | **Uptown**	17
Finn McCool's | **Mid-City**	22
Z 45 Tchoup | **Uptown**	21
Kingpin | **Uptown**	22
Z Loa | **CBD**	24
Molly's at Market | **French Qtr**	21
Monkey Hill | **Uptown**	21
Z Polo Lounge | **CBD**	27

COCKTAIL EXPERTS

NEW Bar Tonique | **French Qtr**	-
NEW Bar UnCommon | **CBD**	-
Bridge Lounge | **Lower Garden**	21
Carousel Bar | **French Qtr**	26
Z Columns Hotel | **Uptown**	27
French 75 | **French Qtr**	25
Z Loa | **CBD**	24
Z Polo Lounge | **CBD**	27
St. Joe's Bar | **Uptown**	20
Z Swizzle Stick | **CBD**	26

DANCE CLUBS

Ampersand | **CBD**	19
Bourbon Pub | **French Qtr**	24
Dungeon | **French Qtr**	22
One Eyed Jacks | **French Qtr**	23
Oz | **French Qtr**	21
Republic | **Warehouse**	16

DANCING

Ampersand | **CBD**	19
Banks St. | **Mid-City**	22
Blue Nile | **Faub Marigny**	23
Bombay Club | **French Qtr**	25
Boot | **Uptown**	14

Bourbon Pub | **French Qtr**	24
Bourbon St. Blues | **French Qtr**	21
Cafe Lafitte | **French Qtr**	21
Cajun Cabin | **French Qtr**	20
Carousel Bar | **French Qtr**	26
Cat's Meow | **French Qtr**	20
Chocolate Bar | **Mid-City**	-
Dungeon | **French Qtr**	22
Hi Ho Lounge | **Faub Marigny**	17
Hookah Café | **Faub Marigny**	21
Maple Leaf | **Carrollton**	25
Z Mid-City Lanes | **Mid-City**	26
One Eyed Jacks | **French Qtr**	23
Oz | **French Qtr**	21
Razzoo | **French Qtr**	18
Republic | **Warehouse**	16
Z Tipitina's | **Uptown**	27
Z Vaughan's Lounge | **Bywater**	27

DIVES

Abbey | **French Qtr**	15
Avenue Pub | **Lower Garden**	20
Checkpoint | **French Qtr**	17
Circle Bar | **Warehouse**	22
Z 45 Tchoup | **Uptown**	21
Gold Mine | **French Qtr**	20
Igor's B&G | **Lower Garden**	19
Johnny White's | **French Qtr**	21
Le Bon Temps | **Uptown**	22
Maple Leaf | **Carrollton**	25
Markey's Bar | **Bywater**	23
Mayfair | **Uptown**	22
Milan Lounge | **Uptown**	17
Molly's at Market | **French Qtr**	21
Ms. Mae's | **Uptown**	17
Saturn Bar | **Bywater**	22
Snake & Jake's | **Uptown**	23
Z Vaughan's Lounge | **Bywater**	27

DJs

Ampersand	**CBD**	19
Blue Nile	**Faub Marigny**	23
Bourbon Pub	**French Qtr**	24
Dungeon	**French Qtr**	22
Handsome Willy's	**CBD**	16
Hookah Café	**Faub Marigny**	21
Le Phare Bar	**CBD**	22
Mimi's	**Faub Marigny**	24
Ohm Lounge	**CBD**	–
One Eyed Jacks	**French Qtr**	23
Oz	**French Qtr**	21
Republic	**Warehouse**	16
Whiskey Blue	**CBD**	23

FINE FOOD TOO

Bombay Club	**French Qtr**	25
Bridge Lounge	**Lower Garden**	21
Mimi's	**Faub Marigny**	24
Ray's Room	**Faub Marigny**	20
Snug Harbor	**Faub Marigny**	26
Z Swizzle Stick	**CBD**	26

GAY/LESBIAN

Bourbon Pub	**French Qtr**	24
Cafe Lafitte	**French Qtr**	21
Corner Pocket	**French Qtr**	–
Good Friends	**French Qtr**	21
Oz	**French Qtr**	21
Phoenix	**Faub Marigny**	–
Rawhide 2010	**French Qtr**	25

HAPPY HOUR

Avenue Pub	**Lower Garden**	20
Balcony Bar	**Uptown**	20
Bridge Lounge	**Lower Garden**	21
Bruno's	**Uptown**	20
Bulldog	**multi.**	24
Circle Bar	**Warehouse**	22
Z Columns Hotel	**Uptown**	27
d.b.a.	**Faub Marigny**	24
Kingpin	**Uptown**	22
Mimi's	**Faub Marigny**	24

Monkey Hill	**Uptown**	21
St. Joe's Bar	**Uptown**	20
Z Swizzle Stick	**CBD**	26

HOTEL BARS

Columns Hotel		
Z Columns Hotel	**Uptown**	27
International House		
Z Loa	**CBD**	24
Loews		
Z Swizzle Stick	**CBD**	26
Loft 523		
Le Phare Bar	**CBD**	22
Monteleone, Hotel		
Carousel Bar	**French Qtr**	26
Renaissance Pere Marquette		
NEW Bar UnCommon	**CBD**	–
Royal St. Charles Hotel		
Ohm Lounge	**CBD**	–
Royal Street Inn		
R Bar	**Faub Marigny**	19
Windsor Court Hotel		
Z Polo Lounge	**CBD**	27
W New Orleans		
Whiskey Blue	**CBD**	23

JAZZ CLUBS

Donna's B&G	**French Qtr**	25
Fritzel's Jazz	**French Qtr**	23
Maison Bourbon	**French Qtr**	26
Z Preservation Hall	**French Qtr**	28
Snug Harbor	**Faub Marigny**	26
Spotted Cat	**Faub Marigny**	25

JUKEBOXES

Apple Barrel	**Faub Marigny**	21
Avenue Pub	**Lower Garden**	20
Balcony Bar	**Uptown**	20
Bruno's	**Uptown**	20
Checkpoint	**French Qtr**	17
Circle Bar	**Warehouse**	22
Cooter Brown's	**Carrollton**	21

Coyote Ugly | **French Qtr**	16
Donna's B&G | **French Qtr**	25
Dungeon | **French Qtr**	22
Fat Harry's | **Uptown**	17
Funky Pirate | **French Qtr**	21
Kingpin | **Uptown**	22
☑ Lafitte's | **French Qtr**	26
Le Bon Temps | **Uptown**	22
Maple Leaf | **Carrollton**	25
Mayfair | **Uptown**	22
☑ Mid-City Lanes | **Mid-City**	26
Molly's at Market | **French Qtr**	21
Ms. Mae's | **Uptown**	17
Old Absinthe Hse. | **French Qtr**	23
☑ Pat O'Brien's | **French Qtr**	25
St. Joe's Bar | **Uptown**	20
Tropical Isle | **French Qtr**	20

LIVE MUSIC

(See also Jazz Clubs)

Apple Barrel | **Faub Marigny**	21
Balcony Music | **French Qtr**	18
Banks St. | **Mid-City**	22
NEW Bar UnCommon | **CBD**	-
Blue Nile | **Faub Marigny**	23
Bombay Club | **French Qtr**	25
Bourbon Pub | **French Qtr**	24
Bourbon St. Blues | **French Qtr**	21
Cafe Lafitte | **French Qtr**	21
Cajun Cabin | **French Qtr**	20
Carousel Bar | **French Qtr**	26
Carrollton Station | **Carrollton**	22
Cat's Meow | **French Qtr**	20
Checkpoint | **French Qtr**	17
Chocolate Bar | **Mid-City**	-
Circle Bar | **Warehouse**	22
☑ Columns Hotel | **Uptown**	27
d.b.a. | **Faub Marigny**	24
Dos Jefes Cigar | **Uptown**	23
Famous Door | **French Qtr**	19
Funky Pirate | **French Qtr**	21
Good Friends | **French Qtr**	21

Handsome Willy's | **CBD**	16
Hi Ho Lounge | **Faub Marigny**	17
Hookah Café | **Faub Marigny**	21
House of Blues | **French Qtr**	23
Howlin' Wolf | **Warehouse**	20
Jimmy Buffett's | **French Qtr**	20
Kerry Irish Pub | **French Qtr**	20
Kingpin | **Uptown**	22
☑ Lafitte's | **French Qtr**	26
Le Bon Temps | **Uptown**	22
☑ Le Chat Noir | **Warehouse**	26
NEW Live Bait | **Bucktown**	-
Maple Leaf | **Carrollton**	25
☑ Mid-City Lanes | **Mid-City**	26
Mimi's | **Faub Marigny**	24
Monkey Hill | **Uptown**	21
Neutral Ground | **Uptown**	19
Old Point Bar | **Algiers**	23
One Eyed Jacks | **French Qtr**	23
☑ Pat O'Brien's | **French Qtr**	25
☑ Polo Lounge | **CBD**	27
Ray's Room | **Faub Marigny**	20
Razzoo | **French Qtr**	18
Republic | **Warehouse**	16
Rivershack Tav. | **Jefferson**	22
Rusty Nail | **Warehouse**	22
Saturn Bar | **Bywater**	22
Snake & Jake's | **Uptown**	23
☑ Swizzle Stick | **CBD**	26
☑ Tipitina's | **Uptown**	27
Tommy's Wine | **Warehouse**	24
Tropical Isle | **French Qtr**	20
☑ Vaughan's Lounge | **Bywater**	27

LOCAL FAVORITES

Apple Barrel | **Faub Marigny**	21
Banks St. | **Mid-City**	22
Bridge Lounge | **Lower Garden**	21
Bulldog | **multi.**	24
Carousel Bar | **French Qtr**	26
Circle Bar | **Warehouse**	22

Z Columns Hotel | **Uptown** 27

Cooter Brown's | **Carrollton** 21

d.b.a. | **Faub Marigny** 24

Donna's B&G | **French Qtr** 25

Dos Jefes Cigar | **Uptown** 23

F&M Patio Bar | **Uptown** 21

Howlin' Wolf | **Warehouse** 20

Igor's B&G | **Lower Garden** 19

Kingpin | **Uptown** 22

Le Bon Temps | **Uptown** 22

Maple Leaf | **Carrollton** 25

Z Mid-City Lanes | **Mid-City** 26

Mimi's | **Faub Marigny** 24

Molly's at Market | **French Qtr** 21

Saturn Bar | **Bywater** 22

Snake & Jake's | **Uptown** 23

Snug Harbor | **Faub Marigny** 26

Spotted Cat | **Faub Marigny** 25

St. Joe's Bar | **Uptown** 20

Z Tipitina's | **Uptown** 27

Z Vaughan's Lounge | **Bywater** 27

NOTEWORTHY NEWCOMERS

Bar Tonique | **French Qtr** -

Bar UnCommon | **CBD** -

Garden District Pub | 19
  Lower Garden

Live Bait | **Bucktown** -

Pravda | **French Qtr** 22

W.I.N.O. | **Warehouse** 24

OLD NEW ORLEANS

(50+ yrs.; Year opened; * building)

1750 | Preservation Hall* | 28
  French Qtr

1772 | Lafitte's | **French Qtr** 26

1800 | Molly's at Market* | 21
  French Qtr

1811 | Cat's Meow* | **French Qtr** 20

1815 | Old Absinthe Hse. | 23
  French Qtr

1831 | Fritzel's Jazz* | **French Qtr** 23

1835 | Dungeon* | **French Qtr** 22

1883 | Columns Hotel* | **Uptown** 27

1886 | Carousel Bar | **French Qtr** 26

1923 | Pat O'Brien's | **French Qtr** 25

1925 | Bar UnCommon* | **CBD** 19

1933 | Cafe Lafitte | **French Qtr** 21

1934 | Abbey | **French Qtr** 15

1947 | Markey's Bar | **Bywater** 23

1956 | Famous Door | **French Qtr** 19

OUTDOOR SPACES

GARDEN

Bombay Club | **French Qtr** 25

PATIO/TERRACE

Balcony Bar | **Uptown** 20

Balcony Music | **French Qtr** 18

Bourbon Pub | **French Qtr** 24

Bruno's | **Uptown** 20

Bulldog | **multi.** 24

Cafe Lafitte | **French Qtr** 21

Cajun Cabin | **French Qtr** 20

Carrollton Station | **Carrollton** 22

Cat's Meow | **French Qtr** 20

Chocolate Bar | **Mid-City** -

Circle Bar | **Warehouse** 22

Z Columns Hotel | **Uptown** 27

Dos Jefes Cigar | **Uptown** 23

F&M Patio Bar | **Uptown** 21

Funky Pirate | **French Qtr** 21

Good Friends | **French Qtr** 21

Handsome Willy's | **CBD** 16

House of Blues | **French Qtr** 23

Z Lafitte's | **French Qtr** 26

Le Bon Temps | **Uptown** 22

NEW Live Bait | **Bucktown** -

Madigans | **Carrollton** 19

Maple Leaf | **Carrollton** 25

Old Absinthe Hse. | **French Qtr** 23

Old Point Bar | **Algiers** 23

Z Pat O'Brien's | **French Qtr** 25

Phoenix | **Faub Marigny** -

NEW Pravda | **French Qtr** 22

Ray's Room	**Faub Marigny**	20
Razzoo	**French Qtr**	18
Rivershack Tav.	**Jefferson**	22
St. Joe's Bar	**Uptown**	20
Tropical Isle	**French Qtr**	20

ROOFTOP

Bourbon St. Blues | **French Qtr** — 21

SIDEWALK

Boot | **Uptown** — 14
Bridge Lounge | **Lower Garden** — 21
Bulldog | **Uptown** — 24
Cooter Brown's | **Carrollton** — 21
Fat Harry's | **Uptown** — 17
NEW Garden District Pub | **Lower Garden** — 19
Igor's B&G | **Lower Garden** — 19
Jimmy Buffett's | **French Qtr** — 20
Z Vaughan's Lounge | **Bywater** — 27

PEOPLE-WATCHING

Bourbon Pub | **French Qtr** — 24
Carousel Bar | **French Qtr** — 26
Circle Bar | **Warehouse** — 22
Z Columns Hotel | **Uptown** — 27
Hookah Café | **Faub Marigny** — 21
Le Phare Bar | **CBD** — 22
Z Loa | **CBD** — 24
Maple Leaf | **Carrollton** — 25
Molly's at Market | **French Qtr** — 21
Z Polo Lounge | **CBD** — 27
Z Swizzle Stick | **CBD** — 26
Whiskey Blue | **CBD** — 23

POOL TABLES

Avenue Pub | **Lower Garden** — 20
Balcony Bar | **Uptown** — 20
Banks St. | **Mid-City** — 22
Boot | **Uptown** — 14
Bruno's | **Uptown** — 20
Cafe Lafitte | **French Qtr** — 21
Carrollton Station | **Carrollton** — 22
Checkpoint | **French Qtr** — 17
Cooter Brown's | **Carrollton** — 21

Dos Jefes Cigar | **Uptown** — 23
Dungeon | **French Qtr** — 22
F&M Patio Bar | **Uptown** — 21
Fat Harry's | **Uptown** — 17
Finn McCool's | **Mid-City** — 22
Gold Mine | **French Qtr** — 20
Good Friends | **French Qtr** — 21
Hi Ho Lounge | **Faub Marigny** — 17
Igor's B&G | **Lower Garden** — 19
Kerry Irish Pub | **French Qtr** — 20
Le Bon Temps | **Uptown** — 22
Madigans | **Carrollton** — 19
Markey's Bar | **Bywater** — 23
Mayfair | **Uptown** — 22
Mimi's | **Faub Marigny** — 24
Monkey Hill | **Uptown** — 21
Ms. Mae's | **Uptown** — 17
Old Point Bar | **Algiers** — 23
Phoenix | **Faub Marigny** — –
Rawhide 2010 | **French Qtr** — 25
R Bar | **Faub Marigny** — 19
Rivershack Tav. | **Jefferson** — 22
St. Joe's Bar | **Uptown** — 20
Tropical Isle | **French Qtr** — 20

ROMANTIC

Bombay Club | **French Qtr** — 25
Carousel Bar | **French Qtr** — 26
Z Columns Hotel | **Uptown** — 27
French 75 | **French Qtr** — 25
Z Lafitte's | **French Qtr** — 26
Z Loa | **CBD** — 24
Z Polo Lounge | **CBD** — 27
Snug Harbor | **Faub Marigny** — 26
Tommy's Wine | **Warehouse** — 24

SPORTS BARS

Boot | **Uptown** — 14
Bulldog | **multi.** — 24
Cooter Brown's | **Carrollton** — 21
Finn McCool's | **Mid-City** — 22
Johnny White's | **French Qtr** — 21

Sites & Attractions Types

Includes attraction names, locations and Appeal ratings.

ARTS/PERFORMANCE CENTERS

Ashé Arts | **Central City** | _-_

Contemporary Arts Ctr. | **Warehouse** | 22

French Quarter Visitor Ctr. | **French Qtr** | _-_

New Orleans Jazz Park | **French Qtr** | _-_

BATTLEFIELDS

Chalmette Battlefield/Cemetery | **Chalmette** | _-_

CEMETERIES

Chalmette Battlefield/Cemetery | **Chalmette** | _-_

Lafayette Cemetery | **Garden** | 25

St. Louis Cemetery | **French Qtr** | 25

HISTORICAL HOUSES

Beauregard-Keyes House | **French Qtr** | 21

Cabildo | **French Qtr** | 23

1850 House | **French Qtr** | _-_

Gallier House | **French Qtr** | 26

Hermann-Grima House | **French Qtr** | 26

Houmas Plantation | **Darrow** | _-_

Longue Vue | **Old Metairie** | 26

Oak Alley | **Vacherie** | _-_

MUSEUMS

Cabildo | **French Qtr** | 23

French Quarter Visitor Ctr. | **French Qtr** | _-_

Historic NO Collection | **French Qtr** | 25

Louisiana Children's Mus. | **Warehouse** | _-_

Louisiana's Civil War Museum | **Warehouse** | 20

NEW Museum/Amer. Cocktail | **CBD** | _-_

Z National WWII Mus. | **Warehouse** | 29

NO Museum of Art | **Mid-City** | 26

Ogden Museum | **Warehouse** | 24

Old U.S. Mint | **French Qtr** | _-_

Presbytere | **French Qtr** | 25

NEW Southern Food/Beverage | **CBD** | _-_

NATURAL HISTORY MUSEUMS

NEW Audubon Insectarium | **French Qtr** | _-_

PARKS/SQUARES

Audubon Park | **Uptown** | 27

Z French Market | **French Qtr** | 23

Jackson Square | **French Qtr** | 27

Jean Lafitte Park | **Marrero** | 26

NO Botanical Garden | **Mid-City** | 26

NO City Park | **Mid-City** | 23

Woldenberg Riverfront | **French Qtr** | 24

RELIGIOUS SITES

Old Ursuline Convent | **French Qtr** | _-_

St. Louis Cathedral | **French Qtr** | 26

ZOOS/ANIMAL PARKS

Z Audubon Aquarium | **French Qtr** | 27

Z Audubon Zoo | **Uptown** | 28

Sites & Attractions Locations

Includes attraction names and Appeal ratings.

New Orleans

CBD (CENTRAL BUSINESS DISTRICT)

NEW Museum/Amer. Cocktail —

NEW Southern Food/Beverage —

CENTRAL CITY

Ashé Arts —

CHALMETTE

Chalmette Battlefield/Cemetery —

FRENCH QUARTER

Z Audubon Aquarium 27

NEW Audubon Insectarium —

Beauregard-Keyes House 21

Cabildo 23

1850 House —

Z French Market 23

French Quarter Visitor Ctr. —

Gallier House 26

Hermann-Grima House 26

Historic NO Collection 25

Jackson Square 27

New Orleans Jazz Park —

Old Ursuline Convent —

Old U.S. Mint —

Presbytere 25

St. Louis Cathedral 26

St. Louis Cemetery 25

Woldenberg Riverfront 24

GARDEN DISTRICT

Lafayette Cemetery 25

MID-CITY

NO Botanical Garden 26

NO City Park 23

NO Museum of Art 26

OLD METAIRIE

Longue Vue 26

UPTOWN

Audubon Park 27

Z Audubon Zoo 28

WAREHOUSE DISTRICT

Contemporary Arts Ctr. 22

Louisiana Children's Mus. —

Louisiana's Civil War Museum 20

Z National WWII Mus. 29

Ogden Museum 24

WEST BANK

Jean Lafitte Park 26

Beyond New Orleans

DARROW

Houmas Plantation —

VACHERIE

Oak Alley —

Hotel Types

Listings cover the best in each category and include hotel names, locations and Room ratings.

BOUTIQUE

Bienville House	French Qtr	_
Bourbon Orleans	French Qtr	18
International House	CBD	20
Maison de Ville	French Qtr	22
Maison Dupuy	French Qtr	22
Prince Conti	French Qtr	17
Provincial, Hotel	French Qtr	_
Soniat House	French Qtr	26
W French Quarter	French Qtr	23

BUSINESS-ORIENTED

Hilton Riverside	CBD	19
Iberville Suites	French Qtr	20
JW Marriott	CBD	19
Le Pavillon	CBD	19
Loews	CBD	26
Monteleone	French Qtr	22
Z Omni	French Qtr	21
Z Ritz-Carlton	French Qtr	25
Royal Sonesta	French Qtr	20
Sheraton	CBD	_
Sheraton Metairie	Metairie	19
Whitney	CBD	20
Z Windsor Court	CBD	24

CONVENTION

Hilton Riverside	CBD	19
InterContinental	CBD	23
Marriott	French Qtr	18
Marriott NO Convention Ctr.	Warehouse	21
Renaissance	Warehouse	_
Westin	CBD	21
W New Orleans	CBD	23
Wyndham	Warehouse	23

Hotel Locations

Includes hotel names and Room ratings.

CBD (CENTRAL BUSINESS DISTRICT)

Doubletree Hotel New Orleans	19
Harrah's	23
Hilton Riverside	19
Hilton St. Charles	-
InterContinental	23
International House	20
JW Marriott	19
Le Pavillon	19
Loews	26
Renaissance Pere Marquette	19
Sheraton	-
Westin	21
Whitney	20
⨉ Windsor Court	24
W New Orleans	23

FRENCH QUARTER

Bienville House	-
Bourbon Orleans	18
Chateau Sonesta	22
Iberville Suites	20
Maison de Ville	22
Maison Dupuy	22
Marriott	18
Monteleone	22
⨉ Omni	21
Prince Conti	17
Provincial, Hotel	-
⨉ Ritz-Carlton	25
Royal Sonesta	20
Soniat House	26
W French Quarter	23

METAIRIE

Marriott Metairie	-
Sheraton Metairie	19

WAREHOUSE DISTRICT

Marriott NO Convention Ctr.	21
Renaissance	-
Wyndham	23

Hotel Special Features

Listings cover the best in each category and include hotel names, locations and Room ratings.

CASINOS

Harrah's | **CBD** [23]

CHILDREN NOT ADVISED

(Call to confirm policy)

Maison de Ville | **French Qtr** [22]

Soniat House | **French Qtr** [26]

CITY VIEWS

Harrah's | **CBD** [23]

Hilton Riverside | **CBD** [19]

InterContinental | **CBD** [23]

JW Marriott | **CBD** [19]

Le Pavillon | **CBD** [19]

Loews | **CBD** [26]

Maison de Ville | **French Qtr** [22]

Maison Dupuy | **French Qtr** [22]

Marriott | **French Qtr** [18]

Monteleone | **French Qtr** [22]

Renaissance | **Warehouse** [-]

Renaissance Pere Marquette | **CBD** [19]

Sheraton | **CBD** [-]

🛛 Windsor Court | **CBD** [24]

OFFBEAT/FUNKY

International House | **CBD** [20]

Le Pavillon | **CBD** [19]

POWER SCENES

🛛 Omni | **French Qtr** [21]

🛛 Ritz-Carlton | **French Qtr** [25]

🛛 Windsor Court | **CBD** [24]

W New Orleans | **CBD** [23]

ROMANTIC

Maison de Ville | **French Qtr** [22]

Prince Conti | **French Qtr** [17]

Soniat House | **French Qtr** [26]

SPA FACILITIES

Harrah's | **CBD** [23]

Iberville Suites | **French Qtr** [20]

Loews | **CBD** [26]

Monteleone | **French Qtr** [22]

🛛 Ritz-Carlton | **French Qtr** [25]

Westin | **CBD** [21]

TRENDY PLACES

International House | **CBD** [20]

Renaissance | **Warehouse** [-]

W French Quarter | **French Qtr** [23]

W New Orleans | **CBD** [23]

WATER VIEWS

Harrah's | **CBD** [23]

Hilton Riverside | **CBD** [19]

International House | **CBD** [20]

JW Marriott | **CBD** [19]

Loews | **CBD** [26]

Marriott | **French Qtr** [18]

Marriott Metairie | **Metairie** [-]

Monteleone | **French Qtr** [22]

🛛 Omni | **French Qtr** [21]

Renaissance Pere Marquette | **CBD** [19]

Sheraton | **CBD** [-]

Westin | **CBD** [21]

🛛 Windsor Court | **CBD** [24]

W New Orleans | **CBD** [23]

Wyndham | **Warehouse** [23]

ALPHABETICAL
PAGE INDEX

ALPHA INDEX

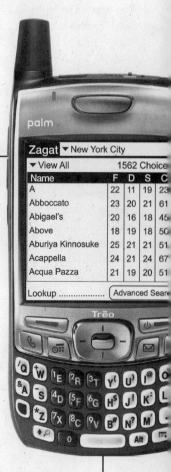

ISBN 978-1-60478-020-8